FROM PHYSICK TO PHARMACOLOGY

From Physick to Pharmacology
Five Hundred Years of British Drug Retailing

Edited by
LOUISE HILL CURTH
Bath Spa University, UK

ASHGATE

Published by
Ashgate Publishing Limited
Gower House
Croft Road
Aldershot
Hampshire GU11 3HR
England

Ashgate Publishing Company
Suite 420
101 Cherry Street
Burlington, VT 05401-4405
USA

Ashgate website: http://www.ashgate.com

British Library Cataloguing in Publication Data
From physick to pharmacology : five hundred years of
  British drug retailing
  1.Pharmacy – Great Britain – History 2.Pharmacists – Great
  Britain – History 3.Pharmaceutical industry – Great Britain
  – History
  I.Curth, Louise
  338.4'76151'0941

Library of Congress Cataloging-in-Publication Data
From physick to pharmacology : five hundred years of British drug
  retailing / edited by Louise Curth.
    p. cm. – (The history of retailing and consumption)
  Includes bibliographical references and index.
  ISBN 0-7546-3597-X (alk. paper)
    1. Pharmaceutical industry–Great Britain–History. 2. Retail trade
  –Great Britain–History. 3. Pharmacy–Great Britain–History.
  I. Curth, Louise. II. Series.
    [DNLM: 1. Drug Industry–history–Great Britain. 2. Pharmacy
  –history–Great Britain.   QV 711 FA1 F931 2006]
  HD9667.5.F75 2006
  381'.4561510941–dc22

                                                    2005037689

ISBN-13: 978-0-7546-3597-0
ISBN-10: 0-7546-3597-X

Printed and bound in Great Britain by Antony Rowe Ltd, Chippenham, Wiltshire.

Contents

General Editor's Preface   *vii*
List of Figures   *ix*
List of Contributors   *xi*
Acknowledgements   *xiii*

1   Introduction: Perspectives on the Evolution of the Retailing of
     Pharmaceuticals   1
     Louise Hill Curth

2   Apothecaries and the Consumption and Retailing of Medicines in
     Early Modern London   13
     Patrick Wallis

3   Medical Advertising in the Popular Press: Almanacs and the Growth
     of Proprietary Medicines   29
     Louise Hill Curth

4   Accessing Drugs in the Eighteenth-Century Regions   49
     Steven King

5   'The Doctor's Shop': The Rise of the Chemist and Druggist in
     Nineteenth-Century Manufacturing Districts   79
     Hilary Marland

6   From 'Bespoke' to 'Off-the-Peg': Community Pharmacists and the
     Retailing of Medicines in Great Britain 1900–1970   105
     Stuart Anderson

7   'A Cascade of Medicine': The Marketing and Consumption of
     Prescription Drugs in the UK 1948–2000   143
     Judy Slinn

Index   *171*

The History of Retailing and Consumption
General Editor's Preface

It is increasingly recognized that retail systems and changes in the patterns of consumption play crucial roles in the development and societal structure of economies. Such recognition has led to renewed interest in the changing nature of retail distribution and the rise of consumer society from a wide range of academic disciplines. The aim of this multidisciplinary series is to provide a forum of publications that explore the history of retailing and consumption.

Gareth Shaw, University of Exeter, UK

List of Figures

3.1   Advertisements in almanacs by type.   34

6.1   Specialization of medicine preparation.   106

6.2   Sources of income of retail chemists 1900–2000.   121

6.3   Principal dosage forms 1900–2000.   129

6.4   Number of prescriptions written by doctors 1900–2000.   132

6.5   Proportion of prescriptions dispensed by doctors and pharmacists 1900–2000.   135

6.6   Prescriptions for branded and generic drugs 1900–2000.   141

List of Contributors

Stuart Anderson is Senior Lecturer in Organisational Behaviour and Teaching Programme Director at the London School of Hygiene and Tropical Medicine. He holds a degree in Pharmacy, and practised as a pharmacist, first in the pharmaceutical industry and subsequently in NHS hospitals, later obtaining an MA in Manpower Studies and a PhD in Organisational Behaviour from the University of London. His principal research interests are organizational studies in health care, and his publications include comparative studies of public and private provision of health care, performance measurement, prescribing at the interface between hospital and general practice, as well as the social history of pharmacy.

Louise Hill Curth is Senior Lecturer in Health Studies at Bath Spa University. She read marketing for her undergraduate degree, followed by an MA in Early Modern English Social History and a PhD in Early Modern Medical History from the University of London. Her principal research interests are in early modern social history of medicine for humans and animals. Amongst her recent publications are *English Almanacs, Astrology & Popular Medicine, 1550–1700* (Manchester University Press, 2007), 'A Remedy for his Beast: Animal Health Care in Early Modern Europe', *Intersections: Representations of Animals, Yearbook for Early Modern Studies* (forthcoming), 'The Medical Content of English Almanacs', *Journal of the History of Medicine and Allied Sciences*, 60 (July 2005), pp. 255–82, and 'The Care of the Brute Beast: Animals and the Seventeenth-century Medical Marketplace', *The Social History of Medicine*, 15(3) (December 2002), pp. 375–92. She is currently working on *'The Care of Brute Beasts': A Social and Cultural Study of Veterinary Medicine in Early Modern England*, which will be published by Brill in 2007.

Steve King is Professor of History, Director of the Centre for Health, Medicine and Society and Assistant Dean for Research in the School of Arts and Humanities at Oxford Brookes University. He read history at the University of Kent, and obtained his PhD from the University of Liverpool. His research interests include the early modern history of European industrialization, with a particular focus on demography and family, British and European poverty and welfare, with a particular focus on the regionality of welfare, the administration of relief and the experience of being poor in the period 1600–1920, medical history of industrial England, the sick poor, the medical marketplace and doctor–patient relationships in the period 1650–1850, and local history. His most recent publications including S.A. King (ed.), *Narratives of the Poor in Eighteenth Century Britain* (Pickering and Chatto, 2006), *Women, Welfare and Local Politics, 1880–1920* (Sussex Academic Press, 2005) and '"It is impossible for our vestry to judge his case into perfection from here": Managing the distance dimensions of poor relief under the old Poor Law', *Rural History*, 16(2) (2005), pp. 161–89.

Hilary Marland is Professor of History and Director of the Centre for the History of Medicine, University of Warwick. She is author of *Dangerous Motherhood: Insanity and Childbirth in Victorian Britain* (Palgrave-Macmillan, 2004), and has published on nineteenth-century medical practice, the history of midwifery and childbirth, alternative medicine, infant welfare and women and medicine. She is currently working on the politics and practices of health in the workplace, 1915–74, the water cure in the English Midlands 1884–1950 and on health advice to young women, 1884–1939.

Judy Slinn is a Lecturer in the Business School at Oxford Brookes University, where she has been Wellcome Research Fellow on strategic innovation in the UK pharmaceutical industry since 1948. Her published work includes 'The growth of the pharmaceutical industry', in S. Anderson (ed.), *Making Medicines: A Brief History of Pharmacy* (Pharmaceutical Press, 2005), pp. 157–74; 'The pharmaceutical industry', in *From Victoria to Viagra: 150 Years of Medical Progress* (Wellcome Trust, 2003), pp. 42–4; 'Innovation at Glaxo and May and Baker: 1945–1965', *History and Technology*, 13 (1996), pp. 133–47; 'Research and Development in the UK Pharmaceutical Industry from the Nineteenth Century to the 1960's', in R. Porter and M. Teich (eds), *Drugs and Narcotics in History* (1996), pp. 168–86, and *Pharmaceuticals and Health Care: A History of Abbott Laboratories* (1999).

Patrick Wallis is Lecturer in Economic History at the London School of Economics. He read history at York and completed his MA and PhD at Oxford. His major research interests are in the history of medicine and disease, particularly epidemics, pharmacy and medical practice, the early modern economy, and cities, particularly London. Recent publications include 'Testing Times: Plague, Courage and Duty in Early Modern England', *English Historical Review*, 121(490) (2006), pp. 1–24; 'Quackery and Commerce in Seventeenth Century London: The Proprietary Medicine Business of Anthony Daffy', *Medical History, Supplement* (The Wellcome Trust Centre for the History of Medicine at UCL, 2005), and P. Wallis and I.A. Gadd (eds), *Guilds, Society and Economy in London, 1450–1800* (Centre for Metropolitan History, 2002).

Acknowledgements

This book has been a number of years in the making, and many thanks are due to the medical and business historians who have provided such excellent contributions to it. I am also very grateful to Tom Gray at Ashgate for his help and support throughout this period.

Chapter 1

Introduction: Perspectives on the Evolution of the Retailing of Pharmaceuticals

Louise Hill Curth

A drug is defined as a chemical substance that is taken to prevent or cure disease or to otherwise enhance physical or mental welfare ... [which] implies a cultural rationale.[1]

Disease is not a human invention, but a biological process which has been created and fostered by the way humans have chosen to live. It is thought that as nomadic hunters and gatherers began to settle permanently in one place, a range of pathogens once limited exclusively to animals transferred to humans. A large number of 'zoonoses', or diseases naturally transmitted between species, probably came from domesticated animals such as dogs and cattle, which manifested themselves as diseases like measles, smallpox or tuberculosis. The early settled populations also became prone to deficiency diseases, most notably anaemia caused by insufficient iron, and parasitic infections caused by the faecal contamination of water. As populations continued to grow, so too did the types and numbers of pathogens.[2]

Although patterns of disease have changed, and will always continue to do so, every culture and society has its own theories about what constitutes 'health' and 'illness' and how to achieve, sustain or cure these bodily states. There are also on-going debates as to how these terms should even be defined. Many modern health professionals tend to view 'health' as a unitary rather than a multidimensional or relative concept.[3] Jacalyn Duffin, however, has suggested that the terms 'illness' and 'disease' are actually two different things. The former relates to what are generally referred to as 'symptoms' or the subjective problems experienced by an individual. 'Disease', on the other hand, describes the way in which these are perceived by society.[4] This definition, however, can be taken further. For example, symptoms may be experienced, described and classified quite differently between groups of people. Furthermore, many diseases have mutated over the centuries, resulting in

---

1   H. Fábrega Jr, *Evolution of Sickness and Healing* (Berkeley, CA, 1999), p. 140.

2   W.H. McNeill, *Plagues and Peoples* (London, 1975), pp. 54–5; A.J. Bollet, *Plagues & Poxes: The Impact of Human History on Epidemic Diseases* (New York, 2004), pp. 4–5.

3   S. O'Sullivan and A. Stakelum, 'Lay Understandings of Health: A Qualitative Study', in I. Shaw and K. Kauppinen (eds), *Constructions of Health and Illness: European Perspective* (Aldershot, 2004), pp. 26–43.

4   J. Duffin, *Lovers and Livers: Disease Concepts in History* (Toronto, 2005), p. 5.

either related or new types of illnesses. What is defined as 'disease' in some societies may not be recognized as sickness in others, and many different types of medical structures of beliefs and practices have developed as a result.[5]

However, despite the many differences, all societies share the drive to produce, maintain or restore such a state of health, generally with the aid of various types of often dangerous, potent organic and inorganic ingredients which fall under the rough heading of 'drugs'.[6] The types of ingredients that are used, their relationship with other treatments and even the way that they are expected to work are also closely linked to the society and culture in which they are used. Although herbal remedies are found in most societies, both the types and quantity of ingredients can differ greatly. Tobacco, for example, was considered to be an 'antidote against all venome and pestilential diseases' during the seventeenth century. Today, it is seen as a 'public danger' from which governments must protect their citizens.[7]

Many differences are also evident in the usage of synthetically made medicines. Antibiotics are widely and enthusiastically consumed in Western Europe in the form of prescriptions and as ingredients in 'over-the-counter' medicines. They are also ingested via the food chain, with large amounts being used to promote growth and prevent infections in animal husbandry and fish farms. As a result, new strains of diseases resistant to antibiotics have developed.[8] There are also many differences between the types and quantities of drugs prescribed within Western countries. For example, in the early 1980s some German doctors were prescribing six to seven times the amount of digitalis-related drugs as those in France and England.[9] There are also differences in the physical attributes of products, with varying preferences for tablets capsules, liquids, transdermal patches or intravenous administration which require different dosages according to factors such as sex, age and weight.[10]

Modern studies on the history of drugs tend to fall into one of four camps, none of which focus specifically on the way in which medicines are sold. The first includes general studies which discuss the murky division between licit and illicit

---

5   V. Nutton, *Ancient Medicine* (London, 2004), p. 22.

6   S. O'Sullivan and A. Stakelum, 'Lay Understandings of Health: A Qualitative Study', in I. Shaw and K. Kauppinen (eds), *Constructions of Health and Illness: European Perspectives* (Aldershot, 2004), p. 27. This is a problematic term which often connotes topics such as abuse and addiction. However, in this context it will be used to refer to psychoactive substances used for medical purposes.

7   G. Everard, *Panacea: or, The Universal Medicine* (London, 1659), sig. A6v; F. Duina and P. Kurzer, 'Smoke in your eyes: the struggle over tobacco control in the European Union', *Journal of European Public Policy*, 11(1) (February 2004), pp. 57–77.

8   D.A. Goldmann, 'The Epidemiology of Antimicrobial Resistance', *Ecosystem Health*, 5 (September 1999), pp. 158–63.

9   L. Payer, *Medicine and Culture: Varieties of Treatment in the United States, England, Germany and France* (New York, 1996), p. 24.

10   T. Munn and J. Williams, 'Formulation of medicines for children', *British Journal of Clinical Pharmacology*, 59(6), pp. 674–6.

drugs, such as narcotics and stimulants.[11] These are followed by histories of specific pharmaceutical companies or monographs on specific types of drugs, such as opioids, hallucinogenics or alcohol.[12] The final category includes collections of essays which cover a range of often loosely related 'drug' themes.[13]

The essays which form *From Physick to Pharmacology* examine the way in which the nature of British drugs changed over the course of five hundred years. At the broadest level, they illustrate basic medical theories and the ways in which they changed over the centuries from a holistic to a biomedical model. These essays also help to illustrate the evolution of drug production and distribution. Perhaps most importantly, however, they illustrate the five main, albeit overlapping, phases in the development of English pharmaceuticals.[14] The first can be called 'kitchen physick', which refers to most remedies being prepared within the home from 'natural' ingredients. This is followed by the mercurial rise of commercialized remedies in the eighteenth century, fuelled by more intensive nation-wide advertising that played on the fears of a hypochondriacal public. The third phase covers an era of rapid population growth and urbanization in the long nineteenth century (roughly 1780–1900), when the number of fixed shops specializing in the distribution of drugs expanded even faster than the rapid growth of the medical profession, and brought with it concerns over the safety of some of the preparations provided. Stage four includes the rise of pathology and microbiology in the late nineteenth and early twentieth centuries, with the final phase concentrating on the era of the giant multinational pharmaceutical companies since the inter-war years. This picture deliberately simplifies the pattern of distribution of medical remedies. Throughout, the most central characteristic has been the immense variety of the channels through which 'patients' have received and acquired 'drugs', and the equally complex strategies of diagnosis and treatment, with self-medication consistently being the most common variety. In some ways the boundaries between these phases are impossible to draw with any precision. Thus, regulation of the sale of drugs begins in our third phase, but really gathered momentum in the fourth. The integration of scientific research into the production of medicines is a characteristic of the fourth stage, but reaches its high point in the

---

11 See, for example, D. Courtwright, *Forces of Habit: Drugs and the Making of the Modern World* (London, 2001), or R.P.T. Davenport-Hines, *The Pursuit of Oblivion: A Social History of Drugs* (London, 2001).

12 Such as R.P.T. Davenport-Hines and J. Slinn, *Glaxo: A History to 1962* (Cambridge, 1992); L. Matthew, *The Billion-dollar Battle: Merck v. Glaxo* (London, 1992);. A. Burnett, *Liquid Pleasures: A Social History of Drinks in Modern Britain* (London, 1999); B. Hodgson, *In the Arms of Morpheus: The Tragic History of Laudanum, Morphine and Patent Medicines* (Buffalo, NY, 2001); M.L. Meldrum, *Opioids and Pain Relief: A Historical Perspective* (Seattle, WA, 2003), and J.H. Mills, *Cannabis Britannica: Empire, Trade, and Prohibition* (Oxford, 2004).

13 R. Porter and M. Teich (eds), *Drugs and Narcotics in History* (Cambridge, 1995); A.H. Maehle, *Drugs on Trial* (Amsterdam, 1999).

14 It should be noted that the availability of 'made-to-order' medicines has accompanied every stage of this process.

big multinational companies of our fifth stage. These categories and boundaries are presented here to try to give a structure to a long period in the development of the production and distribution of medicines. They can no doubt be improved upon.

Naturally enough, this range and complexity of treatment strategies, of medical practitioners and of production and distribution provides a major challenge to the historian. There are, for example, many more levels of complexity and differentiation than are customary in other branches of retail history. While the contributors are necessarily modest about the ability of their researches to uncover the full intricacy and extent of the supply of drugs in their era, this volume breaks new ground in the history of drug retailing. That said, a single volume cannot, of course, hope to serve as a general guide to the topic. It can, however, aim to illustrate the common thread of the relationship between medicinal beliefs, treatments and society.

The first phase, kitchen physick, derived much of its force from classical learning, based on the idea that health and illness were 'organic' or constitutional in the sense of deriving from inner processes, rather than invasive external pathogens. It therefore followed that since all parts of the person were inter-linked, the right frame of mind, composure, control of the passions and suitable lifestyle could either help to prevent or help to cure illness.[15] In this period, the notions of health and disease were linked to Galenic-astrological principles which held that diseases were caused by humoral imbalances, linked to an individual's personal habits or from various environmental effects. Although God was seen as the ultimate source of health or illness, at the same time it was thought that the deity encouraged humankind to make efforts to protect or restore their health with the 'herbes, fruites, rootes, seedes, plantes, gums, precious stones, beasts, foules [and] Fishes' provided for these purposes.[16] In fact, the tradition of using medicinal herbs dates back to Mesopotamian and Egyptian times, a variety of common plants were used for medicinal purposes during the Hittite Empire, which flourished between 1380 and 1200 BC.[17] At the beginning of the early modern period, herbs and other plants were still the foundation of both preventative and remedial medicine.

Although the term 'medical marketplace' can be used to describe later phases covered by this collection, there are doubts about its usefulness in this first phase. Both Margaret Pelling and Andrew Wear have pointed to the limited extent of 'commercial' transactions involving health care and the substantial number of healers who either bartered their services or offered them at no cost, and the even

---

15 R. Porter, 'What is Disease?', in R. Porter (ed.), *The Cambridge Illustrated History of Medicine* (Cambridge, 1996), pp. 82–117.

16 W. Bullein, *A newe Boke of Physicke* (London, 1559), sig. A4r.

17 A. Touwaide, 'Therapeutic Strategies: Drugs', in M.D. Grmek (ed.), *Western Medical Thought from Antiquity to the Middle Ages* (Cambridge, MA, 1998), pp. 259–72; R. Arnott, 'Disease and Medicine in Hittite Asia Minor', in R. Arnott (ed.), *The Archaeology of Medicine: Papers Given at a Session of the Annual Conference of the Theoretical Archaeology Group Held at the University of Birmingham on 20 December 1998* (Oxford, 2002), pp. 41–52.

greater extent of domestic health care taking place in the patient's own home.[18] Two contributions to this volume relate to this period. As Patrick Wallis discusses in Chapter 2, in early modern England, medical potions produced within the household were supplemented by those produced by apothecaries or other merchants. Most were based on easily accessible plants and other organic materials and were often combined with a growing number of imported ingredients.[19] Provincial wholesalers known as druggists also supplied such materials to various types of merchants who all sold a range of goods.[20]

The core texts in use in the early modern period were based on the Greek 'pharmacon'. Strictly defined, this refers to drugs, potions or magical potions, but in the broadest sense refers to the sum of all knowledge pertaining to drugs. This tradition had been built upon by later writers, and as Patrick Wallis shows, there was interest in the early modern period to help standardize remedies which were attributed to ancient writers such as Galen or Avicenna, as well as to the thirteenth-century medical writer Mesue, and then to produce vernacular texts. In England, Nicholas Culpeper translated the Latin *Pharmacoepia*, 'that book by which all Apothecaries are strictly commanded to make all their Physick with' in order to provide his countrymen with 'the liberty of the subject'.[21]

This phase also saw the appearance of pre-made, pre-packaged proprietary nostrums, which were sold in a variety of retail outlets, alongside the more traditional remedies. Although apothecaries had been prescribing, compounding and administering medicines for centuries, the Company of Physicians attempted to stop such activities in the late seventeenth century. Their efforts to halt this competition resulted in what became known as the 'Rose Case', begun by a patient complaint to the Company of Physicians during the winter of 1669–70. Although the College attempted to prosecute Rose for practising medicine, an appeal from the Society of Apothecaries resulted in a judgment in favour of Rose from the House of Lords which resulted in apothecaries being given the legal right to practise medicine.[22]

As Louise Hill Curth shows in Chapter 3, this case gave a green light to growth in the manufacture and distribution of branded, commercially promoted proprietary medicines, which were marketed very vigorously in the contemporary mass media. The development of proprietary medicines had a profound effect on the 'dosing

---

18   M. Pelling, 'Medical practice in Early Modern England: Trade or Profession?', in W. Prest (ed.), *The Professions of Early Modern England* (London, 1987), p. 92; A. Wear, 'Religious Beliefs and Medicine in Early Modern England', in H. Marland and M. Pelling (eds), *The Task of Healing: Medicine, Religion and Gender in England and the Netherlands, 1450–1800* (Rotterdam, 1996), pp. 145–6.

19   W. Bullein, *A newe Boke of Physicke* (London, 1559), sig. A4r.

20   P. Hunting, *A History of the Society of Apothecaries* (London, 1998), p. 29; R. Davis, *The Rise of the English Shipping Industry* (London, 1962), p. 186.

21   N. Culpeper, *A Physical Directory or A translation of the London Dispensatory* (London, 1649), sig. A2r.

22   P. Hunting, *A History of the Society of Apothecaries* (London, 1988), p. 55.

habits' of English consumers.[23] Pre-packaged branded drugs were a novel concept for a people who had spent centuries either preparing potions at home or having them made to order. In a sense, the producers had to 'create' a demand. Anyone could patent a medicine as long as it was a new formula, and they did not have to prove that it worked.[24] Producers were thus free to make any claims that they chose about the effectiveness of their products. As might be expected in these conditions, the majority of advertisements for patent drugs in almanacs were extremely enthusiastic about their virtues. The longest-surviving nostrum was called Daffy's Elixir, which began to appear in almanacs around 1660, and thrived until at least the 1920s.[25] This product was advertised in almanacs, albeit sparingly, but it was sold with a pamphlet to illustrate it efficacy.[26] Anthony Daffy claimed that his 'Elixir Salutis' was a 'most excellent Preservative of Man-kind'. It was said to cure a host of diseases ranging from the gout through to 'languishing and melancholy, scurvy, dropsy and fits of the Mother'.[27]

As the pace of economic and social development quickened in the eighteenth century, there is little doubt that the medical marketplace both broadened and deepened against the background of a wider 'commercial revolution' and evidence of increasing sophistication in retailing, in both large and small market towns.[28] According to Christopher Laurence, differentiation was clearly taking place with the increasing professionalization of certain groups in the medical marketplace and the growth of a concept of 'a disease process distinct from the sufferer' which demanded 'drug' treatments.[29] This is not to suggest that more traditional methods disappeared – far from it – merely that the demand for the services of 'doctors' increased and spread down the social scale. This in turn gave a significant fillip to the trade in drugs, such that in Chapter 4 of this volume, Steven King can identify a rich network of drug suppliers by the later eighteenth century.[30] The historiography has concerned

---

23 Porter, 'People's Health', p. 133.

24 Porter, *Health for Sale*, p. 28.

25 C.J.S. Thompson, *The Quacks of Old London* (London, 1928), p. 255.

26 H. Coley, *Nuncius Sydereus, or the Starry Messenger* (London, 1687 and 1688), sig. C5r.

27 A. Daffy, *Elixir Salutis: The Choise Drink of Health or, Health-bringing Drink* (London, 1674), sig. A1r and pp. 1–6.

28 N. McKendrick, 'The Consumer Revolution of Eighteenth-century England', in N. McKendrick, J. Brewer and J.H. Plumb (eds), *The Birth of a Consumer Society: The Commercialization of Eighteenth Century England* (Bloomington, IN, 1982), p. 9; P. Langford, *A Polite and Commercial People* (Oxford, 1989), p. 2; R.M. Berger, 'The Development of Retail Trade in Provincial England, ca. 1550–1700', *Journal of Economic History*, 40 (1980), pp. 123–8; D. Collins, 'Primitive or Not? Fixed-shop Retailing before the Industrial Revolution', *Journal of Regional and Local Studies*, 13 (1993), pp. 23–38; C. Walsh, 'Shop Design and the Display of Goods in Eighteenth Century London', *Journal of Design History*, 8 (1995), pp. 157–76.

29 C. Lawrence, *Medicine in the Making of Modern Britain* (London, 1994), p. 30.

30 See also R. and D. Porter, 'The Rise of the English Drugs Industry: The Role of Thomas Corbyn', *Medical History*, 33 (1989), p. 280.

itself most with sketching these developments at the national level, Steven King's contribution looks at the way that the medical market place functioned in the regions, contrasting urbanizing Lancashire with rural Northamptonshire and also referring for contrast to the remoter areas of North—West England.

King suggests that there were two countervailing tendencies. On the one hand, there remained specific groups who were cut off, either by socio-cultural factors or because of lack of resources (whether absolute or resulting from suspicion of doctors and the price of their treatments), from the medical marketplace. On the other, the improved transport networks, the faster easier flow of information and the growth of the urban population and incomes made for substantial growth in demand for drugs throughout the eighteenth century. He shows that for both the middling and poorer sorts there was a vibrant and robust sub-regional drugs trade, which was served by a whole range of suppliers, some of whom were paid in the conventional manner (subject to the prevailing constraints of the shortage of small-denomination coin). This constituted the boundary of the eighteenth-century medical marketplace, but the channels of distribution of drugs to the poor also increased during the century, with the rapid development of the voluntary hospital system, some free or cheap treatment from medical practitioners, charitable support from better-off families and the provision of remedies by irregular practitioners. There is comparatively little evidence of major regional differences in the types of drugs available, but Steven King suggests that in the more isolated and rural communities of western England, the supply was more restricted and vulnerable than those of urbanized Lancashire and rural Northamptonshire.

In the third stage, the structure of the drugs trade was profoundly shaped by the speed of population growth, rapid urbanization and the emergence of new ideas on the treatment of the poor. The passing of the New Poor Law in 1834 led to the development of new distributors of drugs, such as dispensaries, infirmaries and the creation of a network of friendly societies, which provided both medicine and financial aid to their members. The nineteenth century was a period of rising concern about issues of public health public health, social hygiene and social medicine, helping to change the basic theories of Western medicine, with diagnosis and treatment resting more heavily on laboratory tests than through clinical symptoms.[31] This period also saw the rise of new medical ideas and treatments based on homoeopathy, mesmerism, hydropathy and medical botany, while at the same time new groups of medical practitioners claimed professional status to differentiate themselves from quacks and healers. Urbanization, improvements in the transport network and the (albeit slow) rise in incomes also fostered substantial change in the retail sector, with the number of fixed shops rising faster than population from roughly 1780 to 1850,

---

31   D. Harley, 'Rhetoric and the Social Construction of Sickness and Healing', *Social History of Medicine*, 3 (1999), p. 416.

while the number of 'traditional' retailers (hawkers, street traders, market sellers) retained a strong foothold in working-class districts, especially of the large cities.[32]

Hilary Marland's contribution in Chapter 5 illustrates many of these themes. According to many historians, the nineteenth century is seen as the period when 'the foundations of modern pharmacology' were laid.[33] Marland shows how the rapid industrialization and urbanization of northern England in the nineteenth century was accompanied by a decline in the number of 'pedlar-druggists' and an even more rapid rise in the number of chemists and druggists operating from fixed, specialist shops.[34] Chemists and druggists fulfilled a major role in the marketing of drugs in the nineteenth century, and by 1850 had become the most numerous suppliers of medical aid, in significant part from the supply of patent medicines. Not only did the numbers of chemists' and druggists' shops expand rapidly, the largest businesses opened a number of branches and followed the grocery trade into multiple retailing.[35] They dispensed prescriptions for qualified doctors, but this role was dwarfed by their functions of preparing medical advice and assistance to the wider public. As Hilary Marland notes, this included 'over-the-counter' prescribing, preparation of family recipes and the sale of a wide range of drugs and patent remedies, and was frequently supported by vigorous advertising and other marketing devices. However, their activities became increasingly subject to criticism as the century progressed and their numbers swelled. Qualified medical practitioners objected to the role that druggists played, especially for the poorer classes, of informal, not always well-informed, over-the-counter diagnosis, while others objected to the sale of opiates and potions designed to induce abortions. The response was the first steps towards professionalization with the formation in 1841 of the Pharmaceutical Society of Great Britain, which aimed to regulate the training and qualifications of those involved in the compounding and dispensing of doctors' prescriptions, but did little to regulate or inhibit their other medical activities.

In Chapter 6, Stuart Anderson takes up the issue of the regulation of the sale of drugs with a potentially harmful impact on the patient, showing how the state and its agents began to define medicinal substances according to how dangerous they were, and began to regulate the claims that manufacturers and retailers of drugs could make about their products. In this process, the nature of the medicinal products underwent a profound change from concoctions made up by the chemist to mass-produced proprietary medicines, and the unfettered access of consumers to the whole

---

32   G. Shaw, 'The Evolution and Impact of Large-scale Retailing in Britain', in J. Benson and G. Shaw (eds), *The Evolution of Retail Systems, c. 1800–1914* (Leicester, 1992), pp. 135–65; J. Benson, *The Penny Capitalists: A Study of Nineteenth Century Working Class Entrepreneurs* (London, 1983).

33   Maehle, *Drugs on Trial*, p. 1.

34   S.W.F. Holloway, 'Regulation of Drugs in Britain before 1868', in R. Porter and M. Teich (eds), *Drugs and Narcotics in History* (Cambridge, 1995), pp. 77–96.

35   On the most famous example, albeit late in the nineteenth century, see S.D. Chapman, *Jesse Boot of Boots the Chemist* (London, 1974).

range of medicines has been severely limited. But that takes us into the fourth and fifth phases of the development of drug retailing.

The fourth phase is characterized by the increasing importance of scientific research in the development of drugs and the analysis of disease – in short, the emergence of modern medicine. Bynum has argued that during the nineteenth century, the conceptual foundations and the practice of medicine were slowly transformed, but the impact was greater on the diagnostic skills of doctors than on their therapeutic capacities.[36] In the late nineteenth and early twentieth centuries, diseases were reconstructed by pathology and microbiology, which gave them the status of entities to be diagnosed in a laboratory, rather than through clinical symptoms.[37] Initially, this allowed medical practitioners to manage patients more effectively than had their predecessors, but the impact on therapeutic care had to await the development of sulphonamides and the establishment of mass-produced vaccines. In the process, the emergence of modern medicine has profoundly affected the public perception of the medical profession, and more crucially for our purposes, the public perception of what medicines can achieve. Patients now expect to be 'cured' by a course of drugs for almost any complaint.

In his very wide-ranging essay, Stuart Anderson discusses the impact of these and related changes on the retailing of medicine in the twentieth century. He argues that the retailing of medicines has undergone its greatest ever phase of transition under the impact of scientific medicine. The range of medicines has increased as a result of pressures on both the demand and supply sides. The demonstration of the power of modern medicines in curing the killer diseases of previous generations has generated unrealistic demands about what drugs might achieve. On the supply side, the development of state welfare in the twentieth century has resulted in a huge increase in the number of prescriptions dispensed by chemists, and has also led to innovations in the form that drugs are dispensed. At the same time, the production and marketing of proprietary medicines has been shaped by a process of concentration by merger and takeover, so that the range of products has diminished, but with heavy promotion of the commercially more successful lines. This has encouraged the makers of proprietary medicines to search for new ways to sell their products, and has seen the emergence of the supermarket, probably the most dramatic retailing development of the second half of the twentieth century, as a major channel for the sale of non-prescription medicines.

Stuart Anderson's contribution takes us well into the fifth phase, and the age of biomedicine and giant multinational pharmaceutical companies who produce both over-the-counter drugs and those only available by prescription from a licensed medical practitioner. The biomedical model is based on a number of assumptions that would not have been recognized in the earliest phases. The first is that the mind and

---

36   W.F. Bynum, *Science and the Practice of Medicine in the Nineteenth Century* (Cambridge, 1994).

37   D. Harley, 'Rhetoric and the Social Construction of Sickness and Healing', *Social History of Medicine*, 3 (1999), p. 416.

body can be treated separately, and that the body can be repaired like a machine, with doctors acting like engineers to mend the dysfunctioning part. The biomedical model thus tends to explain disease in terms of biological changes to the relative neglect of social and psychological factors, linked with the nineteenth-century development of the 'germ theory' that every disease is caused by a specific, identifiable agent (a disease entity).[38] This model has accumulated critics, who claim that the merits of technological interventions are sometimes overplayed, but these came relatively late into the period. At first, there was almost unbounded optimism that the scientific approach (epitomized in the developments in physiology and pharmacology) began in the inter-war years to provide a therapeutic revolution to match that in diagnostics in the late nineteenth century.

The success of the sulphonamides was followed by the development of penicillin and other antibiotics during the Second World War and its aftermath. As Judy Slinn's contribution in Chapter 7 shows, the ability to protect by patent the right to produce these drugs, albeit for a limited period, helped to reinforce the dominant paradigm of the pharmaceutical industry, with a heavy commitment by successful companies to research and development, and patent protection giving monopolistic profits, which in turn helped to finance more research, more new products and a further flow of monopolistic profits. But successful companies also need to exploit the period of patent-protected profit *margins* with high sales to create the profit *streams* to finance more research, so modern drug companies have become increasingly sophisticated in sales and marketing to match their research efforts. Thus, the big drug companies have been in the vanguard of globalization as they have striven to develop and exploit international markets, and have had to restructure on a global scale, with pharmaceutical companies becoming among the largest in the world.

This system is, however, inordinately expensive, and has resulted in an industry where, in 2003, the ten largest international drug firms had profits equal to 14 per cent of sales, compared to a median of 4.6 per cent for other industries.[39] Both Judy Slinn and Stuart Anderson have explored the efforts of the British government to curb the costs of prescription drugs, and the impact on retail chemists. Judy Slinn also explores the tightening of licensing and testing rules to limit the likelihood of another thalidomide scandal, but notes that the more extensive testing and safety rules ensure that the cost of new drug development continues to rise and underwrites the concentration of the production side of the industry and the continuing pressure on the costs of the retailers. That said, the drugs industry in the twenty-first century has been accused of a variety of evils, including:

---

38   S. Nettleton, *Sociology of Health and Illness* (Cambridge, 1996), p. 3.

39   M. Angell, 'Excess in the pharmaceutical industry', *Canadian Medical Association Journal*, 171(12) (7 December 2004), pp. 1451–3; A. Relman, 'Separating continuing medical education form pharmaceutical marketing', *Journal of the American Marketing Association*, 285 (2001), pp. 2009–12.

Overselling its products, of disease mongering, of trying to encourage a therapy culture in society by convincing every human being that for every moment of pain, boredom, distress, anxiety they feel in their life, they should take a pill of some kind.[40]

Such criticism is not, however, unique to the modern drug trade. As this book shows, the production and distribution of commercially produced medicines has aroused considerable controversy over the centuries. There have been enormous changes in the way that drugs have been produced and in the underlying approach to the approach to the diagnosis and treatment of patients, but there are also obvious continuities. Stuart Anderson concludes his essay by drawing attention to the most striking: the human desire to take medicine knows no bounds, and 'the public appetite for unconventional remedies harks back to previous generations, who were so ready to believe the claims of any hawker promoting quack remedies'. In addition, the consumer remains relatively ignorant of the nature and potential effectiveness of the product, and dependent upon the producer's assessment of what the consumer needs. Throughout the period covered by this volume, the retailing channels through which drugs have been sold or otherwise made available have been extremely diverse. Even in the fifth phase, when the marketing of prescription drugs has been dominated by retail chemists, the number of channels through which 'medicines' can be obtained is huge, from the supermarket to the carefully worded advertisement in the Sunday newspaper, from the local market to the Internet. In the face of this variety and range, is it surprising that the retailing of drugs has been such an elusive topic for historians?

---

40 See <www.publications.parliament.uk/pa/cm200304> (accessed March 2005), *House of Commons Hansard Debates for 10 November 2004*, Col. 250WH.

Chapter 2

Apothecaries and the Consumption and Retailing of Medicines in Early Modern London

Patrick Wallis

I do remember an apothecary –
And hereabouts a dwells – which late I noted
In tatter'd weeds, with overwhelming brows,
Culling of simples. Meagre were his looks,
Sharp misery had worn him to the bones,
And in his needy shop a tortoise hung,
An alligator stuff'd, and other skins
Of ill-shap'd fishes; and about his shelves
A beggarly account of empty boxes,
Green earthen pots, bladders and musty seeds,
Remnants of packthread, and old cakes of roses
Were thinly scatter'd to make a show.[1]

The apothecary's shop in *Romeo and Juliet* appears far distant from the clinical, white spaces of modern medicine. It is full of the skins of odd fish, a tortoise, and, most bizarre of all, a stuffed alligator. Empty boxes, pots and ancient cakes of roses are thinly scattered about. As a theatrical device, the disordered appearance of the shop signifies the failing livelihood that induces the apothecary to sell an illegal poison to Romeo. Yet the exotica that seem most distinctive to readers today were indicators of occupation, not the signifiers of dark quackery and imposture that they may appear to be. This chapter explores the contemporary context against which Shakespeare sketched his description of this unhappy Veronese apothecary: medicine in early modern London. It seeks to examine several aspects of the range, depth and organization of medical retailing in the metropolis. Such an exercise necessitates a consideration of demand as much as supply, both because our knowledge of the employment of medicines, particularly across different social levels, remains weak, and because the characteristics of demand impinge heavily on the form taken by the mechanisms of supply, most notably within the retailing relationship. This entanglement of factors shaped the structure and nature of medical retailing in London. Indeed, I would argue that the intimate relationship apparent in the scene

---

1 *Romeo and Juliet*, Act V, Scene 1, lines 37–48.

in *Romeo and Juliet* between dubious consumption, honesty and the apothecary's shop interior – which we might take as a representative of the range of material sites and objects and performative strategies that encircled and accompanied medical work – was an essential element of early modern medicine. Not all early modern consumption was as dangerous as that of young Romeo and his Juliet, but obtaining medicines could none the less be problematic, demanding the cautious assessment and negotiation of price, quality and reputation.

Consumption of all kinds, not just medical, did of course present commonplace risks. These included the obvious dangers of any commercial transaction, particularly the chance that the purchaser might be the victim of fraud and imposture. However, in early modern England, shopping also became a focus of anxieties about illicit or improper association in the less regulated spaces of the shop or market, of dangerous sociability, even improper dalliance. Anxieties about consumption were extended to apply to vendors as much as their products. Shopkeepers' wiles and arts were notorious. His conscience, as the seventeenth-century satirist John Earle put it in his description of the 'apothecary', seemed to be 'a thing, that would have layde upon his hands, and he was forc't to put it off', and all the while, 'He tels you lyes by rote.'[2]

All these generic anxieties applied within medicine. However, the dynamics of health care exaggerated and intensified them to an unusual degree. For few other products were purchasers as ill equipped to judge the quality of the items they received. This was not just the difficulty of determining the quality and proper price of a medicine before buying it from a medical practitioner, grocer or apothecary. The use-to-destruction inherent in the literal consumption of pills, drinks, plasters and unguents left no trace to examine after the fact, while the efficacy of a therapy was – as it remains – notoriously difficult to discern. Little wonder that vernacular medical texts written for a lay readership put such an emphasis on attaining something of the skills of pharmacy. In a similar vein, in 1676 Gideon Harvey set out the wholesale prices that simples and compounds were sold for by druggists in order that his readers could avoid being exploited and judge 'what the *Apothecary* deserve for his pains'.[3]

---

2   J. Earle, *Micro-Cosmographie, or, a Piece of the World Discovered* (London, 1633), sig. M12r. For similar cautions about deceit and fraud, see W. Scott, *An Essay of Drapery, or the Complete Citizen* (London, 1636). In the 1720s, Bernard Mandeville also commented that the shopkeeper: 'By precept, Example and great Application he has learn'd unobserv'd to slide into the inmost Recesses of the Soul' and discovers their 'Blind Side'; 'A Search into the Nature of Society', essay appended to the 1723 edition of *The Fable of the Bees* (Oxford, 1924 [1714]), i, p. 351. General concerns about consumption are discussed in I.W. Archer, 'Material Londoners?', in L.C. Orlin (ed.), *Material London, ca.1600*, (Philadelphia, PA, 2000), pp. 175, 178; L. Hutson, 'The Displacement of the Market in Jacobean City Comedy', *London Journal*, 14 (1989), pp. 3–16; N.C. Cox, *The Complete Tradesman: A Study of Retailing, 1550–1820* (Aldershot, 2000).

3   G. Harvey, *The Family Physician, and the House Apothecary* (London, 1676), sig. A2r.

This focus on the relationship between vendor and purchaser may seem oddly anachronistic for the seventeenth century. In some histories of medicine, and even more so in many modern popular accounts, it is still not uncommon to regard this period as one in which we can, at most, observe the birth pangs of commercial health care amidst a sea of household or non-commercial provision. However, this is seriously to underestimate the degree of engagement of early modern Londoners in commercial medicine. As Charles Webster, Margaret Pelling and Hal Cook amongst others have shown, people living in London in the seventeenth century had a range of sources of medical care.[4] At some point in their lives, many people paid for advice from medical practitioners. The large numbers of medical practitioners in London in this period implies that demand for their services was substantial. That said, medicine, like charity, did still begin at home. After self-treatment, the advice and help that their family and friends could supply was the resource most readily drawn upon by the sick: lay care was the first, and often the last, port of call in many cases. The balance between lay and commercial sources of medical advice is replicated in the treatments employed.

Treatments, be they self-imposed or directed by friends, family or regular or irregular practitioners, frequently drew on domestic resources such as everyday foodstuffs or herbs that were freely available either wild or in gardens; even London contained numerous gardens and green spaces within the city or nearby. There was no obvious division between rich and poor over the use of common herbs and ingredients, although price inevitably instituted a division in the use of exotic ingredients. Many vernacular medical books of the period described the use of locally available plants as simples and in compound remedies.[5] As Mary Fissell has pointed out, numerous of the simples Culpeper described in his *The English Physician Enlarged* were so commonly known that the reader did not even require a description.[6] Similar – if less extensive – instructions were contained in the even more widely circulated form of almanacs, several hundred thousand of which were published each year by the mid-

---

4   M. Pelling and C. Webster, 'Medical Practitioners', in C. Webster (ed.), *Health, Medicine and Mortality in the Sixteenth Century* (Cambridge, 1979), pp. 165–235; C. Webster. 'William Harvey and the Crisis of Medicine in Jacobean England', in J.J. Bylebyl (ed.), *William Harvey and His Age: The Professional and Social Context of the Discovery of the Circulation* (Baltimore, MD, 1979), pp. 1–27; M. Pelling, *The Common Lot: Sickness, Medical Occupations and the Urban Poor in Early Modern England* (London, 1998); M. Pelling, *Medical Conflicts in Early Modern London: Patronage, Physicians, and Irregular Practitioners 1550–1640* (Oxford, 2003); H.J. Cook, *The Decline of the Old Medical Regime in Stuart London* (Ithaca, NY, 1986); H.J. Cook, *Trials of an Ordinary Doctor: Joannes Groenevelt in Seventeenth-century London* (Baltimore, MD, 1994).

5   P. Slack. 'Mirrors of Health and Treasures of Poor Men: The Uses of the Vernacular Medical Literature of Tudor England', in C. Webster (ed.), *Health, Medicine and Mortality in the Sixteenth Century* (Cambridge, 1979), pp. 237–73.

6   M.E. Fissell, *Patients, Power and the Poor in Eighteenth-century Bristol* (Cambridge, 1991), p. 40.

seventeenth century.[7] Medical practitioners might themselves make use of remedies based on domestic resources rather than arcane or exotic ingredients. In treating sore breasts, for example, the irregular practitioner Mrs Fletcher used either a medicine of saffron, white wine and thistle, or one of the herbs smallage and parsley, with white bread and milk, ingredients more common in the kitchen or garden than the grocer's or apothecary's shop.[8]

However, these local sources were regularly combined or supplemented with medicinal simples and compound drugs obtained from apothecaries, druggists, proprietary medicine sellers, distillers, herb-women or surgeons. There was nothing to prevent laymen using the entire range of learned, commercially produced medicines under their own direction, and this, it seems, is what they did. Indeed, it is virtually impossible to draw a line between 'lay' or 'folk' herbal remedies and those of learned medicine.[9] The extensive and elaborate medical manufactures carried out by Lady Grace Mildmay in sixteenth-century Northamptonshire, for example, rivalled those of a well-equipped apothecary.[10] More commonplace examples of this overlap can be found in the numerous recipes that circulated widely in Stuart England. During the plague of 1607, for example, when Maria Thynne wrote from Wiltshire to advise her husband in London of 'an approved medicine', the home-made medicine she described relied on shop-bought ingredients, being a mix of dragon water with some theriac or mithridatium and some 'redding', a red ochre used for marking livestock. In addition, she wrote, as a preservative against the plague he was to eat three or four rue leaves put into some raisins every morning – this time a medicine which used just common grocery wares.[11] This mixed approach can also be seen in other cases, such as the orders Daniel Fleming put in several times in the 1660s and 1670s for apothecaries' simples from Kendal – galingale, cubebs, cardamoms and melilot flowers – in order to make up aqua mirabilis at his Westmorland home.[12]

As the widespread communication of prescriptions suggests, information on making and using these remedies passed freely between commercial practitioners and laymen.[13] Alongside such direct person-to-person transmissions of knowledge,

---

7   B. Capp, *English Almanacs, 1500–1800: Astrology and the Popular Press* (Ithaca, NY, 1979).

8   She was examined by the College of Physicians in 1613: London, Royal College of Physicians, MS Annals, iii, 51 (hereafter abbreviated to CPL, Annals).

9   Fissell, *Patients*, p. 38.

10   L.A. Pollock, *With Faith and Physic: The Life of a Tudor Gentlewoman, Lady Grace Mildmay 1552–1620* (London, 1993), pp. 98–103.

11   A.D. Wall (ed.), *Two Elizabethan Women: Correspondence of Joan and Maria Thynne 1575–1611* (Wiltshire Record Society, Vol. 38, 1983), p. 36.

12   J.R. McGrath (ed.), *The Flemings in Oxford: Vol. 1, 1650–1680* (Oxford Historical Society, Vol. 154, 1903) pp. 449, 462, 475, notes 6–475. Like cardamom, galingale and cubeb were both imported from the East Indies (*OED*), however melilot was grown in England in the sixteenth century; M. Grieve, *A Modern Herbal* (London, 1974).

13   The letters of John Symcotts offer good examples of such interchanges, with Symcotts receiving recipes as well as sending them; F.N.L. Poynter and W.J. Bishop, *A Seventeenth*

medical books were widely bought, and when the opportunity arose, there seems to have been a general interest in observing medicines and their manufacture, which was closely related to the contemporary fascination with natural history and curiosities. Witnessing the making of theriac in Venice was a regular part of travellers' itineraries. John Evelyn, who had a particular interest in such matters, noted a similar spectacle in London in 1659:

> I went to see the severall *Drougs* for the confection of *Treacle* [theriac], *Diascordium* &
> other *Electuaries* which an ingenious *Apothecarie* had not onely prepared, & ranged upon
> a large & very long table, but covered every ingredient with a sheete of paper, on which
> was very lively painted the thing, in miniature very well to the life, were it plant, flower,
> Animal, or other exotic drough.[14]

In parallel with the diffusion of information about learned medicine ran the diffusion of demand for its drugs, a process already well advanced by the start of the seventeenth century.

As this indicates, some laymen and women were undoubtedly highly skilled in physic, but domestic medicine did not necessarily require a high level of medical knowledge. As is the case today, self-treatment did not require much understanding of learned diagnostics or therapeutics. The most obvious example of unlearned self-treatment is the use of proprietary medicines, with their applicability to numerous ailments. Apothecaries' receipts seem to support this. They offer a picture of the sick often buying pre-made medicines for commonplace purposes – compound drugs described simply as purges, cordials, vomits and the like – and only occasionally concerning themselves with the particular ingredients of a medicine or purchasing simples to use in home-made therapies.

Medicines named for their application rather than their ingredients were qualitatively little different to branded proprietary medicines. Arguably, proprietary medicines were simply a specialized version of such compositions: for example, the proper name of Daffy's Elixir was 'Elixir Salutis', a generic name for a health-giving drink. However, using medicines was in itself a source of knowledge about them. From the experience of purchasing non-specific medicines, laymen and women might gain the knowledge to make a more refined and particular choice in the future. Something of this process can be seen in the experience of one Londoner from Ave Maria Lane, who came to Henry Dickman's shop in 1612 asking for 'vomiting cakes', and was then convinced by Dickman's apprentice that he would be better off with 'tabulas stibiatus' (an antimony preparation).[15] In this case, Dickman's apprentice

Century Doctor and His Patients: John Symcotts, 1592?–1662 (Streatley, 1951), pp. 11–12, 21–2.

14   J. Evelyn, *The Diary of John Evelyn* (Oxford, 1955), iii, pp. 235–6. Evelyn had also seen theriac being made in Venice in 1645, and seems to have been generally interested in medicines, taking a course in chemistry in Paris under le Febvre, who later became Charles II's chemist; ibid., ii, p. 451; ibid., iii, p. 373–4.

15   CPL, Annals, iii, p. 40.

was manipulating a commercial transaction in directing the man towards a specific remedy, but he was also simultaneously creating a more informed customer.

Not all treatments, it should be emphasized, involved taking medicines. In 1604, John Saunders, agent to the Somerset gentleman John Trevelyan, wrote to explain to his employer that his recent silence was because of a sickness about which he had obtained 'the opinion of a phisition touching the kind & cause of my disease (but have taken no phisycke)'.[16] The importance of the non-naturals, particularly diet, meant that giving treatment might involve manipulating aspects of lifestyle or advising the use or avoidance of certain foods and drinks rather than employing drugs.[17] Because many surviving casebooks are composed of collections of prescriptions, they can give a misleading impression of practitioners' uses of medicines. When fuller material survives, a different picture can emerge. Although he was not perhaps representative, the astrological physician Simon Forman prescribed therapies (including bloodletting) for only 35 per cent of cases, mostly purges or vomits, and only 12 per cent received a potion or pill.[18] Drugs might be consciously avoided because of worry about the dangers of interfering with nature. For example, Sir Justinian Isham recounted to his friend Bishop Duppa how, when a violent flux had affected his family, 'we only tooke some Cordialls at the beginning not daring any way to stop what Nature (though very violently) drave forth'.[19] Bishop Duppa was himself an avoider of medicines, commenting at one point that the alkermes he had been advised to take 'is yet a stranger to me', although he commended the use of Jesuit's bark against epidemic fever in 1658.[20] The physician and philosopher John Locke noted one case of prodigious abstinence: Alice George, a poor woman of 108 years who claimed to have taken physic only once, 40 years before, a pennyworth of Jalap which had wrought sufficiently to remove her vapours ever since.[21]

For the many who did resort to taking medicines bought from apothecaries and their peers, the financial costs could vary greatly. Surviving apothecaries' bills sometimes reveal the consumption of large volumes of drugs over short periods. Between 28 August and 30 October 1633, an apothecary supplied one Mr Wimkells with 31 items at a total of £3 3s. 6d. (an average of 2s. ½d. a piece). The medicines included diets, cordial potions, purges and plasters, and varied in price from 8d. for a 'fume for the head' to 2s. 6d. for 'a bottle of diet [drink]'. Wimkell's bill evidently reflects the course of a single illness; in contrast, the same anonymous apothecary

---

16   M. Siraut (ed.), *The Trevelyan Letters to 1840* (*Somerset Record Society*, Vol. 80, 1990), p. 68.

17   H.J. Cook, 'Good Advice and Little Medicine: The Professional Advice of Early Modern English Physicians', *Journal of British Studies*, 33 (1994), pp. 14–17.

18   L. Kassell, 'Simon Forman's Philosophy of Medicine: Medicine, Astrology and Alchemy in London, c. 1580–1611' (DPhil. Thesis, University of Oxford, 1997), pp. 152–53.

19   G. Isham (ed.), *The Correspondence of Bishop Brian Duppa and Sir Justinian Isham 1650–1660* (Northamptonshire Record Society, Vol. 17, 1951), p. 160.

20   Ibid., pp. 162–3.

21   P. Laslett, *The World We Have Lost* (London, 1965), p. 110.

drew up an account for one Mr Street which shows the requirements of a household over a longer period, the eight months between October 1637 and June 1638. The medicines were much the same as supplied to Mr Wimkells: cordial potions at 2s. 6d. a dose, opening pills at 2d. a piece, juleps at different prices. At the close of the account, the total was £4 17s., for which 37 batches of medicines (some of two or more doses) had been supplied for the use of Street's wife, his daughter, a Mistress Laurence and a Mistress Margaret (averaging 2s. 7d. an item).[22] The medicines used in navy service could be a little cheaper: from March to September 1653, the medicines for 42 sick and wounded English seamen cost £88 18s. 7d., or just under £2 a head.[23] Elsewhere, bills totalling several pounds seem commonplace: the Earl of Huntingdon was sent a bill by a Loughborough apothecary, Mr Cowper, in 1644 for £3 18s. 11d.[24] Similarly, in 1639, Culpepper Clapham's annual bill (for October 1639–October 1640) to the Earl of Bath came to £4 13s. 2d. for 46 items (average 1s. 10d. an item), including two fees for a day's attendance at 10s., and several small quantities of exotics, compounds and simples: 1 oz of 'troches Alhandal' for 2s. 6d.; 2 oz of 'syrup of stacados'; 1 oz of 'sem foeniculi dulci' for 3d.; oil of cloves at 6d.[25] Thirty years later, accounts were much the same. Even the prices were unchanged – although inflation meant that in real terms they had fallen: for example, Samuel Barnard's bill for 49 medicines supplied between 23 December 1675 and 2 February 1676 to Major Gunstone came to £5 9s. (average 2s. 3d. an item), whilst Mr Fleming charged Mayhew Watts £2 4s. 6d. for 24 medicines from 25 December 1674 to June 1676 (average 1s. 10d. an item).[26]

The costs of commercial medicines set out in these bills are similar to those given in the College of Physicians' records. Really large charges were normally reserved for cures involving advice as well as medicines. Cures costing several or even tens of pounds appear regularly in the archives. For example, the apothecary Henry Dickman charged £4 for one cure and £20 for another in the 1630s, while Richard Mason charged £20 for a cure of dropsy in 1640.[27] For these large sums, it is worth emphasizing, patients might receive a great deal over an extended period,

---

22 London, Public Record Office, E 101/634/5 (hereafter PRO).

23 PRO, *Calendar of State Papers Domestic, 1653–4* (London, 1875), pp. 178–9.

24 Huntingdon Library, California, HAF Box 15 (32). I am grateful to Dr Andrew Boyle for this reference.

25 T. Gray, ed., *Devon Household Accounts, 1627–59*, 2 vols (Devon and Cornwall Record Society, New Series, Vols 38–9, 1995–96), pp. xxxix, 307–8. 'Stacados' is Stoechados or Stechados, or French lavender; 'sem foeniculi' is fennel seed; 'troches Alhandal' are based on coloquintida, oil of roses, gum Arabic, tragacanth and bdellium: a recipe is included in: College of Physicians, *Pharmacopoeia Londinensis* (London, 1618).

26 London, Society of Apothecaries, E7 (Samuel Barnard to Major Gunstone, 1676); British Library, MS Add. 38854, f. 190. Inflation seems to have continued in London in the second half of the seventeenth century, diverging from the rest of the country; J.P. Boulton, 'Food Prices and the Standard of Living in London in the "Century of Revolution", 1580–1700', *Economic History Review*, 53 (2000), pp. 455–492.

27 CPL, Annals, iii, pp. 274, 489, 513–14.

including all drugs, visits, and sometimes even accommodation. As the surgeon Edward Harryes protested when John Smyth sought to avoid paying him the £20 he owed for a cure for syphilis, he had both laid out money for all the necessaries, 'and tooke greate paynes with him and bestowed much tyme and was verie industrious and Carefull about the same'.[28]

It is easiest to get a sense of the amounts spent by aristocratic and gentry families for whom household accounts and bills most often survive. Their wealth, and possibly also their education and social status, made them the most likely group to use commercial medicine on a regular basis. None the less, medicine was commercialized for a much broader section of society than the gentry alone. Medicines ranged from a penny to a couple of shillings in price. In the 1630s and 1640s, usable quantities of theriac were available for a penny even as far away from London as Devon.[29] These are sums that members of the middling sort and artisans – for whom it is particularly difficult to find evidence – could have afforded. Even some who were not likely to have had much surplus money – maids, servants, wet nurses, gardeners – do appear as the patients of apothecaries in the records that survive from the London College of Physicians' attempts to prevent illicit medical practice, though the presence of servants raises the question of whether their masters or mistresses, or local authorities, may have paid.[30] The clergyman and astrological physician Richard Napier treated a similarly wide range of patients in the 1610s and 1620s, including many servants and artisans. His fees reflected this, beginning as low as 12d. Most of his patients paid two to four shillings, including the medicines they were given, with members of the nobility paying substantially more.[31] Despite such sliding charges, funding treatment, particularly over a long period, might have serious consequences for the marginally prosperous, who were sometimes willing to spend more than they could afford on such important needs.[32]

Undoubtedly, the prices of such medicines remained substantial or impossible amounts for the poor, particularly when they might need to be taken repeatedly. Even a pill costing a penny becomes far less affordable when it took a course of 12 to treat a sickness. The extended credit common to the economy facilitated this to some extent, but the poor might be able to raise money for expensive medical care from guilds, charitable sources or parish relief, or obtain care for free from philanthropic physicians (although, outside of plague times, London had no town physicians, unlike Chester, Ipswich and Newcastle).[33] For many, though, medicines

---

28   PRO, REQ 2/307/38, f. 2.

29   CPL, Annals, iii, pp. 312; *Devon Household Accounts*, i, p. 54.

30   CPL, Annals, iii, pp. 120, 165, 210, 443.

31   M. MacDonald, *Mystical Bedlam: Madness, Anxiety, and Healing in Seventeenth-century England* (Cambridge, 1981), p. 51 and note 118.

32   Pelling, *Common Lot*, p. 64.

33   Ibid., pp. 83-4, 88; A. Wear, 'Caring for the Sick Poor in St Bartholomew's Exchange: 1580–1676', in R. Porter and W. Bynum (eds), *Living and Dying in London* (*Medical History*, Supplement 11, 1991), pp. 49–51; I.W. Archer, *The Pursuit of Stability: Social Relations in Elizabethan London* (Cambridge, 1991), pp. 193–4. Parish provision is particularly noticeable

must have been restricted to what they could put together with their own resources and ingredients, or perhaps the help of someone in the neighbourhood. Exotic and imported simples would remain firmly out of the reach of the poor, as underlined by their inclusion in the preservatives for the 'richer sort' but not in the general 'inward medicines' given in the *Directions* printed by the College of Physicians during plagues.[34]

With these exceptions in mind, it is possible to speak of a highly developed commercial side to medicine in London throughout the seventeenth century. Large numbers of apothecaries were supplying significant and increasing volumes of medicines to the gentry and middling sort, both on their own account and on the prescription of medical practitioners. If this activity still often excluded the poor, it should not be dismissed as a relatively minor or irrelevant phenomenon. For many people, health care was dependent on the services of apothecaries as practitioners, advisers and suppliers of medicines.

Thus far we have emphasized the use and availability of Galenic medicines. These were, of course, only one aspect of medical treatment. Outside orthodox medical circles, some healers offered religious, magical or astrological solutions which might require very different processes or practices, although the scale of religious healing is less well documented in England than in other European countries.[35] Alternative medical theories were also expanding in number and variety in this period. It should be emphasized that whilst often being fiercely critical of Galenic pharmacy as well as theory, most of those who advocated rival medical ideas, whether Paracelsian, Helmontian or the various empirical or mechanical medical philosophies of the later seventeenth and eighteenth century, served in practice to extend and expand upon the ramshackle pharmacopoeia that was the legacy of several millennia of accumulation.[36] At most, these heterodox medical practitioners shifted the emphasis between substances, or added new ones, notably chemical essences and extracts, that presented many of the same issues of danger, dirt and value that were apparent around more established medicines. Individual efforts to refine the therapeutic armoury seem to have had little overall effect in the absence of any regulatory agency that could enforce such reforms. It need hardly be stated that modern pharmacy faces many of

during epidemics: London, Guildhall Library, MS 4525/4, ff. 11, 43–4, 52 (hereafter GL); University of London, Centre for Metropolitan History, Records of Churchwardens' Accounts. It might be less substantial at other times; St Brides' churchwardens made very few payments, and then only a few pence to pay for children's physic: GL MS 6552/1, ff. 228v, 247v. I am grateful to Dr Paul Griffiths for this last reference.

34   College of Physicians, *Certaine Necessary Directions for the Prevention and Cure of the Plague* (London, 1665), paras xiii, xvii.

35   See, in particular, D. Gentilcore, *Healers and Healing in Early Modern Italy* (Manchester, 1998).

36   A. Wear. 'Medical Practice in Late Seventeenth- and Early Eighteenth-century England: Continuity and Union', in R. French and A. Wear (eds), *The Medical Revolution of the Seventeenth Century* (Cambridge, 1989), pp. 294–320.

the same problems of proving that its profits are justified and that its medicines are safe and effective.

Demonstrating that demand for commercially provided medicines was widespread during the sixteenth and seventeenth centuries does not, of course, preclude the possibility, or indeed the likelihood, that the scale of demand changed substantially over this period; given the broader changes that were occurring in the English economy, we should expect some such shift to be occurring. None the less, we must be cautious about leaping to easy conclusions about how dramatic this transformation was, and even more hesitant in labelling particular watersheds in the growth of medical commerce. London's significance as the nation's greatest centre of consumption was long established by the sixteenth century.[37] The extensive early reliance of Londoners on the commercial market for obtaining even the most basic commodities was mirrored in their consumption of medicine. Hence, while much has been made of an expansion in consumption of medical services in England from the Restoration into the eighteenth century, there is relatively little clear evidence about the timing and scale of shifts in supply or demand within London.[38] Many of the most prominent changes were oriented more towards provincial rather than metropolitan consumers, such as the enthusiastic adoption of print advertising by proprietary medicine sellers, the rise of spa towns, and the creation of dispensaries and voluntary hospitals. As this list of developments indicates, certain aspects of medicine may well have experienced a growth in consumption as part of a widening of access to leisure and luxury commodities and a desire to emulate the elite. None the less, great care needs to be taken in interpreting indications of changes in the *way* medicines and medical care were supplied as proof of shifts in the *volume* consumed.

Establishing any detailed measurement of the scale and rate of change of the consumption of medicines in early modern London is certainly very difficult, although Ian Mortimer's recent success in charting growing demand in seventeenth-century Kent may yet be replicable for the city.[39] Some indications can be inferred from other sources. The presence of significant numbers of medical practitioners in the city, estimated at 1 practitioner to every 400 individuals in the late sixteenth century, implies that they must have obtained a range of drugs, as well as other therapies, from somewhere, and that there was sufficient demand to provide them with some employment – although many were, of course, combining medicine with

---

37 F.J. Fisher, *London and the English Economy, 1500–1700* (London, 1990).

38 G. Holmes, *Augustan England: Professions, State and Society, 1680–1730* (London, 1982); I. Loudon, *Medical Care and the General Practitioner 1750–1850* (Oxford, 1986); A. Digby, *Making a Medical Living: Doctors and Patients in the English Market for Medicine, 1720–1911* (Cambridge, 1994).

39 I.J.F. Mortimer, 'Medical Assistance to the Dying in Provincial Southern England, c 1570–1720' (PhD Thesis, University of Exeter, 2004). Mortimer has also published an article summarizing his findings: 'The Triumph of the Doctors: Medical Assistance to the Dying c. 1570–1720', *Transactions of the Royal Historical Society*, 15(1) (December 2005), pp. 97–116.

other trades.[40] Numbers of apothecaries can only be roughly estimated before 1617. On its establishment, the Society incorporated 122 freemen by charter, although a number of these did not in practice join the new company. By the end of 1620, another 52 apothecaries had joined under the terms of the charter that obliged apothecaries, even if not named, to enter the new company. Using estimates for survival of freemen and counts of subsequent new entrants, the number of apothecaries can be calculated for the century. Over the seventeenth century, absolute numbers of apothecaries in London grew steadily, but relative to the city population, they remained at just over 1 per 2,000 inhabitants.

Averages of this kind do not properly convey the character of the structure and organization of the retailing system through which Londoners obtained their medicines. Margaret Pelling has shown that barber surgeons were relatively dispersed across the built area of the city. Apothecaries, however, were far more clustered, reflecting their intimate connection with the mercantile sector of the city; they had, after all, been part of the Grocers' Company until 1617. The main area where apothecaries were found was Cheapside and Bucklersbury, the street that ran from the west end of Cheapside to the Poultry. This had been the centre of the trade by 1300, at the latest. In the 1660s, 1 in 5 householders in the small parishes of St Benet and St Stephen Walbrook were druggists or apothecaries, and nearly all of these were based on or immediately adjacent to Cheapside itself.[41] This remarkably dense huddle of apothecaries led one Venetian visitor to note that a quarter of the city was 'full of apothecaries' shops on either side of the way'.[42] Businesses in this area often persisted beyond the working lifetime of a single craftsman. In one case, a shop in Bucklersbury passed through the hands of at least four apothecaries, beginning with George Haughton in 1617, and then moving via William Shambrooke and John Lorymer to the partnership of Zachary Bertrand and Thomas Child, who would rebuild it after the Great Fire.[43] The poor eastern suburb of St Botolph Aldgate offers a striking contrast, with only two apothecaries known to be based there during the century: John Banner at the Three Cranes in the Minories, and John Whyt who lived in Ship Alley. Similarly, few apothecaries seem to have been based in the poorer parishes along the river.[44]

40　Pelling and Webster, 'Medical Practitioners', p. 188. This figure includes apothecaries (100 of 500 practitioners in the city). If apothecaries are excluded, the figure falls to 1 practitioner per 500 individuals.

41　D. Keene, 'The Walbrook Study: A Summary Report' (typescript, Institute of Historical Research, University of London, 1987), p. 13.

42　PRO, *Calendar of the State Papers and Manuscripts Relating to English Affairs, existing in the Archives and Collections of Venice*, 38 vols, (London, 1864–1940), Vol. for 1617–19, p. 257.

43　D. Keene and V. Harding, *Historical Gazetteer of London before the Great Fire: Part I, Cheapside* (Cambridge, 1987), Part 105/26E.

44　M. Carlin, 'Historical Gazetteer of London before the Great Fire: St Botolph Aldgate' (typescript, Institute of Historical Research, University of London, London, 1987), Parts 43/7/9Aii, 43/7/7A.

Cheapside was not the only location where apothecaries were found.[45] The distribution of apothecaries matched the pattern of wealth across the city itself, so that they remained most densely clustered in the areas where the richer citizens of the city and its visitors were found. By the 1640s, apothecaries were already established in force along the main thoroughfares to the west of the city which ran toward Westminster, such as the Strand, and on Fleet Street, Holborn and around the Old Bailey, drawn by the demand for medicines from the wealthy western parts of the city that were growing rapidly under the influence of the court.[46] A number had also established shops in the east of the city, particularly on major roads in the parishes of All Hallow's Staining and St Andrew Undershaft, long an area where apothecaries had been based. In the 1690s and before, clusters can also be found in Cornhill and on London Bridge.[47]

From within these shops, London's apothecaries met the medical demands of a wide swathe of London. As the connection between apothecaries and wealth apparent in this mapping exercise indicates, they were most concerned about drawing in customers from the middling and upper tiers of society. None the less, their products reached a broader cross-section of the metropolis than this might at first suggest. This is not simply because apothecaries, while marketing themselves primarily towards the well-to-do, do not seem to have excluded the poor: business was business, and the reputation they gained as physicians of the poor, while often grossly exaggerated by later historians, has some basis in reality. Beyond this direct relationship, less visible connections of supply tied apothecaries as retailers, wholesalers and manufacturers of medical products with an extensive portion of the medical practitioners who sought patients within all quarters of the city, both rich and poor.

Just as apothecaries combined the production and sale of medicines with other aspects of medical practice throughout the sixteenth and seventeenth centuries, it was common for other kinds of medical practitioners to supply medicines as part of the cure. This elision of the traditional intellectual boundaries that cut across medicine could produce conflict, particularly at an institutional level. However, commercial linkages of supply and demand held across even the fiercest political fault lines. Thus, many practitioners obtained the drugs they themselves gave patients from apothecaries who acted as medical wholesalers. For example, the irregular Dutch physician Dr Arnold Boet, had Susan Lyon, widow of the apothecary William Reeve, and her new husband make up medicines that 'he himself bought ... to sell'.[48] Others – including a number of fellows of the College of Physicians – organized or supervised their manufacture personally. Indeed, this practice was

---

45 R. MacKenney, *Tradesmen and Traders: The World of the Guilds in Venice and Europe, c.1250–c.1650* (London, 1993), p. 89.

46 PRO, SP/16/539, Part 1, Section 72, f. 155; M. Pelling, 'Appearance and Reality: Barber-surgeons, the Body and Disease', in A.L. Beier and R. Finlay (eds), *London, 1500–1700* (London, 1986), p. 85.

47 C. Spence, *London in the 1690s: A Social Atlas* (London, 2000), p. 142.

48 CPL, Annals, iii, 329 (16 February 1631), 349 (4 July 1632).

to prove controversial at times in the seventeenth century, particularly when some physicians began to extol its virtues for the intellectual and practical advantages it could offer to them as experimental philosophers.

The demand for medicines was therefore met from a wide variety of sources. The systems for the supply and production of medicines necessary to sustain this supply at the point of consumption were not restricted to the individual workshops of apothecaries, but had developed to form a web of manufacturing and wholesaling medical producers in a structure characteristic of artisan craft production.[49] Whilst the individual production of drugs on demand was still presented as the ideal in corporate regulations and medical writing, in practice manufactured medicines were often sold in bulk by apothecaries and other producers. Some apothecaries had become little more than retailers, relying on others to carry out the majority of the processing of medicines. Others specialized in particular parts of manufacturing. This kind of specialization was well suited to a medical system utilizing the traditional pharmacopoeia. When the official listing of authorized medicines was published by the College of Physicians in 1618 to accompany the establishment of the Society of Apothecaries, it described 936 recipes using 1,190 simples.[50] However, even this catalogue of therapeutic substances was meant to restrict apothecaries only: physicians could and did create new medicines or vary old ones as they thought necessary. For any one apothecary, even possessing the ingredients to produce every medicine was therefore difficult. Having the time, capital and labour to engage in the production of more than a selection of the more complicated medicines was even more unlikely.

The consequences that this diversity of ingredients and prescriptions had for retailing and supply is evident in surviving shop inventories from the later part of the seventeenth century. Eight apparently complete inventories for London apothecaries' shops in the 1660s and 1670s offer a privileged window on their trade.[51] The first impression is of the sheer variety of different drugs and simples that apothecaries sold. Three of the eight kept forty or fifty different commodities, but the remaining

---

49 M. Sonenscher, *Work and Wages: Natural Law, Politics and the Eighteenth-century French Trades* (Cambridge, 1991); M. Sonenscher, *The Hatters of Eighteenth-century France* (Berkeley, CA, 1987); J.R. Farr, *Artisans in Europe, 1300–1914* (Cambridge, 2000).

50 G. Urdang (ed.), *Pharmacopoeia Londinensis of 1618, Reproduced in Facsimile* (Madison, WI, 1944), p. 34.

51 The inventories come from three sources. In the case of those surviving in the probate records of the prerogative court of Canterbury and the Orphans Court of the City of London, the inventories were drawn up after death. The remaining four were drawn up while the subject was alive as part of debt cases heard before the Mayor Court of the City of London: PRO, PROB 4/2838 (William Clement, 1673), PROB 4/11990 (Richard [Didier?] Foucant, 1666), PROB 4/17465 (Christopher Gore, 1666); City of London Record Office, London (hereafter CLRO), Orphans Inventory, 1050 (Henry Atkinson, 1675); CLRO, Mayors Court, MC1/177.141 (William Wade, 1671), MC1/199B.38–40 (William Townson, 1682), MC1/230.154 (James Gopp, 1676), MC1/189.161 (William Ford, 1674).

five all stocked more than a hundred, and two had more than two hundred.[52] (The sheer labour of recording so many items perhaps helps explain the scarcity of such inventories.) Roughly two-thirds of the items these eight inventories together contain can be identified with some degree of certainty. This identified portion consists of variations around 279 individual substances, each of which was available prepared in a variety of ways – as syrups, seeds, spirits – confirming the impression of diversity given by the number of items.[53] A few commodities are commonplace, appearing in several of the inventories, and often in more than one batch. Sandalwood (both red and white) is the most common, featuring 18 times, as the apothecaries frequently had several separate batches of it. Aloes, turpentine, coral, vitriol, hartshorn and mastic are also frequently listed. But only two substances, mastic and coral, are present in all eight inventories. Over two hundred items only appear only once or twice, kept by just one or two of these apothecaries. On the evidence of these listings, at least, there seems to have been no large core of medicinal substances that every apothecary would possess.

This elaborate combination of medical, manufacturing and commercial roles may seem a long way from the shabby chaos of the Veronese apothecary's shop with which we began. Yet the characteristics highlighted by Shakespeare in *Romeo and Juliet* were, in a less impoverished form, shared by most apothecaries' shops. Apothecaries were, as the enumeration of *materia medica* just given suggests, faced by a significant practical problem of storage, compounded by the valuable and sometimes corrosive and dangerous qualities of the substances involved. However, they were also faced by a broader set of culturally constructed problems that derived from negative perceptions of their product, profits and piety.

Medicines were, for many contemporaries, a highly suspect category of goods, in a marketplace packed with dubious products. The lists of medical ingredients that spread colourfully over the pages of learned and popular texts were a thicket of dangers for the consumer. Pharmacy remained entwined in a close relationship with poison; accidental as much as deliberate harm was a chance accepted in any treatment; fraudulent substitutions or adulterations were easy to make and almost impossible for even experts to spot, while the bills patients received seemed often to bear no relation to the price of the ingredients. The problems of identifying even unprepared herbs or other drugs were significant. The ambiguous and indiscernible identity of medicines can be measured by their use as a forceful political analogy by Queen Elizabeth, who compared her advisers hiding the harmfulness of monopolies from her to physicians gilding drugs before administering them.[54]

---

52   These figures do include a limited amount of double counting, as separate batches of the same commodity often had distinct values (often due to age). However, this represented only a small proportion of the total.

53   The main sources for identifying items in the inventories were the *Oxford English Dictionary*, the 1618 second edition of the *Pharmacopoeia Londinensis*, and Grieve, *Modern Herbal*.

54   D.H. Sacks. 'The Countervailing of Benefits: Monopoly, Liberty and Benevolence in Elizabethan England', in D. Hoak (ed.), *Tudor Political Culture* (Cambridge, 1995), pp.

This combination of commercial problems, essentially rooted in consumers' unwillingness, often with good reason, to trust apothecaries in a weakly regulated market, induced apothecaries to invest considerable resources in placating the worries of their customers. Apothecaries' shops, like those of goldsmiths, were marked out from the majority of retailing spaces by the large effort they made to convey messages about their trustworthiness, skill and reliability through shop design. They were in the vanguard of a wave of developments in retail that occurred in the late sixteenth and seventeenth centuries. One notable aspect of this was the large numbers of elaborate painted drug jars that apothecaries displayed in their shops. Another was the collections of exotica – fish, serpents, crocodiles and the like – that some had on display. Together with other technologies of display, these helped make apothecaries' shops into carefully constructed and distinctive retail sites.[55]

Metropolitan medicine in early modern London cannot be conveniently sliced into tidy sectors: production sat cheek by jowl with retailing; customers might seek to purchase anything from a full package of healing services to a few ingredients for a remedy they were making up and administering in their own home. Apothecaries' shops formed one of the central arenas in which this disparate medical economy operated. However, if the medical economy cannot easily be parsed, neither can medicine be conveniently separated from other areas of economic life. Thus, it is important to recognize that apothecaries – and their rivals and peers in other parts of medicine – participated in the development of some of the distinctive devices of 'modern' commerce and retailing, such as shop design and advertising, that would come to be of ever-increasing importance in subsequent centuries. It is ironic that one of the apothecaries' lineal successors, the modern pharmacist, has developed a commercial style that stands at arm's length from other branches of retail, seeking an iconographic alliance with the hygienic spaces of the clinic rather than the glistening fabric of the arcade, for the pharmacies of early modern London were among the most vigorous of commercial innovators of the period.

278–9.

55 P. Wallis, 'Medicines for London: The Trade, Regulation and Lifecycle of London Apothecaries, c.1610–c.1670' (DPhil. Thesis, University of Oxford, 2002), pp. 293–322.

Chapter 3

Medical Advertising in the Popular Press: Almanacs and the Growth of Proprietary Medicines

Louise Hill Curth

Introduction

The history of retailing is a topic that has attracted increasing attention over the past two decades. Much of this has focused on the role that distribution and consumption have played in the evolution of modern economic and cultural systems, generally based on documentation such as trade reports, articles in the trade press, business records or other archival material.[1] Unfortunately, there are relatively few surviving sources of this kind for the early modern period. As a result, the retailing of early proprietary drugs in England is a topic that has received little serious academic attention.[2] While some inventories or other merchants' accounts have survived, they omit any references to stocks of proprietary drugs. There are a large number of contemporary advertisements for proprietary drugs, however, that provide insights into the way in which they were distributed and sold.

This chapter will focus on the distribution of proprietary drugs in the seventeenth century, an area that has been comparatively ignored by recent scholarship. The majority of modern studies on the growth of 'medical consumerism' generally link it to the 'consumer revolution' of the eighteenth century.[3] As numerous studies by Roy

---

1   S. O'Connell and D. Porter, 'Cataloguing Mail Order's Archives', *Business Archives: Sources and History*, 80 (2000), pp. 44–55; G. Shaw, A. Alexander, J. Benson and J. Jones, 'Structural and Spatial Trends in British Retailing: The Importance of Firm-level Studies', *Business History*, 40(4) (1998), pp. 79–83; A. Godley and S.R. Fletcher, 'International Retailing in Britain, 1850–1994', *The Service Industries Journal*, 21 (2001), pp. 31–46; S. Strasser, G. McGovern and M. Judt (eds), *Getting and Spending: European and American Consumer Societies in the Twentieth Century* (London, 1998); J. Benson, *The Rise of Consumer Society in Britain, 1880–1980* (London, 1994); J. Benson and G. Shaw, The *Evolution of Retail Systems, c. 1800–1914* (London, 1992).

2   The main exception are apothecaries' records, which are discussed in Chapter 1.

3   See, for example, B. Coward, *Social Change and Continuity in Early Modern England 1550–1750* (London, 1988), pp. 79–81; J. DeVries, 'Between purchasing power and the world of goods: Understanding the household economy in early modern England', in P. Sharpe (ed.), *Women's Work: The English Experience 1650–1914* (London, 1998), p. 215; P. Langford, *A Polite and Commercial People* (Oxford, 1989), p. 2; R. Porter, 'Consumption: disease of the consumer society?', in J. Brewer and R. Porter (ed.) *Consumption and the World*

Porter have shown, this was an important period in the commercialization of English medicine, where 'the contemporary prominence of hypochondria', aided by shrewd and highly visible publicity of their benefits, led to a dramatic rise in proprietary medicines.[4] Whilst not disputing that medicine became increasingly commercialized in the eighteenth century, this section will illustrate the important changes occurring in the previous century. The evidence from advertisements in almanacs, which were cheap, annual publications distributed on a national basis, clearly show that proprietary drugs were being promoted and distributed to a national and even international groups of consumers by the second half of the seventeenth century.

In order to provide a context for the remainder of this chapter, the first section will provide an overview of the genre of almanacs and the role they played in early modern advertised. The second section will focus on the types of pre-made, pre-packaged and branded proprietary medicines that were advertised in the popular press. This will be followed by a discussion of the way in which these products were distributed in late seventeenth-century London, the provinces and abroad.

Almanacs

Although there has been a recent, growing interest in early modern advertising, most studies have tended to focus on eighteenth-century newspapers, although an increasing number have utilized a collection of some five hundred medical handbills at the British Library.[5] This is a positive step in the study of early modern medical

---

of Goods (London, 1993), p. 63; N. McKendrick, 'The Consumer Revolution of Eighteenth-century England' in N. McKendrick, J. Brewer and J.H. Plumb (eds), *The Birth of a Consumer Society: The Commercialization of Eighteenth Century England* (Bloomington, IN, 1982), p. 9.

   4   See, for example, R. Porter, *Health for Sale: Quackery in England 1660–1850* (Manchester, 1989); D. and R. Porter, *Patient's Progress: Doctors and Doctoring in Eighteenth-century England* (Oxford, 1989); R. Porter, 'Civilisation and disease: Medical ideology in the Enlightenment', in J. Black and J. Gregory (eds), *Culture, Politics and Society in Britain 1660–1800* (Manchester, 1991), and R. Porter, *The People's Health in Georgian England* (London, 1995), p. 126.

   5   J. Crellin and J.R. Scott, 'Lionel Lockyer and his pills', *Proceedings of the XXIII International Congress of the History of* Medicine, 2 vols (London, 1972), pp. 1 182–6; P.S. Brown, 'Medicines advertising in eighteenth-century Bath newspapers', *Medical History*, 20 (1976), 152–68; J. Barry, 'Publicity and the public good: Presenting medicine in eighteenth century Bristol', in W. Bynum and R. Porter (eds), *Medical Fringe and Medical Orthodoxy 1750–1850* (1987), pp. 29–39; P. Crawford, 'Printed advertisements for women medical practitioners in London 1680–1710', *Society for the Social History of Medicine Bulletin*, 25 (1984), pp. 66–70; Porter, *Health for Sale*; R. and D. Porter, 'The Rise of the English drugs Industry: The Role of Thomas Corbyn', *Medical History*, 33 (1989), pp. 277–95; F. Doherty, 'The anondyne necklace: a quack remedy and its promotion', *Medical History*, 34 (1990), pp. 286–93; P. Isaac, 'Pills and Print', in R. Harris and M. Myers (eds), *Medicine, Mortality and the Book Trade* (London, 1998), pp. 25–49; L.F. Cody, '"No cure, no money" or the

advertising, as these flyers contain a vast amount of information about practitioners, their products and how they were distributed – and, indeed, their patients. However, although almanacs were the greatest form of mass media in this period, modern studies have tended to ignore the advertising they contained. This is a serious omission, as unlike handbills, almanacs had the power to reach a wide, national range of consumers, earlier and more diverse than early newspapers could ever hope to reach.

While newspapers and handbills are excellent sources of information, the advertisements contained in almanacs have three unique benefits. In the first place, almanacs were the first true British mass media which were printed in their hundreds of thousands every year and which began to carry advertisements in the late sixteenth century. The first advertisements in newspapers, on the other hand, are generally agreed as appearing in the 1620s.[6] Secondly, advertisements in almanacs had a long life span, for unlike handbills or newspapers they would remain in use for an entire year. This meant that individual advertisements might be seen a number of times by the same reader, which is an important tool in creating both demand and brand awareness for commercialized medicines. Finally, the distribution of almanacs meant that their advertisements had the potential to reach a local, regional, national and even international audience.

Almanacs, which still exist as astrological publications in the twenty-first century, are thought to have evolved over thousands of years. There is some debate as to the actual meaning of the word, with some experts arguing that it comes from the Arabic word for calendar, brought into Spain by the Moors while other believe that it originated from the Latin *manacus* or *manadius*, which refers to the circle in a sundial.[7] Nevertheless, the earliest known astrological almanac is a papyrus edition believed to date from the period of Ramses II (1304–1168 BC) at the British Library.[8] The nature of almanacs continued to change over the centuries, and by the early Middle Ages generally took the form of 'clog almanacs', simple constructions made of sticks or rods marked by a series of notches and symbols, representing the lunar

invisible hand of quackery', *Studies in Eighteenth Century Culture*, 28 (1999), pp. 103–30; E.L. Furdell, *Publishing and Medicine in Early Modern England* (2002), esp. pp. 134–54; K.P. Sienna, *Venereal Disease, Hospitals and the Urban Poor: London's 'Foul Wards', 1600–1800* (Rochester, NY, 2004), esp. pp. 41–59; BL 551.A32 and BL C.112.f9.

6   J. Frank, *The Beginnings of the English Newspaper 1620-1660* (Cambridge, 1961), p. 155; M. Harris, 'Timely Notices: The Uses of Advertising and its Relationship to News during the Late Seventeenth Century', in J. Raymond (ed.), *News, Newspapers and Society in Early Modern Britain* (London, 1999), p. 141; Furdell, *Publishing,* p. 135; E. Bosanquet, 'English Seventeenth-century Almanacks', *The Library*, 10(4) (March 1930), pp. 361–97. The only almanac by Bourne that I have been able to locate dates from ten years earlier.

7   C. Camden Jr, 'Elizabethan Almanacs and Prognostications', *The Library*, 10 (1932), p. 84.

8   B. Katz, *Cuneiform to Computer: A History of Reference Sources* (London, 1998), p. 97.

cycle and the Christian feasts.[9] By the high Middle Ages, manuscript almanacs were more common, being generally referred to as 'kalendaria'. In addition to calendars, this form of almanac included important ecclesiastical information, and they were generally used by clergymen. During the fourteenth century, the friars John Somer and Nicholas of Lynn expanded these works with information on eclipses, medical and other matters of interest. Unlike the earlier versions for clergymen, they were aimed to appeal to a wider audience of students and physicians.[10]

Johannes Gutenberg was responsible for the first printed almanac in 1448, eight years before he produced his famous Bible. By the 1470s, large numbers of almanacs were being printed in various countries on the Continent.[11] Although many of the earliest almanacs were printed as broadsheets, most eventually appeared in booklet form, which were more popular especially in Germany and the Netherlands.[12] The evolution of almanacs in England, however, proved much slower, with the first domestically printed edition only appearing in 1537.[13] It was not until the 1550s, however, that significant numbers of almanacs began to be printed in London, almost all of which were translations of European editions, such as the series attributed to the German doctor Simon Heuring of 'Hagenaw' (Hagenau), Arnould Bogaert, 'Doctour in medecyne, resident in Bruxles', Mychal Nostradamus, 'Doctour of Phisicke of Salon of Craux in Provence', and Paul Fegenhauer from the Netherlands, whose English version appeared under the name of 'Adam Foulweather'.[14] Although some almanacs by English writers began to appear during the 1560s, they floundered over the following decade, and only became the norm in the mid-1580s. According to E. Bosanquet, the first advertisement appeared in William Bourne's almanac of 1581, promoting his four books 'extant in print'.[15]

The numbers of English almanacs began to grow dramatically in the late 1580s after Richard Watkins and James Roberts obtained the privilege of printing almanacs which they enjoyed for over a decade. [16] Advertisements also started to become

9   D. and J. Parker, *A History of Astrology* (London, 1983), p. 152.

10   P.M. Jones, 'Medicine and Science', in L. Hellinga and J.B. Trapp (eds), *The Cambridge History of the Book in Britain*, Vol. II (Cambridge, 1999), p. 439.

11   B. Capp, *Astrology and the Popular Press: English Almanacs, 1500–1800* (London, 1979), p. 25.

12   R. Houston, *Literacy in Early Modern Europe* (London, 1988), p. 180.

13   R.C. Simons, 'ABC's, almanacs, ballads, chapbooks, popular piety and textbooks', in J. Barnard and D.F. McKenzie (eds), *The Cambridge History of the Book in Britain*, Vol. IV (Cambridge, 2002), p. 56.

14   S. Heuring, *An Almanack and Prognostication* (London, 1551); A. Bogaert, *A Prognostication* (London, 1553); M. Nostradamus, *An Almanack* (London, 1563); A. Foulweather, *A Wonderfull, Strange and Miraculous Astrologicall Prognostication* (London, 1591).

15   Bosanquet, 'English Seventeenth-century Almanacks'.

16   W. Gregg, *Some Aspects and Problems of London Publishing between 1550 and 1650* (Oxford, 1956), p. 100.

more of a regular feature, particularly those for books.[17] Over the following decade, additional privileges, or patens, were acquired by members of the Stationers' Company, which eventually led to the acquisition of monopolistic rights to produce almanacs in 1603. In addition to almanacs, privileged members of the Company formed a new joint-stock operation to produce and wholesale what became known as the 'English Stock', which included 'private prayers, prymers, psalters and psalmes in English or Latin'. Although other elements of the English Stock also sold in large numbers, almanacs were arguably the most profitable publication, as unlike more expensive works where a single copy or two might suffice, there was an annual demand for new almanacs.[18] One of the Company's earliest decisions was to restrict the production of almanacs to London, where it could be more easily monitored. However, they were grudgingly forced to acknowledge Cambridge and Oxford's rights to produce them, as well.[19]

Most surviving late sixteenth- and seventeenth-century almanacs were made up of two major sections. The core of the first section always consisted of a calendar marking upcoming astronomical and astrological events for the coming year. Generally, this would be presented in a monthly format over two adjoining pages. As one writer explained, every month would contain 'the Common aspects and configurations of the planets'.[20] These were generally further divided into two sections, with the first containing daily listings of astral movements on the left-hand side of the page. Depending on the author, the facing side might either be left blank to use for personal notes or pre-printed with various types of information, including genitures of famous people or medical recipes.[21] The second section of almanacs was generally called the 'prognostication'. This part usually contained material that was not very 'time-sensitive', such as medical information and advice. Joseph Blagrave, for example, offered the 'Time and Manner of curing Diseases by Sympathy and Antipathy, Rules for husbandry, dayly Predictions of the Weather, and many other Things beneficial for Phisitians and Young Students'.[22] Although there are some exceptions, advertisements tended to be placed either on the last page or two of the prognostication.

One of the main reasons why almanacs were such a powerful tool for advertising was the huge range of different titles written to appeal to readers with varying levels of literacy, wealth and sophistication. Some almanacs appeared to have targeted purchasers with low levels of literacy, while others appealed to more erudite readers.

---

17 For example, R. Westhawe, *An Almanack* (London, 1594), sig. B3r.

18 M. Nicholson, 'English Almanacs and the New Astronomy', *Annals of Science*, 4 (1939), p. 2; A. Johns, *The Nature of the Book: Print and Knowledge in the Making* (Chicago, IL, 1998), p. 260.

19 M. Mendle, 'De Facto Freedom, De Facto Authority: Press and Parliament 1640–1643', *The Historical Journal*, 38(2) (June 1995), pp. 307–22.

20 V. Wing, *An Almanac and Prognostication* (London, 1643), sig. A2r.

21 J. Gadbury, *Ephemeris or a Diary Astronomical, Astrological, Meteorological* (London, 1692), sig. A4r–B8r; W. Salmon, *The London Almanac* (London, 1691–1700).

22 W. Blagrave, *Blagrave's Ephemeris* (London, 1659), sig. A1r.

Furthermore, although most almanacs were printed in London, many targeted specific, regional audiences. These included towns from Dover all the way up to Durham, making almanacs the first periodicals with national coverage. Other titles differentiated themselves by targeting specific occupational groups. Although several titles were written for 'country-men', others focused on chapmen, weavers, seamen, shepherds, farriers or constables. Readers who had strong religious convictions, or prejudices, could have chosen to purchase almanacs intended for either a Protestant or Catholic audience. As with modern periodicals, the ability to provide a diversified range of almanacs allowed the Stationers' Company to offer something of interest to most readers. The result of their success showed in the contemporary saying that almanacs were 'readier money than cake or ale'.[23]

Figure 3.1 illustrates two distinct periods of growth in advertising during this study, with each bar referring to the number of individual advertisements for each item. The figure shows that non-medical books were the most heavily promoted categories, followed by patent drugs, popular medical books, medical paraphernalia and services, and other miscellaneous products.

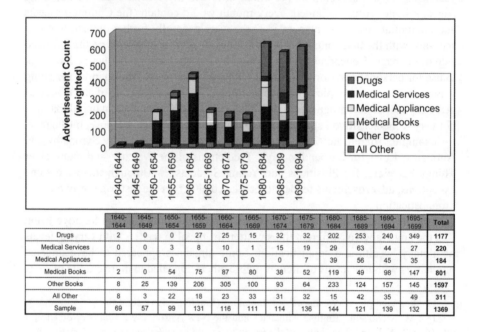

	1640-1644	1645-1649	1650-1654	1655-1659	1660-1664	1665-1669	1670-1674	1675-1679	1680-1684	1685-1689	1690-1694	1695-1699	Total
Drugs	2	0	0	27	25	15	32	32	202	253	240	349	**1177**
Medical Services	0	0	3	8	10	1	15	19	29	63	44	27	**220**
Medical Appliances	0	0	0	1	0	0	0	7	39	56	45	35	**184**
Medical Books	2	0	54	75	87	80	38	52	119	49	98	147	**801**
Other Books	8	25	139	206	305	100	93	64	233	124	157	145	**1597**
All Other	8	3	22	18	23	33	31	32	15	42	35	49	**311**
Sample	69	57	99	131	116	111	114	136	144	121	139	132	**1369**

Figure 3.1   Advertisements in almanacs by type.

---

23   M. Plant, *The English Book Trade* (London, 1962), p. 48.

The first column shows an almost total absence of advertisements, possibly related to the economic depression in 1641–42, followed by years of civil war which resulted in reduced manufacturing and trade, compounded by a series of poor crop yields.[24] As a result, there would have been few consumer products to advertise, and even less disposable income available to pay for them.

A dramatic rise in advertising followed during the more prosperous years of the interregnum. The most heavily promoted items during this period were books, a trend which continued through most of this study. Between 1650 and 1654, advertisements for proprietary drugs are almost non-existent, although they show a slight rise in the following five-year period while 'medical services and appliances' began to make a showing during the first part of the 1650s. This category encompasses a variety of items. In the first place, it refers to medical services such as general consultations offered either by the almanac writer or other healers.

The number of advertisements experienced a decline after 1665, and remained comparatively small until 1680. It can be seen that the percentages of products offered were also rather stagnant. This may, in part, be linked to the Great Fire of 1666, which seriously affected both industry and retail sales in the capital. In addition to many other consumer goods, almanacs and a number of products that they advertised were either produced or sold in London. As Samuel Pepys reported on 26 September 1666:

> I hear the great loss of books in St. Paul's churchyard, and at their [Stationers' Company] hall also – which they value at about 150000 [pounds]; some booksellers being wholly undone.[25]

Paradoxically, English shipping was experiencing a period of great expansion during this time. This was partially due to the need to import timber to rebuild London, as well as other building materials. As a result, increasingly larger ships traded with Norway, the Mediterranean, Virginia and the Indies in the last decades of the century.[26] The rising quantities of imported goods of all sorts were joined by a rapid expansion in the manufacturing of cheap consumer goods, such as pottery or Midlands hardware, as well as ribbons, lace and vegetable dyes.[27] One of the greatest

---

24 B. Manning, *The English People and the English Revolution* (London, 1991), p. 173; T. Raylor, 'Samuel Hartlib and the Commonwealth of Bees', in M. and R.T. Taylor (eds), *Culture and Cultivation in Early Modern England: Writing and the Land* (Leicester, 1992), p. 94.

25 S. Pepys, *The Diary of Samuel Pepys*, Vol. VII, ed. R.C. Latham and W. Matthews (London, 1983), p. 297.

26 R. Davis, *The Rise of the English Shipping Industry* (London, 1962), p. 17.

27 B. Coward, *Social Change and Continuity in Early Modern England 1550–1750* (London, 1988), p. 58.

areas of expansion, however, was in the production, wholesaling and retailing of all types of English books.[28]

Whilst books were widely promoted in all forms of print, the earliest advertisements for these publications appeared in almanacs in 1581 and 1594, and soon became a regular feature.[29] Arthur Hopton used his preface of 1610 to inform readers that the astrological book he had been working on was finally in press and available at the Signe of the Crowne in Paules Churchyard, and William Pratt's newly published *Arithmeticall Jewell* was advertised in 1619 and 1621.[30] Such advertisements increased dramatically in parallel with the dramatic growth in publishing in the 1640s.[31] The highest number of advertisements for books appeared between 1660 and 1665, followed by mass commercial disruption as the result of the Plague of 1665 and the Great Fire of 1666. In fact, annual book production in 1666 and 1667 fell back to pre-Civil War levels, and only began to recover after 1670. [32] The evidence in almanacs, however, suggests that as normality returned to the capital, the numbers of advertisements for books rose once again.

After books, proprietary medicines were the second most frequently advertised commodity in almanacs, which will be discussed in the following section. The third category of medical advertising centred on medical services such as consultations for a range of illnesses or other complaints, followed closely by medically related appliances. Daniel Woodward promised his readers both a consultation, and if necessary, 'Lodging, Medicines and Attendance in my house, till well', which presumably included the chance to purchase his branded pills.[33] Other advertisements were for more traditional healers with special talents for curing specific diseases. The widow Sarah Matthews claimed that she could rectify hunched backs. She was willing to treat any child under 16 years old. Her method included setting them 'once a Month in a Mathematical Chair, where they are exactly measured' and eventually cured.[34]

Some advertisers provided what might be called medical appliances such as false teeth, artificial eyeballs and spectacles. John Wads offered to produce and 'set in' authentic-looking artificial teeth. He boasted that they were so 'exact that they may

---

28 G. Mandelbrote, 'Workplaces and living spaces: London book trade inventories of the late seventeenth century', in R. Myers, M. Harris and G. Mandelbrote (eds), *The London Book Trade: Topographies of Print in the Metropolis from the Sixteenth Century* (London, 2003), pp. 21–43.

29 Bosanquet, 'English Seventeenth-century Almanacks'; R. Westhawe (1594), sig. B3r.

30 A. Hopton, *An Almanack* (London, 1610), sig. B2v; J. White, *A New Almanack* (London, 1619), sig. A2v; J. Johnson, *An Almanack* (London, 1621), sig. C4r.

31 W. , *News from the Starres* (London, 1680), sig. C8v; J. Riolanus, *A Sure Guide or the Best and Nearest Way to Physick and Chyrugery*, trans. N. Culpepper (London, 1671), p. 2.

32 Mandelbrote, 'Workplaces and living spaces', pp. 24–5.

33 D. Woodward, *Ephemeris Absoluta* (London, 1698), sig. C8v.

34 H. Coley, *Merlinus Anglicus Junior* (London,1686), sig. C8r.

be eat upon, and not discovered by the nicest Observor'.[35] William Boyse advertised artificial eyeballs, 'the like was never seen in England', while others offered spectacles, which were fairly common in the second half of the seventeenth century. Unlike modern spectacles, they were constructed without hinged supports over the ears. Instead, they were meant to grip the nose, or to be made as a pince-nez that could be gripped by a strong linking bar. John Yarwell promised to make 'spectacles for most sights and ages'. He claimed that these eyeglasses were 'wrought to the greatest Perfection', and that they had even been 'approved of by the Royal Society'. John Marshall could not make that same claim, although he promised 'very neat Leather Frames for Spectacles, which are not subject to break as Horn or Tortois Shell'.[36]

Proprietary Medicines

The tendency to equate proprietary medicines with quacks has led to a skewed view of the makers of these products. Although there is some disagreement as to the best definition of the term itself, it is generally accepted that it was a derogatory description. Unfortunately, this debate is outside the scope of this chapter, which will use one of the least value-ridden definitions by Roy Porter, which stated that quacks 'transgressed what those in the saddle defined as true, orthodox or "good" medicine'.[37] While such a label is appropriate for many contemporary healers, it does not, however, hold true for the proprietary drug makers who advertised in almanacs.

On one hand, it is clear that contemporaries believed that many manufacturers of proprietary drugs were simply 'cozering quacksalvers' and 'false juggling deceivers'.[38] The most systematic attempts to stop such people, however, came from the College of Physicians, which carried out what Margaret Pelling has called regular 'censorsorial activity' against irregular medical practitioners.[39] It is therefore somewhat surprising to find that many producers were actually members of the College themselves. Although such an affiliation was likely to have impressed many almanac readers, not all advertisers were willing to put their names in print. One anonymous advertiser of 'Pilulae Londinenses or the London Pill', for example, claimed to be 'a Physician of long standing in the College of Physicians, London'.[40]

---

35   G. Parker, *A Double Ephemeris* (London, 1700), sig. A3r; S. Rider, *Rider's British Merlin* (London, 1696), sig. A2v.

36   S. Pepys, *Diary*, Vol. VIII, p. 486; J. Dreyfus, 'The Invention of Spectacles and the Advent of Printing', *The Library*, 10 (1988), p. 97; G. Parker (1697), sig. E8r; A. Williams (1698), sig. C8v.

37   R. Porter, *Quacks*, p. 11.

38   E. Gardiner, *Phisicall and approved Medicines* (London, 1611), sig. A2r.

39   M. Pelling, *Medical Conflicts in Early Modern London: Patronage, Physicians and Irregular Practitioners 1550–1640* (Oxford, 2003), p. 50.

40   W. Andrews, *Newes from the Stars* (London, 1688), sig. B8r.

Others such as John Archer, 'one of his Majesties sworn Physicians', were less
reticent. Archer promoted his products both in almanacs and in his own books. He
promised potential customers that 'those that make trial of My Medicines, shall
be Gods grace find them very effectual'. Archer also vouched for their safety by
assuring readers that he personally produced these medicines, and would 'not entrust
any to prepare them, nor the delivery of them from my own house'[41]

Roy Porter has suggested that there were two main types of products,
consisting of 'cure-alls' or pills to treat specific illnesses.[42] Advertisements in
almanacs, however, tended to focus mainly on those in the first category. 'Spirits
of Scurvy Grass' was the most commonly advertised type of proprietary product,
which was manufactured and distributed under a number of brand names. The most
frequently mentioned brand name was Bateman's Scurvy Grass, which appeared
in 151 advertisements between 1680 and 1700, followed by Clarke's Scurvy
Compound, Pordage's Scurvy Grass and Parker's Elixir of Scurvy Grass.[43] As
with many successful nostrums, Bateman was regularly plagued by counterfeiting
attempts, including those by the 'Whiffling Emperick' who called himself 'Sieur de
Verantes', who donned 'this Outlandish Mask to counterfeit my Spirits', and 'the
late pretenders' who tried to cheat Bateman's loyal customers.[44] Bateman advised
potential purchasers to always check for his seal showing his 'Coate of Armes, the
Half Moon and Ermins'. This served both as decoration and as an attempt 'to prevent
the Designs of some Pretenders, who sell about the City their Counterfeit ware'.[45]
Although Bateman continued to struggle with counterfeiters, his product was so
successful that it continued to be marketed for many years after his death through his
'sole Executrix'.[46] Although it is not known when Bateman died, by 1690 Bateman's
Scurvy Grass was being produced 'at the house he lately dwelt in, in St. Paul's Lane,
London, nor Sold by any but such as have it from thence'.[47] It may even be that
the Georgian 'Bateman's Pectoral Drops' had evolved from the original Bateman's,
although it might simply have been an effort to capitalize on a well-known brand
name.[48]

---

41   W. Andrews, *Newes from the Stars* (London, 1684), sig. C8v; J. Archer, *Every Man
his own Doctor* (London, 1671), p. 114.
42   R. Porter, *Quacks: Fakers and Charlatans in English Medicine* (Stroud, 2001), p.
172.
43   T. Gallen, *An Almanac* (London, 1683), sig. C8v; H. Coley (1687), sig. C8v; G.
Parker, *Merlinus Anglicanus* (London, 1694), sig. E8r.
44   L. Coelson, *Speculum Perspicum Uranicum* (London, 1686), sig. C8r; BL C112,
advertisement 83; C.J.S. Thompson, *The Quacks of Old London* (London, 1928), p. 176.
45   M. Crimp, *The Market Research Process* (London, 1990), p. 4; W. Andrews (1670),
sig. C8v; J. Partridge, *Mercurius Coelestis* (London, 1681), sig. C8v; H. Coley (1697), sig.
C8v; G. Wharton, *Hemerologium: or a Register* (London, 1656), sig. C8r.
46   W. Andrews, *Newes from the Stars* (London, 1700), sig. C8v.
47   Fly, *A Prognostication* (London, 1690), sig. C8r.
48   Porter, *Health for Sale*, p. 45.

Another heavily advertised proprietary medicine was Buckworth's Lozenges, which appeared in almanacs a total of 64 times between 1656 and 1700. Interestingly, the longer the product was advertised, the more illnesses it claimed to be able to treat. In 1657, readers were promised that 'approved of for the cure of all diseases of the Lungs, and a great antidote against the Plague, are made by Mr Edmund Buckworth at his house'.[49] Two years later, the claims had grown to include 'the cure of Consumptions, Coughs, Catharrs, Astma's, Hoarsnesse and all other Diseases incident to the Lungs, and a soveraign Antidote against the Plague, and all other contagious Diseases, and obstructions of the stomach'.[50] Interestingly, in the year following the Great Plague of 1665, Buckworth's Lozenges are not advertised in almanacs at all, perhaps because they were in fact ineffective when put to the test of an epidemic. Buckworth presumably died some time before the 1680s, when James Shipton began to manufacture the pills under what became a well-known brand name. Buckworth's continued to enjoy success under Shipton, having gained the stamp of success from the 'Chief Physicians of the Colledge' (of Physicians) by 1697.[51]

One of the best-known nostrums was a cordial drink called Daffy's Elixir, which was invented around 1660, and thrived until at least the 1920s.[52] Although the drink did not include a list of its ingredients, a late seventeenth-century manuscript 'boke of physick' provided the following instructions 'to make Dafyes Elixir':

Take 3 quarts of aqua vitae of the second stilling of rubarb and sena 3 ounces in an ounce of coriande seed of saffran half a dram campanae powder, 2 drumms of Liqoriesh 2 ounc of coriander seeds 2 pounds of raisons of the sone stoned the Liquorish and rubarb sliced the sena and seed brused, put it all into the 3 quarts of aqua vitae let it stand to gather form a week stirring sometimes, then strain it, through a fine cloth, squees the cloth hard, into these engredients put 3 quarts more the licor, lett it stand a week as the former strain it through a brown paper through a funnel stir it every day when it is first made bin it over with a bladder.[53]

Interestingly, this was still 'a favourite quack medicine' in the 1870s, when the recipe appeared in *The Family Doctor*. Although the instructions had been simplified somewhat, the ingredients had changed very little over two hundred years. The late nineteenth-century version consisted of:

Senna leaves, 5 ounces; Guaiacum shavings, dried Elecampane Root, Aniseeds, Corianders, Caraways, and Liquorice Root, and according to some, red Sanders wood,

---

49 J. Booker, *Celestial Observations* (London, 1657), sig. B8v.

50 G. Johnson, *An Account Astrological* (London, 1659), p. 20.

51 H. Coley, *Merlinus Anglicus Junior* (1687), sig. C5v; H. Coley, *Merlinus Anglicus Junior* (1697), sig. C8v.

52 Thompson, *Quacks*, p. 255.

53 Royal College of Surgeons, London, MSS 42 d.18, 'Elizabeth Isham Book of Physick', early seventeenth to eighteenth centuries, p. 108.

of each 2 ½ ounces; stoned Raisins, 8 ounces; Proof Spirit, 6 pounds: macerated for a fortnight and filter[ed].[54]

Proprietary drugs were accompanied by instruction manuals, sometimes also used as promotional materials or as part of the wrapping. Although they omit any references to ingredients, there were frequent accusations that producers simply used the same recipes from the Pharmacopeia Londiniensis as apothecaries.[55] Surviving booklets do, however, provide other types of information. For example, most began by identifying the types of illnesses the nostrum could treat. The accompanying literature for Nendick's Pills claimed that they were most useful for treating scurvy, 'the Original and most Chronick Disease'. In common with other instruction booklets, this was followed by instructions on dosages, which would differ according to the sex and age of the patient. Woodward's Cordial Pills called for 'discretion in the Dose ... take as the Body can bear, or Disease require them', while Whalley's Pills could be administered up to four times daily, down to once every third or fourth day.[56]

Many booklets also contained testimonials of satisfied patients. In many cases, these appeared to be 'common folk' who had suffered chronic pain for years, such as a grocer in Canterbury or 'the Countess of Lincoln's Gardiner'. [57]

William Sermon, who gained his reputation by treating plague victims in Gloucester in 1666, was able to boast that his medicine had saved the life of George Monck, the Duke of Albermarle, in 1669, and Monck's subsequent recovery led to the king awarding a mandated MD from Cambridge. In 1671, Sermon, 'Doctor of Physick and one of his Majesties Phisicians in Ordinary', began to advertise that although Monck was no longer living, Sermon's potion had saved him, as well as 'many hundreds beside'.[58] This advertising device was used in another almanac printed that year, in a somewhat facetious manner to advertise McColly's Golden Purging Pills, which 'only want an operation upon an Earl or a Duke to commend them to the world'.[59]

Testimonials by everyday people, on the other hand, probably helped to convince potential customers that the medicines were value for money. After all, most were relatively expensive, and would have been a major investment for many. Part of this was based on the quantities sold, with most being offered in fairly large amounts. As a result, many producers tried to convince readers that they were making an investment in a product that would 'retain its Vertues several Years', and that it was more economical to buy a larger size, such as 'Pilu Alnomenes Morbos', which cost

---

54 A Dispensary Surgeon, *The Family Doctor* (London, *c.* 1870), pp. 179–80.

55 Porter, *Quacks*, p. 33.

56 H. Nendick, *Book of Directions*, sig. A1v; D. Woodward, *Woodward's Cordial Pills*, p. 3; J. Whalley, *Directions for the Use of Whalley's Pills and Elixir* (Dublin, 1710), p. 4.

57 H. Nendick, *Book of Directions*, sig. A1v and A2r.

58 H. Cook, *The Decline of the Old Medical Regime in Stuart London* (London, 1986), p. 47; J. Gadbury, *Ephemeris, or a Diary of the Celestial Motions* (London, 1671), sig. C8v.

59 R. Neve, *Merlinus Verax* (London, 1671), sig. C8r.

3s. for a small bottle, or 80 pills for only 6s.[60] Others took a more direct approach, arguing that those who did not buy his product clearly preferred 'Money before Health'.[61] In theory, proprietary drugs that were made in large quantities might have been slightly cheaper than individually prepared prescriptions. However, home-made medicines would have been more economical than either of these. In many cases, this appears to have been true even when individual ingredients had to be purchased. For example, according to *The Family-Physician and the House-Apothecary*, 'Aqua Epidemica, or the London Plague-Water' was sold by apothecaries for between 3s. 6d. and 4s. a pint. If made at home, the total cost would come to 7d. a pint.[62]

Of course, special prescriptions prepared by an apothecary would have been even more expensive. The Earl of Bedford's servants were given drugs prepared by a local apothecary in the 1670s. These items also appear rather expensive at 3s. for just three doses of cordial pills or cordial juleps. A box of stomach pills also went for 3s., and a box of purging pills only slightly cheaper at 2s.[63]

Distribution

Keith Thomas has suggested that there were three overlapping spheres of commercial activity in early modern England. The first involved small-scale dealing, or even 'quasi-commercial' trading between inhabitants of specific neighbourhoods or areas. This was followed by rural–urban or inter-urban trading focusing on the food and other raw materials. The third sphere involved the relationship between market towns and the surrounding areas, and the distribution of food, raw materials, manufactured goods and luxury items. [64] This model is supported by the advertisements in almanacs, which represent local, provincial and even national trading networks.

The proprietary drugs advertised in almanacs all appear to have been produced in London, generally from the manufacturer's home. It seems likely that nostrums that were only sold at the producer's house were prepared in fairly small quantities. As production levels increased, the nostrums would be made available via a wider chain of distribution. At the lowest level, this would include products such as Welden's Balsamick Spirit, which could be purchased either at Welden's lodgings in 'Lambart-Street in Goodman's Fields' or at Mr R. Collin's house 'at the Bell in St. Joan's-Court, in Clerkenwell Parish'.[65] Potential profits would clearly increase if sufficient quantities could be produced and distributed on a national basis. In his early advertising, Edmund Buckworth noted that his lozenges were only available at

---

60 J. Gadbury, *A Diary of the Celestial Motions* (London, 1672), sig. C8r; D. Woodward (1690), sig. C6v.

61 S. Winter, *Directions for the Use of My Elixir* (London, 1664), sig. A1r.

62 G. Harvey, *The Family-Physician and the House-Apothecary* (London, 1678), p. 19.

63 G.S. Thomson, *Life in a Noble Household 1641–1700* (London, 1937), pp. 313–14.

64 K. Wrightson, *Earthly Necessities: Economic Lives in Early Modern Britain, 1470–1750* (London, 2002), pp. 93–8.

65 M. Hobbs, *Chaldaeus Anglicanus* (London, 1693), sig. C8r.

his house 'in the great Piazza in Convent-garden' and 'for more convenience to those that live remote in the City' with Mr Richard Lownds, a Bookseller, at the White Lyon in St Pauls Churchyard, near the little North door'.[66] While many proprietary drugs were only available from the producers' home, most could be purchased from other 'temporary' or 'permanent' retail outlets, or through the post.

The term 'temporary' outlet includes a range of travelling salesmen such as 'hawkers', 'pedlars' or 'petti-chapmen' who offered 'small Wares and commodities' advertised either 'by crying it in Cities and Market Towns or by offering it from door to door all about the Contrey'. [67] Such men also often visited fairs and markets, the most traditional forum for purchasing consumer goods, and also important distribution points for nostrums.[68] Many almanacs provided notices of the dates of other fairs, to help consumers and travelling salesmen avoid appearing at a venue either 'too soone' or 'when it is doone'. [69] Some editions even informed readers about the presence of proprietary drugs, such as the advertisement from 1688 that promised that Buckworth's Lozenges would be available at four fairs at Weldon, Northamptonshire, on the first Wednesday in February, May, August and September.[70] Markets, on the other hand, were a weekly occurrence which required regular visits for both sellers and buyers of animals, produce and other goods.

Nancy Cox has argued that it was 'fixed' shops in provincial towns and villages that had the greatest impact on early modern consumer growth. Until fairly recently, the commonplace that the nationwide distribution of consumer goods was an eighteenth-century phenomenon linked to improvements in road conditions, the rise of more navigable rivers and construction of canals and the emergence of a nationwide carrier system was widely accepted. Cox and others, however, illustrate that early modern population growth was linked to the earlier 'intensification of internal trade of all kinds'. [71] A late seventeenth-century book claimed that every village of ten or more houses had at least one shop which often carried 'as many

---

66   G. Johnson, *An Account Astrological* (London, 1659), p. 20.

67   N.H., *The compleat tradesman, or, the exact dealers daily companion* (London, 1684), p. 44.

68   M. Spufford, *Small Books and Pleasant Histories: Popular Fiction and its Readership in Seventeenth-century England* (Cambridge, 1981), p. 115; R.A. Houston, *Literacy in Early Modern England* (London, 1988), p. 172; J.A. Sharpe, *Early Modern England: A Social History 1550–1750* (London, 1992), pp. 141–2. J. Tanner, *Angelus Britannicus* (London, 1678), sig. C8r; T. White, *A New Almanacke* (London, 1685), sig. C8v; W. Dade, *A New Almanacke* (London, 1685), sig. C8v.

69   Anon., *An Answer to the Pretended Reasons of some Drapers, Mercers, Haberdashers, Grocers and Hosier, &c against Pedlars, Hawkers & Petty-Chapmen* (London, 1675), sig. A1v; H. Alleyn, *An Almanacke* (London, 1607), sig. C8v.

70   W. Andrews, *Newes from the Stars* (London, 1688), sig.C8v.

71   N. Cox, *The Compleat Tradesman: A Study of Retailing 1550–1820* (Aldershot, 2000), p. 59; H.C. Mui and L. Mui, *Shops and Shopkeeping in Eighteenth-century England* (Basingstoke, 1989), p. 12 ; Wrightson, *Earthly Necessities,* p. 93.

substantial Commodities as any do that live in Cities and Market Towns'.[72] By the early seventeenth century, the linkage of all towns on the main highways with branch services meant that there were regular services for goods, passengers and letters on either a daily, weekly, bi- or tri-weekly basis between London and provincial towns like Wakefield, Preston, Halifax, Chester, Reading, Cambridge, Salisbury, Leicester and Exeter. By 1637, over two hundred towns had at least a weekly service to and from London. Small packages containing proprietary medicines would have been easy and fairly cheap to transport to the growing numbers of retail shops found in both large and small market towns, most of which began to stock a range of wares by the middle of the century.[73]

Advertisements in almanacs show that the stock of many of these provincial shops would have included proprietary drugs. Woodward's Pills, for example, could be purchased from grocers in two different towns, a coach harness maker, a girt web maker, a baker and a nurse.[74] . The same held true for Russell's Spirit of Scurvy Grass, found at 'his House at the Blew Posts against Grays-Inn, Holborn, and in most great market Towns', while John Piercy's lozenges for the cure of 'Consumptions, Coughs, Catarrhs, Astmaes, Tiffick, Colds old and new' were sold in Exeter, Norwich, Yarmouth, Worcester, Bristol, Oxford, Bury St Edmunds and Lincoln.[75] Many of these same great provincial cities were stocked with Stoughton's Elixir Magnum, who boasted that his medicine was also 'much enquired after and approved of beyond sea, especially in our plantations abroad'. Stoughton also assured readers that he had sufficient stock to supply:

> Any Captain or Seman, Bookseller, stationer, shop keeper, coffee-man and any keeper of a Publick House, wants any quantitites to dispose of, or sell again, they may be Furnished (with good Allowance) by Letter or otherwise.[76]

Although Peter Isaac has suggested that the book trade was 'perhaps the most important distribution network for proprietary medicines in the late seventeenth century', many other types of London retailers also sold proprietary medicines.[77] The main distributor for John Partridge's Elixir Stomachicum was a Mr Levingston, who was a Fruiterer at the Royal Exchange, although it was also available for 'the Chief Coffeeshouses in and about London' and three booksellers.[78] This is not to negate the important role that the printing industry played in the growth of commercialized

---

72   N.H., *The compleat tradesman*, p. 39.

73   E. Kerridge, *Trade and Banking in Early Modern England* (Manchester, 1988), p. 9; C. Shammas, *The Pre-industrial Consumer in England and America* (Oxford, 1990), p. 235; N. Cox, 'The Distribution of Retailing Tradesmen in North Shropshire 1660–1750', in J. Benson and G. Shaw (eds), *The Retailing Industry* (London, 1999), p. 322.

74   D. Woodward, *Vox Uranie* (London, 1685), sig. C8v.

75   J. Bowker, *An Almanack* (London, 1684), sig. C8v; J. Tanner, 1694, sig. C8V.

76   BL, 551.A32, no. 60.

77   Isaac, 'Pills and Print', pp. 25–49.

78   J. Partridge, *Merlinus Liberatus* (London, 1696), sig. C8v.

medicine. As with most types of shops, stationers or booksellers generally carried a range of other products, such as pictures or mathematical instruments.[79] There were, of course, a number of booksellers or stationers who offered such items, such as Mr Richard Lownds at the White Lyon near the little door of St Paul's Church.[80] However, almanac advertisements show that such retailers were generally only one out of several possible places to purchase proprietary medicines.

'Drinking houses', such as alehouses, taverns or inns, were known not only for being centres for business and social activities, but also as retailers for tobacco and pre-packaged nostrums. According to one popular medical book, 'Taverns, Inns, Ale houses [and] victuallers' were the best places to purchase tobacco which could either be taken as snuff, smoked or made into a potion that could help to 'avoid Rhume, break winde, and keep the body open'.[81]Advertisements in almanacs show that many producers chose drinking houses as the major suppliers of their proprietary drugs. The Elixir Proprietatis, for example, could only be purchased from one of nine London pubs or a single stationer's shop, while Lancelot Coelson's suppliers included three pubs and a strong water house in Wapping, West Smithfield, Spittlefields and the Royal Exchange.[82] 'Dr. Turners famous Dentifrices, which make the breath sweet, fasten the teeth, making them as white as Ivory, and cure the tooth-ach, are sold by Tho Tooks at the Lamb at the East end of St. Pauls', who also offered 'the best Ink for Records' and 'copie-books'. As the craze for coffee swept England in the 1650s and 1660s, an increasing number of coffeehouses opened in the capital and became increasingly popular as social and business venues.[83] Coffeehouses were also well represented as vending outlets, including 'Dukes' in 'Salsbury Court near Fleet Street' as well as all 'the Chief Coffeehouses' in London.[84] As with other types of drinking houses, they became known as suppliers of other types of consumer goods, such as tea or tobacco. [85]

Many advertisements offered to supply medicines through the post. William Salmon, for example, suggested that 'any one that sends to me for them may have

79   Johns, *The Nature of the Book,* p. 116.

80   S. Jinner, *An Almanack* (London, 1659), sig. C8v; W. Lilly, *Merlini Anglici Ephemeris* (London, 1670), sig. F8r.

81   G. Everard, *Panacea: or, The Universal medicine, Being a Discovery of the Wonderfull Vertues of Tobacco* (London, 1659), sig. A3r; K. Digbie, *The Closet of the Eminently Learned Sir Kenelme Digbie Knight Opened* (London, 1669), p. 208. W. Rumsey, *Organon salutis: An instrument to cleanse the stomach* (London, 1659), sig. B3v.

82   W. Lilly, *Merlini Anglici Ephemeris* (London, 1670), sig. F7v; L. Coelson, *Speculum Perspicuum Uranicum* (London, 1680), sig. C8v.

83   Anonymous, *The Character of a Coffeehouse with the symptoms of a town wit* (London, 1673), sig. A2r.

84   L. Coelson, *Speculum Perspicuum Uranicum* (London, 1680), sig. C8v; W. Lilly, *Merlini Anglici Ephemeris* (London, 1670), sig. F7v; J. Gadbury, *Ephemeris* (London, 1684), sig. A2r.

85   W.D. Smith, *Consumption and the Making of Respectability, 1600–1800* (London, 2002), p. 146.

them sent to them, in what part of the Kingdom soever'.[86] Another. producer suggested that out-of-town customers could obtain his drugs 'by engaging the Carriers who come from their respective Countreys, or some of their Friends in Town, to come to me for them'. Alternatively, readers could send an order to London, and obtain the drugs via the postal service.[87] Potential customers who were planning to travel overseas were also targeted by advertisements in almanacs.

In 1694, for example, Daniel Woodward advised readers that his Cordial Pills were particularly suitable for those travelling by sea to the East or West Indies so that they would not 'miserably perish for want of so choice a medicine'.[88] An advertisement for Nendick's Pill's, on the other hand, suggests that Captain John Collins saved the life of the ship's doctor, as well as numerous passengers, whilst travelling to Jamaica.[89] Stephan Freeman's Pox Medicine, on the other hand, could be purchased in (unnamed) towns in Jamaica and America, in addition to 10 outlets in London and 16 in the provinces.[90]

Although there are many inherent problems in studying early modern drug retailing in England, these problems are intensified when examining distribution in colonial America. Trade statistics show that large quantities of consumer goods were imported during the late seventeenth century. The largest proportion of these included grain products, drink and cloth or clothing, accompanied by books and other consumer durables.[91] Unfortunately, the absence of seventeenth-century colonial advertising makes it difficult to identify potential retail outlets.

Unlike their English counterparts, American almanacs did not carry medical advertisements in until the early nineteenth century.[92] James Harvey Young has claimed that the first colonial newspaper which carried an advertisement for an imported proprietary medicine was the *Boston News Letter* in October 1708, while John Boyd used the *Maryland Gazette* to advertise when a fresh supply of English proprietary medicines arrived at his 'medicinal store' in Baltimore.[93]

---

86   V. Wing, *An Almanack* (London, 1672), sig. C8v; W. Salmon, *The London Almanack* (London, 1692), sig. B8r.

87   J. Partridge, *Merlinus Liberatus* (London, 1686), sig. C8r; S. Rider, *British Merlin* (1689), sig. B8r; V. Wing, *An Almanack* (London, 1672), sig. C8v; W. Salmon, *The London Almanack* (London, 1692), sig. B8r; N. Comben, 'Snape's Purging Pill for Horses – 1692', *Veterinary Record*, 84 (1969), p. 434; P. Brassley, A. Lambert and P. Saunders, *Accounts of the Reverend John Crankanthorp of Fowlmere 1682–1710* (Cambridge, 1988), p. 215.

88   D. Woodward, *Vox Uranie* (London, 1694), sig. C8v.

89   H. Nendick, sig. A2r.

90   Sienna, *Venereal Disease, Hospitals and the Urban Poor*, p. 48.

91   Shammas, *The Pre-industrial Consumer*, p. 199.

92   T.A. Horrocks, 'Rules, Remedies and Regimens: Health Advice in Early American Almanacs', in C.E. Rosenberg (ed.), *Right Living: An Anglo-American Tradition of Self-help Medicine and Hygiene* (Baltimore, MD, 2003), pp. 112–46, p. 115.

93   J.H. Young, *The Toadstool Millionaires* (Princeton, NJ, 1961), p. 7; G.B. Griffenhagena and J.H. Young, 'Old English Patent Medicines in America', *Contributions from the Museum of History and Technology, U.S. National Museum Bulletin*, 218 (1959), pp. 155–83.

Conclusion

In the past, academic interest in the relationship between the growth of consumerism and advertising has tended to focus almost exclusively on eighteenth-century newspapers, which were the major mass media of their day. While this has provided valuable information and insights, such studies have failed to examine earlier relationships between consumerism and advertising as illustrated by almanacs, previously unrecognized as the leading form of mass media in the seventeenth century. As this essay has shown, the first advertisements in almanacs date from the 1580s and 1590s, with rising numbers through the following centuries.[94] The major focus of these advertisements was on books, many of which covered medical topics, followed by mostly medical products and services.

The content of the advertisements are important both for what they included as well as what they omitted. Pre-packaged brand drugs were a novel concept for a people who had spent centuries either preparing potions at home or having them made to order. The growing number of advertisements for branded commercial medicines which were available in both urban and provincial retail outlets, by post or through itinerant merchants, illustrates the gradual erosion of traditional kitchen physick and other types of 'non-commercial' medicine. This is not to suggest that it was ever replaced totally, but simply to demonstrate the beginnings of a movement that would result in a demand for proprietary drugs that resulted in overflowing eighteenth-century domestic medicine chests that would make modern ones appear almost austere.[95]

It is also interesting to note the absence of advertisements for other types of domestic material culture generally linked to the 'consumer revolution', such as curtains, china and clocks. Advertisements for products such as beer or food are also absent in almanacs.[96] I would argue that this says more about the cost of advertising than about the actual consumption of such goods. What might be classed as 'ordinary' as opposed to 'luxury' goods might have been considered to be too expensive to advertise in almanacs. Whilst a newspaper advertisement might be seen once or twice, the long life span of an individual almanac meant that an individual advertisement might be a number of times over the course of a year. While such advertisements were likely to have been cost-effective for proprietary drugs, which were probably fairly cheap to produce and yet sold at relatively high prices, the same may not have held true for more utilitarian products.

The continuing presence of advertisements for branded medicines implies success, whether this was because the medicines were actually effective, or at least perceived to be. By purchasing these drugs, readers were obtaining a medicine that, in theory,

---

94 Bosanquet, 'English Seventeenth-century Almanacks'; R. Westhawe (1594), sig. B3r.

95 R. Porter, 'The Patient in England, c. 1660–c. 1800', in A. Wear (ed.), *Medicine in Society* (Cambridge, 1992), p. 106.

96 Shammas, *The Pre-industrial Consumer*, pp. 157–94.

should always contain the same unadulterated ingredients in identical amounts. The two main ways purchasers could be sure of obtaining the real thing was through a mixture of package design and distribution points. As modern marketing methods still show, the presentation of a product can add to its perceived value.[97] It may be that the high percentage of alcohol or opiates in many products made people forget their troubles, or perhaps success was due to the placebo effect. If people believed that their medications would work, they may actually have done so.[98]

As this chapter has shown, the growing acceptance, popularity and subsequent demand for proprietary medicines in the seventeenth century changed the face of the English medical marketplace forever. It also illustrates the beginnings of the 'booming health culture' of the eighteenth century, which encompassed a preoccupation with health and fascination with proprietary medicines.[99]

---

97 Crimp, *Market Research,* p. 4.

98 Porter and Porter, *Patient's Progress*, p. 24; K. Thomas, *Religion and the Decline of Magic* (London, 1991), pp. 248–9.

99 Porter, 'Consumption', p. 69.

Chapter 4

Accessing Drugs in the Eighteenth-Century Regions

Steven King

Introduction

It is well known that treatment of medical conditions was often not drug-related for most of the eighteenth century. Leeches/bloodletting, lifestyle solutions and doing nothing were, as Roy Porter has shown, an eighteenth-century commonplace.[1] For much of the eighteenth century, diseases, and hence their cure, were seen as unique to the sufferer, and even by the late eighteenth century medical education in leading universities 'stressed the importance of practising medicine within a system'.[2] This said, and as Louise Curth has pointed out in Chapter 1 of this volume, much of the eighteenth-century literature dealing directly or tangentially with the development of the medical marketplace shows a rise in demand for doctoring services. The clear need for doctors to garner more of the market, to professionalize and distinguish themselves clearly from others in the medical marketplace, meant rising demand was probably linked to a tendency to adopt more by way of remedy-based medical care. Crudely, doctors had to be seen to be 'doing something'. This was particularly true of the emerging surgeon-apothecary grade of practitioner, key players in the evolution of 'The idea of a disease process distinct from the sufferer'.[3] In turn, apothecaries, druggists and early chemists were more directly dependent for their continued prosperity on the formulation and distribution of remedies to order or on speculation.

---

1   R. Porter, 'Spreading medical enlightenment: the popularization of medicine in Georgian England and its paradoxes', in R. Porter (ed.), *The Popularization of Medicine 1650–1850* (London, 1992), pp. 218–23; C. Lawrence, *Medicine in the Making of Modern Britain* (London, 1994), p. 12.

2   C. Lawrence, 'Ornate physicians and learned artisans: Edinburgh medical men 1726–1776', in W.F. Bynum (ed.), *William Hunter and the Eighteenth Century Medical World* (Cambridge, 1985), p. 156.

3   Lawrence, *Medicine in the Making of Modern Britain*, pp. 28–30; but see I. Inkster, 'Marginal men: aspects of the social role of the medical community in Sheffield 1790–1850', in J. Woodward and D. Richards (eds), *Health Care and Popular Medicine in Nineteenth Century England* (London, 1977), p. 130, who argues that at the end of the eighteenth century there was no inevitable connection between London and provincial practice. See also R. Porter, 'The people's health in Georgian England', in T. Harris (ed.), *Popular Culture in England c.1500–1859* (London, 1995), p. 134.

These features of the medical environment, plus the continuance of self-dosing, aristocratic doctoring of the locality and the tendency for access to quacks and doctors to work its way down the social scale, must have made the late eighteenth and early nineteenth centuries an age of pills and potions. Indeed, Christopher Lawrence suggests that as well as physicians, surgeons and surgeon-apothecaries, 'A multitude of other healers … swarmed through eighteenth century society … flamboyantly selling their wares.'[4] In practice, the dividing line between trained and registered practitioner and untrained 'quack' was often not as distinct as the rhetoric of contemporary debate suggested, but the key point for this chapter is that there was a rich network of drug *suppliers* in place by the later eighteenth century.[5] Some of them (doctors, quacks, chemists, medical irregulars) produced drugs on a commercial basis. Others (some middling families and medical irregulars in particular) produced and dispensed drugs on a non-profit basis. Some drugs came free. Doctors might prescribe free to the poor or middling as a loss leader, for instance, whilst middling and aristocratic families in many places appear to have dispensed both advice and medicine to the impoverished. And, of course, family archives are littered with commonplace books which testify to production and self-dosing of medicines at domestic or family level.[6] Yet characterization of the drugs available to eighteenth-century families from this network of suppliers – before 'the infusion of science into medical practice' – has generally been severe. Edward Shorter, for instance, refers to 'endless lists of syrups, spirits, infusions and extracts'. He warns that: 'For the traditional patient, therefore, access to medicine meant really procuring a prescription for some complex purgative the patient could not compound.'[7] Weatherall is similarly dismissive, noting the 'chaotic state of therapeutics' and the tendency for doctors to supply 'complicated prescriptions containing many supposedly active drugs'.[8] Useless, or indeed positively harmful, quack remedies loaded with addictive drugs are a commonplace in the historiographical literature, and more widely, Loudon points to a concerted attack on the drug and ingredient services offered by druggists after 1790.[9]

---

4   Lawrence, *Medicine in the Making of Modern Britain*, pp. 15 and 37.

5   I. Loudon, 'The vile race of quacks with which this country is infested', in W.F. Bynum and R. Porter (eds), *Medical Fringe and Medical Orthodoxy, 1750–1850* (London, 1987), p. 106; R. Porter, *Quacks* (Stroud, 2000), pp. 161–92; D. Porter and R. Porter, *Patients Progress* (Cambridge, 1989), p. 100; C. Thompson, *The Quacks of Old London* (London, 1928).

6   But see M. Weatherall, 'Drug therapies', in W.F. Bynum and R. Porter (eds), *Companion Encyclopaedia of the History of Medicine* (London, 1993), p. 916, who notes that there was little in print about drug preparation standards.

7   E. Shorter, 'The History of the doctor–patient relationship', in Bynum and Porter (eds), *Companion Encyclopaedia of the History of Medicine*, pp. 783–7.

8   M. Weatherall, 'Drug therapies', in Bynum and Porter, *Companion Encyclopaedia of the History of Medicine*, p. 917; my emphasis.

9   Loudon, 'The vile race of quacks with which this country is infested', p. 108.

These abstract dimensions of eighteenth-century drug supply are relatively easy to trace. Yet they are based upon slim empirical and theoretical foundations. Notwithstanding the excellent work of Hilary Marland, Mary Fissell and others, we are desperately short of systematic regional studies of the medical marketplace or patient strategies.[10] The implicit research agenda posed by Anne Digby on the economics of doctoring (and by implication, drug supply) has not been followed up.[11] Detailed family case studies remain deeply unfashionable. Hence, in the context of this chapter, important questions that remain unasked or unanswered will be addressed. How did different groups in different regions put together the potential avenues (or how they were put together for them) for securing drugs to refine a treatment strategy? Were the sorts of drugs made and sold the same in each region, or were there specific regional recipes and dosing strategies? Were regions insular medical marketplaces, or did medicines from other areas and even the metropolis seep into them? How robust was the production and marketing of drugs? Were drugs always to be had when wanted, either by patients or professionals? Within any locality, could the market for drugs withstand the loss to death, bankruptcy or migration of a major player? How long did it take to replace such major players? To what extent was there collusion or competition amongst drug suppliers on a regional basis? Were drugs sought by or imposed on patients? How were new drugs introduced to the medical marketplace? How were the experiences of the comfortable and poor similar or different? What were the cost dynamics of drugs in the emerging medical marketplace?

Obtaining answers to these questions is a formidable wish list, and clearly beyond the scope of a single chapter. That said, this chapter uses sources from two regional contexts – Lancashire and Northamptonshire – with other regional examples to explore the medical and drug strategies of the middling and the poor.[12] The two regions provide an important socio-economic contrast that should allow us to identify regional nuances in medicine if they existed. Eighteenth-century Lancashire had an early dependence upon rural industry, and by the later eighteenth century was home to a thriving cotton trade and a growing urban population. By contrast, eighteenth-century Northamptonshire was largely agricultural, was racked by enclosure, and had a small urban population.

---

10   H. Marland, *Medicine and Society in Wakefield and Huddersfield 1780–1870* (Cambridge, 1987); M. Fissell, *Patients, Power and the Poor in Eighteenth Century Bristol* (Cambridge, 1991).

11   A. Digby, *Making a Medical Living: Doctors and Patients in the English Market for Medicine* (Cambridge,1994).

12   Arguably, it was the medical demands of these groups, rather than the aristocrats and higher gentry, that drove the development of a medical marketplace.

Eighteenth-Century Drug Supply: A Framework for Understanding

Any attempt to dissect the supply of medicines in regional England of the eighteenth century must initially discuss the framework of opportunity and constraint faced by patients and suppliers. These framework conditions were complex, and are often missed in medical historiography. Thus, road and canal development in the eighteenth century notionally made England a smaller place and facilitated the spread of medical knowledge and medical personnel. The Rev. John Penrose, for instance, went to Bath to take the water for his gout in 1766, and on his way he and his wife encountered:

> A young Gentleman one Mr Cook, who is going to set up business (which is that of an Apothecary) here at Bath, his Mother is the person Mrs Walker taulk's so much of. It was very happy for us that we met with so agreeable a companion for he was very useful to Papa on the road. [13]

On another occasion, in 1767, Penrose met a gaggle of doctors and apothecaries fleeing fever in Banbury, who advised him to bypass the place. More generally, Penrose seems to have found no problem obtaining drugs and medical attention in towns linked by the emerging network of turnpike roads. Even in places such as Camelford, he was able to consult 'Mr Murray, a Druggist of this place'.[14] The analogue is that living in outlying rural counties probably posed serious problems to sick residents throughout the eighteenth century. In the 1787 census of Westmorland, not a single apothecary was recorded, and few doctors/surgeons. John Nickleson was a doctor in Cliburn, Hugh Docker was a surgeon in Morland parish, and Michael Parker was a surgeon in Shap.[15] Substantial medical provision was to be found only in Kendal, and in these more distant locations a few doctors remained suppliers of drugs to patients over a very wide area throughout the eighteenth century. In October 1781, for instance, Dr Bickerstall submitted his bill (19s. 6d.) for treatment of the Robinson family of Bignall in Cumbria between 28 July and 6 October. The list contained: 'A small bottle of acid drops, A parcil of strengthening powders, A quart infusion of bark in wine, A larger bottle of drops, Pill for the teeth, the drops *requested* double quantity, the powders *requested*, an astringent draught, a large opening mixture and a box of opening pills'.[16] It is interesting here that as well as supplying his own medicines as part of a treatment programme, Bickerstall supplies medicine to order, suggesting both a vigorous self-dosing regime and some background medical knowledge. In such spatially marginal communities, both characteristics are perhaps to be expected. Lancashire and Northamptonshire were

---

13   B. Mitchell and H. Penrose (eds), *Letters from Bath 1766–1767, by the Rev John Penrose* (Stroud, 1983), p. 24.

14   Ibid., p. 166.

15   L. Ashcroft, *Vital Statistics* (Curwen Archives Texts, Berwick, 1992).

16   Cumbria Record Office Kendal (hereafter CRO) WD/Big/1/147, 'Bill'; my emphasis.

hardly spatially marginal. Lancashire, for instance, was home to the most vibrant of integrated turnpike and canal networks. None the less, both counties had places – The Fylde and north Lancashire or East Northamptonshire, for instance – where the physical presence of doctors and other medical personnel was very limited. Similar observations might be made about counties such as Cornwall or areas such as the West Country. Access to drugs and doctors at sub-regional level might not always, therefore, have been either easy or certain.

One of the knock-on effects of better transport was an improvement in the flow and density of information. In terms of the communication of general medical knowledge and the specifics of drug formulation and dosing, this sort of information revolution offered profound opportunities to the sick. Roy Porter has demonstrated that the *Gentleman's Magazine* was packed with medical information, at least some of it contributed by medical men themselves.[17] That readers took some account of such information can be seen in a recipe copied from the *Gentleman's Magazine* by a member of the Cavendish family of Lancashire and inserted into their family recipe book. It read:

> As I think no person should keep to himself the knowledge of what may prove beneficial to mankind, I publish in the following manner the medicine which I know from much experience may be relied on to cure the worst kind of Thrush in women Tho indeed I could make a secret of it.[18]

Ginnie Smith and others have concentrated upon self-help manuals, diagnosis books and descriptions of the medicinal properties of plants, suggesting that such publications empowered consumers and allowed them to seek out their own particular package of medical care from the locality and elsewhere.[19] Moreover, as Mary Fissell points out, not only did almanacks and self-help manuals carry plenty of 'Choice receipts in physick and surgery', but the eighteenth-century practice of reading out loud fostered dissemination of knowledge far beyond the printed medium.[20] Presumably, too, this culture would have allowed servants to acquire and disseminate knowledge. However, we see the information revolution played out most keenly in the process by which local home-brewed remedies achieve regional or

---

17   R. Porter, 'Laymen, doctors and medical knowledge in the eighteenth century: the evidence of the Gentleman's Magazine', in R. Porter (ed.), *Patients and Practitioners* (Cambridge, 1985), pp. 283–314.

18   Lancashire Record Office (hereafter LRO), DDCa 17/234, 'A cure for Thrush'. This may have been an attempt to elevate the local standing of a quack or practitioner.

19   G. Smith, 'Prescribing the rules of health: self-help and advice in the late eighteenth century', in Porter, *Patients and Practitioners*, pp. 250–55. For an advert dealing with *Blackwell's Herbal*, 2 volumes containing 500 prints 'of the most useful plants used in the practice of Physick ... to which are added 125 explanation plates giving a description of the plants with their uses in Physick', see *Manchester Magazine* (24 November 1741).

20   M.E. Fissell, 'Readers, texts, and contexts: vernacular medical works in early modern England', in Porter, *The Popularization of Medicine*, pp. 72 and 94; E. Furdell, *Publishing and Medicine in Early Modern England* (New York, 2002).

national visibility. Thus, in Lancashire, the women of the Parker/Shackleton family brewed their own rabies medicine, and by the late eighteenth century people were travelling hundreds of miles to purchase it.[21] Elizabeth Shackleton's diary of early 1781 records the following instances:

> 13th January Miss Chippendale from Skipton came to take the medicine and Nelly
>   Nutter came whincing about her son Robert to take the medicine from a lick he
>   had from John Rileys dog supposed to have gone off mad.
> Weds 14th February A man came for a shot into Rippondale he took it.
> Monday 19 February A man from Dumfries in Scotland came for 4 meds one for a
>   woman that was bit with a cat.
> Thursday 22 Feb Betty dairymaid from Marsden came to take the medicine.
> Friday March 1 A gentleman and two servants from Malton came and took the
>   medicine.[22]

The family had founded a very promising drug supply venture and we return to them later in this chapter. More widely, with the advent of trade directories, newspaper advertising, business cards[23] and easier communication by letter, it is clear that one of the greatest stimuli to the development of a sales network for drugs must have been this improvement in the speed and depth of information flow.

Not all, though, were in a position to take advantage of the dissemination of medical knowledge or the increasing supply of medical practitioners. Indeed, the eighteenth century was dotted with groups of people who were cut off from (or who cut themselves off from) wide access to drugs and doctors. The rapidly growing Moravian community at Fulneck near Leeds was physically separate from surrounding communities, and its registers suggest no resident medical personnel.[24] The Quakers of north-east Lancashire or west Northamptonshire were equally cut off from an emerging medical marketplace. Lancashire Catholics also found themselves in an anomalous position. The biggest group of Catholics in England, they formed almost a majority of the population in some places before the rapid population rises of the last decades of the eighteenth century. Catholic access to medicine was, however, limited. The general population had a long history of turning to the local Catholic gentry to provide medicines and medical treatment.[25] Even by the mid- and late eighteenth century, Catholic gentry were playing an active role in medical provision and there was a pronounced tendency to prefer Catholic doctors. Yet, as the 1776 survey of the Catholics in Lancashire makes clear, Catholic doctors were thinly

---

21   The eighteenth-century concern with rabies was profound. For even earlier Lancashire evidence, see 'A cure for the bite of a mad dog, publish'd for the benefit of mankind by a person of note', *Manchester Magazine* (11 August 1741).

22   LRO DDb 81/39, 'Diary'.

23   For an early example, see Manchester Central Library (Hereafter MCL), M35 5/17/13, 'Bill and trade card'.

24   Public Record Office RG4 3062 1-E, 'Moravian births and baptisms 1753–1781', and RG4 3 343 1-E, 'Moravian births and baptisms 1742–1783 and burials 1749–1783'.

25   S.A. King, *A Fylde Country Practice* (Lancaster, 2002).

spread and failing to reproduce themselves. Thus, in Wigan, Mr Bryan Hardson was a midwife-doctor aged 60 who had lived in Wigan for forty years; Ralph Thickness was a doctor of Physick aged 48 who had lived in Wigan for fourteen years; Peter Marden was a doctor of 70 who had lived in Wigan for fifteen years; Joseph Cooling was an apothecary of 57 who had lived in Wigan for 44 years and lived with an apprentice, John Cropper aged 23, who had been in Wigan three years. Mr Thomas Harden was an apothecary, but younger, at 48. He had none the less lived in Wigan for twenty-seven years. This may be evidence of a stable drug/doctoring supply, but it is also evidence of a medical corpus that lacked long-term critical mass. Indeed, only Mr Thomas Scott, a surgeon of 29, was a recent addition to the Wigan medical scene, having lived there for just one year. In turn, if we look at the rest of the Catholic census of 1776, we see no Catholic medical men at all in Pemberton, Haigh, Abram, Ince, Aspull, Hindley, Billinge, Upholland, Orrell, Dalton or Walton Le Dale. In Kirkham town, Thomas Swarsbreck, aged 40, was an apothecary who had lived there for fifteen years, but there were no Catholic medical men in Newton with Scales, Freckleton, Westby, Plumpton, Weeton, Eccleston, Greenal, Medlar, Treales, Warton, Bryning or Ribby.[26] Nor is there evidence of extensive numbers of Catholics from this area feeding through to the case books of the local Anglican doctor, Dr Loxham.[27] In short, several thousand people must have found their access to doctors, drugs and the middling and upper reaches of the practitioner spectrum constricted by notions of religion and custom.

Others found themselves drowned out of the medical marketplace and the market for drugs by issues of cost. Whilst there is evidence of an emerging poor underclass who were perpetually dependent upon poor relief and charity from the late eighteenth century onwards,[28] this is not simply a rich versus poor dichotomy. Many middling and wealthier families railed against the cost of medical care and drugs and/or refused to call doctors or go to apothecaries for themselves or their servants except in cases of dire necessity. The Rev. John Penrose found his stock of ready cash rapidly depleted within two weeks of coming to Bath. He wrote pointedly to his housekeeper in Cornwall on 22 April 1766:

> I would have you prepare, as well as you can, to set out for Bath immediately on our coming home: for you will do anything I'm sure for the good of the Family; and what can be more so, than for you to set up here as a Nurse-Keeper? They have a Guinea a Week. As you are so expert in that profession, and can be strongly recommended for industry and honesty, you will certainly make more of it.[29]

His temper had improved by 23 April, when he wrote: 'I hate for gouty folks to lie at home grunting when so cheap a Remedy as Water is within 200 miles of them.'

26 M. Orrell, *The Catholic census of Lancashire 1767* (London, 1987).
27 King, *A Fylde Country Practice*.
28 S.A. King, *Poverty and Welfare 1700–1850: A Regional Perspective* (Manchester, 2000).
29 Mitchell and Penrose, *Letters from Bath*, p. 46.

By 8 May, however, he had received more bills and he styled his doctor bitterly as 'One of Ten Thousand', whilst by 24 May he was looking forward to paying his bills and getting out of the grip of the leeches of Bath.[30] He at least could pay. Other middling people periodically found medicine, or at least certain types of medicine in certain areas, outside their grasp. In 1702, Margaret Weld wrote from London to her father, Sir James Simeon, at Stone in Staffordshire. Pregnant, sick and faced by a 'very mortall' smallpox outbreak in London, she reflected on the fact that she could not afford to seek medical treatment there – 'the charge will be intolerably great' - and she would have to leave it until they got back to the family home in Lulworth, Dorset.[31] The straitened circumstances continued. In a letter of 4 May 1706 to her father, Margaret notes:

> Two of our maid servants have been very ill this fortnight of a feaver that goes about in the country, they were let blood and blistered for four days. I thought they would have dyed, we were *forc'd* to send for a doctor, who only approv'd of what had been done'.[32]

Several important points spring from this brief extract. First, that the medicine initially tried was treatment by the lady of the house. Second, that Weld was as unwilling to call a doctor for others as she was for herself. Third, that it may have been cheaper at home because doctoring was less professional than in the City. Finally, that the doctor called either did not have the social standing to contradict Weld, or had no drugs in his armoury to give in the context of the fever raging in the country. At the opposite end of the eighteenth century, the Brierley family of Kirkham, near Preston, were equally unwilling to deal with doctors or to use drugs due to the cost.[33] In turn, Joan Lane has generalized this sort of individual example to suggest that even for the middling sorts, the doctor and his drugs were a court of last resort.[34]

Yet whilst some middling people may have absented themselves, and their servants, from the market for medicine, others who really could not afford it none the less engaged. The independent labouring poor and labour aristocracy, for instance, would often call in doctors or apothecaries to meet illness and then seek to pay for treatment and drugs in instalments or in kind. Such was the experience of Dr Loxham of Poulton on the Lancashire Fylde, who saw payments in cash and kind dribble in from such patients often over several years.[35] Even those who were in poverty or on its verges might resort to the doctor or the apothecary and then apply to the poor law to pay the bill. In both Lancashire and Northamptonshire, for instance, vestries faced a constant battle with paupers who thought they had a right to call in

---

30 Ibid., pp. 51 and 141.
31 Bodleian Library (hereafter BDL) Weld Mss C.13/5/8, 'Letter, London 1702'. I am grateful to Elizabeth Hurren for this reference.
32 BDL Weld Mss C. 15/5/23, 'Letter 4 May 1706'; My emphasis. I am grateful to Elizabeth Hurren for this reference.
33 King, *A Fylde Country Practice.*
34 J. Lane, *The Making of the English Patient* (Stroud, 2000), p. 43.
35 LRO DDPr 25/6, 'An account book of a doctor on the Fylde'.

the doctors and medical men, who concurred or who were badgered into providing care when the poor turned up on their doorsteps.[36] Questions of costs versus income thus work in subtle ways on the nature of engagement with the medical marketplace and the market for drugs at a regional level.

Other framework conditions also have a subtle impact. Thus, irrespective of notional incomes or costs, we must realize that eighteenth-century England experienced a chronic shortage of the small coinage needed to pay for drugs.[37] It is much too easy to take the advertisements of quacks or the account books of apothecaries at face value and assume that prices mediated through to payment. Whilst 6d. or 1s. for a bottle of Daffy's Elixir might not have been very much in nominal terms, finding the cash for the quack or the apothecary was a completely different matter. We have already seen that some of the labouring patients of Dr Loxham sought to pay in instalments. However, his very worst payers were the gentry, who had competing demands for clothing, food, estate management, travel and rates on their purses at the same times as their income tended to flow in quarterly from rents.[38] Shortages of coin were most severe in the eighteenth-century industrial districts such as Lancashire or West Yorkshire, where bartering for goods, services and medicines was common, but even in rural Northamptonshire, the seasonality to the rural economy was probably reflected in a seasonality to the availability of coinage.[39] The problem of liquidity may have been least severe in larger urban areas, and urbanization is a further framework condition that we must review briefly.

Hence, whilst it is true that the first decades of the nineteenth century were home to the most rapid English urbanization, it is also true that in the eighteenth century, many provincial towns, Northampton for instance, made steady gains in terms of absolute population size. Other towns, particularly in the emerging industrial areas, experienced substantial percentage population growth, whilst some flourished briefly and brilliantly before deflating and stagnating. These sorts of urban context provided both opportunities and constraints for the supply of, and demand for, drugs. On the supply side, larger or rapidly growing urban areas would have given impetus to the formation of nascent medical districts, where doctoring and drug making were combined in the same physical area, of the sort that would develop substantially in the nineteenth century. Even smaller urban areas might support a surprising range of medical people.

Without the ubiquitous trade directories of the nineteenth century to link to medical directories, it is difficult to locate precisely the role of urban areas in eighteenth-century regional medical networks. However, if we use the flotsam and

---

36   S.A. King, 'Stop this overwhelming torment of destiny': Negotiating Medical Relief under the English Old Poor Law 1800–1840', *Bulletin of the History of Medicine*, 79 (2005), pp. 228–60.

37   On this issue, see J.C. Muldrew and S.A. King, 'Cash, wages and the economy of makeshifts in England 1650–1800', in P. Scholliers and L. Schwarz (eds), *Worlds of Wages* (Cambridge, 2004).

38   King, *A Fylde Country Practice*.

39   Muldrew and King, 'Cash, wages and the economy of makeshifts'.

jetsam of county record offices – deeds, mortgages, releases and indentures – it is possible to begin to appreciate the impact that even modest urbanization might have on the visibility of medical people, and presumably their drugs and cures. By way of example, we might look very briefly at towns in Northamptonshire. Thus, surviving deeds and rental lists for Spratton indicate that the town got its first resident surgeon apothecary, Robert Hawkins, in the late 1770s.[40] Oundle appears to have got its first resident apothecary at the same date.[41] Towcester certainly had at least one apothecary by the early eighteenth century. The apothecary Backhouse Harris gave his neighbour William Davis a right of way to his house in November 1737.[42] And such documents reveal that Northampton itself had at least four apothecaries and a range of other practitioners operating in the early and mid-eighteenth century.[43]

Whilst a minority of people lived in towns by 1800, their importance as a focus for a doctor's 'circuit' and a location for the fixed shops and consulting rooms of apothecaries and others who dispensed drugs is clear. Little surprise, then, to find that at the very end of our period, the Hensman family of Pytcheley were drawing on a wide range of urban practitioners for their medical needs.[44] Yet it would be wrong to think that the impact of urbanization on the supply of medical services and drugs was inevitably positive. Anne Digby has shown that urban doctors frequently formed cartels to protect their margins and suppress market clearing, the effect of which must have been to constrain access.[45] Moreover, as urban doctors and drug suppliers enriched themselves, they tended to diversify their economic interests into land and other ventures, encouraging them to put time and resources into non-medical activities. Thus, Harry Stile of Thame, apothecary, often appears to have been in Syresham, Northamptonshire, to oversee leases of farms on his estate there in the 1770s.[46]

Much more could be said about framework conditions. The key point, however, is that drug supply in the eighteenth century is likely to have been influenced by a complex regional melting pot of socio-economic and cultural continuity and change. We can begin to unpick this complex picture by concentrating on the drug procurement strategies of two groups of people – the comfortable middling sort, and the poor on relief.

---

40 Northamptonshire Record Office (hereafter NRO) ZA 907, 'Abstract of deeds: Robert Hawkins of Spratton'.

41 NRO ZA 1 345, 'Lease, January 1784'.

42 NRO ZA 4 439, 'Right of way release'.

43 NRO ZA 681, 'Apprenticeship indenture'; ZA 1058, 'Assignment of mortgage'; ZA 1897, 'Deed to specify the uses of a fine'; ZA 4497, 'Mortgage'; ZA 4580, 'Lease and release'.

44 NRO ZA 2 110–13, 'Account books, 1801–1850'.

45 Digby, *Making a Medical Living*.

46 NRO ZA 833, 'Indentures and feoffment'. From a different angle but to the same effect, see the Colne Parish Registers, where we find the entry 'Baptised 14th July, 1737, Barton Barton, son of Joshua Barton of Darwen or Manchester, Apothecary, and Margaret Baldwin of Colne, Illegitimate'. Barton had come a long way indeed in search of his sex life.

Medicines and the Middling Sort

It is now well established that the middling sort were the great success story of the eighteenth and early nineteenth centuries. They were also important drivers of domestic demand in the Industrial Revolution, and a vital conduit for the process of the commercialization of medical services and drug supply. Yet whilst these conclusions might be plain in broad outline, there are relatively few family or regional studies at the disposal of the medical historian. We might thus begin our analysis of the drug supply strategies of the middling sort with a Lancashire family case study.

On 23 November 1816, just outside our period, Dr William St Clare wrote from Preston to Mrs Whitacker of Moorfield, near Clitheroe in Lancashire. She was approaching the final stages of pregnancy, and his letter said:

> My Dear Madam, As the period approaches, a good deal of attention has to be paid to the bowels. I don't mean however that it will be necessary to go beyond the measure of just keeping them moderately open. This may be answered by occasionally taking a neat spoonful of castor oil; or two or three aperiant pills, as prescribed on the other side, as may be found most agreeable. It will be advisable to continue to go out a little in the open air every day as long as you can bear it; using the exercise very easily, so as not to fatigue or over heat. Great caution will now become necessary in walking up or down stairs as a failure of the limbs is apt to take place, which has often occasioned unpleasant falls. When any stitch, great uneasiness, pain or bearing down occurs, it will be provident to change the posture by lying down a while either on the couch or a bed, or by turning from one side to the other. With regard the diet no particular regime seems necessary. Most anxiously wishing you a happy moment and every other blessing, I remain ever dear madam Most Faithfully yours, Wm St Clare
>
> R extract Colocynth c., aloes spic, sod. sub. carbon [d], extract anthernid [d], ol. carni [d], mucilary qs vt ft mass and ri [d], sign, capt [d] vit [d] hor somm, pro [rom], sign normine proprio.[47]

St Clare's letter demonstrates very well the complexity of doctor–patient relationships in the provinces, as well as showing how much doctors continued to rely on advice as a medical and social tool. In the context of this chapter, however, it is significant for another reason. St Clare had been doctor to the Whitacker family for well over thirty years, and this was the first time that he had issued a prescription to be made up locally rather than sending medicines or bringing them directly himself.[48] Breaking the habit of decades was clearly not a one-off. Over the next four years he sent prescriptions for effervescing medicine, aperient mixture and a medicine 'to soothe during pain and keep off miscarriage', as well as recommending that the Whitacker family secure a supply of James's Powder, a clear indication that a national drugs market

---

47 LRO DDWh 4/92, 'Letter, 23 November, 1816'.

48 For previous and subsequent letters, see the large number of items in LRO DDWh 4, 'Correspondence 1770s to 1820s'.

intruded on the regional.[49] This change of attitude might reflect the fact that St Clare was no longer in need of family patronage, that the range of illness the Whitackers faced had changed, or that St Clare had wormed his way into the social circle of the family sufficiently to adopt a more distant attitude. A more subtle interpretation, and the one preferred here, is that St Clare had, for the first time, been able to build up a close working relationship with a local apothecary. Certainly his letters after this one in 1816 begin to refer to Mr Hardy, an apothecary from Whalley on the Preston side of the Whitacker residence and directly on the line of communication between St Clare and his patient. Thus, in a letter of September 1820, he notes that Mr Hardy had come with medicine, and that 'Should the drowsiness continue Mr Hardy might probably think it prudent to apply half a dozen leeches to the temples or perhaps a blister to the nape of the neck, besides paying particular attention to the bowels.' In November 1820, he notes that 'Mr Hardy will not fail to warn you of the approach of fever', whilst on 6 May 1821 he recommends Mrs Whitacker to send a message to Mr Hardy's shop for medicine.[50] St Clare's change of approach to his more distant patients may reflect the first stages of a transformation in the preparation and selling of medicines at sub-regional level, a theme taken up by Hilary Marland in Chapter 5 of this volume. It probably also prefigures the development of medical districts within and between towns, as I have argued elsewhere.[51]

For the purposes of this chapter, however, the St Clare story demonstrates keenly how complex access to medicines must have been for the middling sort in the eighteenth century outside the metropolis, county towns and medical hot spots like Spa towns. St Clare was based in Preston, and clearly had an extensive and well-established circuit of patients whom he visited in person and diagnosed and prescribed by letter. His circuit must have overlapped with those of other, more local, doctors. Thus, whilst the Whitacker family chose to go to St Clare, Elizabeth Shackleton, who lived not very far from them in the late eighteenth century, consulted doctors Turner and Midgeley from Colne.[52] Such overlapping circuits were common elsewhere in Lancashire,[53] and their existence and operation confirms the core–periphery model of the doctors' circuit advanced by Digby.[54] Yet if we know plenty about the doctor's circuit, what do we know about the complementary, doctor-based, drug circuit? We have seen that until the nineteenth century, St Clare chose to bring his medicines direct to the Whitacker family, or to send them by post. Indeed, he requested that the family confirm that medicines had arrived on all occasions. This was not through

---

49   For an explanation of what went into various medicines and pills, see Royal College of Surgeons, London (hereafter RCS) Mss Add 104, 'Ashton family domestic remedies', pp. 1–3, or LRO DDx 1554/9, 'Dr Willeses Domestic Medicine'.

50   LRO DDWh 4/104 and 107, 'Letters'.

51   King, *A Fylde Country Practice.*

52   LRO DDb 81/39, 'Diary'.

53   King, *A Fylde Country Practice.*

54   Digby, *Making a Medical Living.* St Clare, for instance, was frequently forced to send diagnoses and remedies by post to the Whitackers because more pressing (that is, nearer) concerns over took him.

want of local apothecaries to make up his prescriptions or local doctors to dispense on his behalf. The parish registers of Colne reveal that Dr Samuel Coates was baptising and burying children in the 1740s, and that John Barnes, an apothecary, was burying his children at the same date.[55] By the later eighteenth century, as we have already seen above, Elizabeth Shackleton was consulting doctors from Colne. It is perhaps unsurprising that St Clare would not turn to other doctors in the locality. More surprising is the fact that he did not turn to the apothecaries in Colne in the later eighteenth century. The parish registers reveal that William Midgley, apothecary, died (presumably after practising in the town) in April 1759. John Parr, apothecary, died in January 1763, and Henry Bird, apothecary, died in May 1784. Why St Clare would want to conduct his own drug supply business by post or in person is open to speculation. Drug supply at a distance may have increased his professional authority by promising something that could not be obtained locally, for instance. The point for this chapter is that he did, and that drug supply retained an element of the personal in the eighteenth century. This must have meant medicines from Preston criss-crossing with medicines from Colne and other towns in north-east Lancashire in a complex local drugs market punctuated, as we have seen, with the presence of nationally available remedies such as James's Powder.

Two brief case studies of other doctors confirm this situation. Edward Sabine of Towcester, Northamptonshire, was operating as a surgeon in the late eighteenth century, and apparently making a good living.[56] His prescription book for 1797–98 survives, and contains almost 2,600 prescriptions, no less than 504 in April 1797 alone.[57] Some of these prescriptions were for the parish poor and the labouring poor. Others were for sickness clubs and friendly societies, and still more for travellers passing through Towcester on their way to or from Northampton.[58] The majority, though, appear to have been destined for middling families in, and for some distance around, Towcester. Indeed, some 450 entries appear to be repeat prescriptions for such middling patients issued on a regular basis, suggesting a robust local drug supply mechanism. Moreover, it is clear that it was Sabine himself who made up many of the prescriptions. On 9 April 1797, he wrote himself a memo to one of

55   J. Bentley, *Colne Parish Registers 1734–1774* (Colne Parish Register Society, 1990), p. 7.

56   See, for instance, his part in NRO ZA 4406, 'Conveyance and assignment of a mortgage, 4 April 1787'.

57   NRO YZ 1770, 'Prescription book of Dr Sabine of Towcester, 1797–8'. The book contains the date of the prescription, the person for whom it is intended, dosage and the prescription itself.

58   Towcester was on the A5, and he would have found it easy to pick up business from middling patients on the road. The location would also have made it easier for Sabine to tap into medical gossip and new medical knowledge. Note here the resonance with the Rev. John Penrose, who frequently consulted medical men while on the road.

the prescriptions, noting: 'Miss Lovell's medicines to be got ready to go again on Tuesday.'[59]

Of course, sources like this are problematic in many ways. Thomas Giordano Wright illustrates the potential pitfalls of relying on them when he says that: 'having seen in my tour on a moderate calculation about a score of patients and with my brain full of prescriptions ready for delivery into the day book'.[60] Given the gap between the delivery of the prescription or the medicine and its recording, we must be wary of taking prescription books at face value. None the less, even in a very general sense, Sabine's prescription book must testify to a very substantial local network of medicines and instructions centred about late eighteenth-century Towcester. Since we know that there were surgeon-apothecaries in Northampton, Brackley, Syresham and Evenly, all presumably with overlapping prescription networks of the same order, it must be the case that medicines criss-crossed Northamptonshire as much as they did north-east Lancashire. Since some of these prescriptions were clearly destined for domestic execution, there is at least a *prima facie* case for suggesting that there must have been equally complex networks for the procurement of ingredients, though no doubt somewhat less formalized than the networks of chemists and druggists that were to emerge in the nineteenth century.

We might draw similar conclusions from the account book of Dr Loxham of Poulton, in Lancashire, who was practising during the 1750s–1780s.[61] Whilst this account book does not always record the exact composition of drugs, it does list some 3 000 drug interventions over thirty years. Drawing up a definitive list of discrete drugs is complicated by the fact that Loxham frequently bundles therapies together in one accounting entry, but as we might expect from the historiography, it is possible to generate a potentially very long list of infusions, decoctions, syrups. pills and embrocations. Thus, between 1750 and 1769, his most popular medicines were: Julep Cordial, purges, Anodyn mixture, vitriol, Balsam, Calem, Mercury, Camphor and tinctures. In terms of patient experiences, this might translate over even a short period into a very complex drugs bill. Hence Loxham attends the daughter of John Cummins on account of her hysterics for the first time on 30 May 1758. His prescribing then takes the following form:

---

59   NRO YZ 1770, 'Prescription book of Dr Sabine of Towcester 1797–8', 9 April 1797.

60   A. Johnson (ed.), *The Diary of Thomas Giaordani Wright, Newcastle Doctor 1826–1829* (Newcastle, 2001), p. 83.

61   LRO DDPr 25/6, 'An account book of a doctor on the Fylde'.

30 May 58	to vin ipec [dose]
29 Jun 58	to advice during a course of mercury[62]
	to a visit to her
	to pul purge [dose]
14 Jul 58	to vin naleb [dose
	to pul emet
22 Oct 59	to elect februfig cum nitro
9 Nov 59	to decoct cart cum acidus [dose]
26 Nov 59	to julep februfig [dose]
	to pul linat

Such drug treatment could be expensive, as illustrated by Loxham charging the middling Hornby family £2 10s. 6d. for medicines and £1 13s. 6d. for attendance in 1762. In most cases the balance is reversed, but still this is testimony to a vibrant drug market. As with Sabine in Towcester, some of the medicines were made up by Loxham himself. Thus, on 22 January 1762 we see an entry for the son of William Shaw, Carpenter of Marton, which says: 'to potio purg [dose] in phial'. This is a familiar entry, and suggests that Loxham had ingredients to hand. He certainly carried medicines with him. Thus, on 21 January 1763 we find an entry for the wife of David Atkinson, 'relating her fractured leg, setting [ditto] applications and c.', suggesting perhaps that Loxham had been summoned and grabbed the medicines most likely to be of use given the detail in the summons. However, Loxham, like the other doctors reviewed so far, also sent medicines in the post. On 7 June 1759, he makes up a phial of 'sal tartar [dose] emet distillant qq fort [dose] rq sac [dose] bolus e syr croci [dose', but 'to [ditto] repeated ye 1st being broken' when it went by post. Clearly, then, drug supply on the rural Fylde of Lancashire was every bit as complicated as it was around Colne, Clitheroe and Towcester. A further complication is that Loxham also had a relationship with a local apothecary, James Hull, who often called him in for problematic cases. On 6 August 1765, we see Loxham attending Henry Fisher for '2 visits to his daughter (one pr Jas Hull) …', whilst on 8 August 1763, 'Wm Cowell of Staining, a visit in a peripneumonary pr Hull'. At times, Loxham attended patients at the apothecary's house. On 27 February 1762, he charges Edward Jolly £1 1s. for attendance on his daughter 'for a week at Jas Hull's'. Such relationships led to further complexities in terms of supplying drugs. Thus, sometimes patients paid Loxham for drugs through James Hull, who then had to settle up with Loxham, as on 18 July 1762, when we see 'rec'd 13s. in part of ye above from Jas Hull'. Sometimes, too, the relationship worked in the opposite direction, as on 19 June 1758, when Loxham went to see Widow Ellen Whiteside to give 'advice to herself relating an intermittent complaint', and while there, he paid 'Mr Hull on her account for pills'.[63]

---

62 Supervised administration of medicine was relatively common for Loxham.
63 LRO DDPr 25/6, 'Account book of a doctor on the Fylde'.

In short, the localized activities of doctors and other medical professionals in a series of overlapping spatial networks must have meant the generation of a dense network of medicines and prescriptions at sub-regional level on eighteenth-century roads. Moreover, the fact that such networks were overlapping probably underpinned a robust drug supply for middling patients willing to switch between providers with very little compunction. The situation is made more complex by the fact that many middling families also consulted doctors and took their medicines from much further afield than their immediate locality. Elizabeth Shackleton, for instance, was inveigled by her relatives on 19 May 1781, who 'insisted I wo'd send for Doctor Edward Hall' from Manchester. He subsequently arrived, and 'We then began to talk of my disorder, he said it was the scurvy, beg'd I wo'd take a very slight vomit, then to take some med's he wo'd order, whatever I did to keep my body open.' His medicines duly arrived by post, and on 24 May: 'I had a painful night and took the new pills this morning order'd by Dr Hall.' Then, on 9 June, 'a most civil, obliging letter from Doctor Hall with a prescription'.[64] Not only was Shackleton locked into a north-east Lancashire network of medical supply, but she also had networks that spread as far as Manchester. Families in other regions were similarly locked into longer-distance medical networks. The Walker family of Ludlow in Shropshire, for instance, called upon local doctors, but also corresponded with Dr William Thomson of Worcester. One of the letters from Thomson is particularly illuminating. It dispensed advice, sought information and promised: 'As for the complaint on your skin, you know I shall be very shy of doing anything to repel your eruptions, but *if I can contrive a medicine* that will correct the acrimony and render its consequences less troublesome, I shall be very glad to *attempt it.*'[65] In this letter, then, we find definite evidence that doctors brewed their own remedies and that some families were tied into a longer-distance, commercialized, drug supply trade.

However, concentrating on drugs supplied by doctors or prescriptions to be made up by apothecaries only scratches the surface of the network of commercial drug supply. Apothecaries and chemists, for instance, were also called upon directly by middling families. Thus, on 17 August 1781, Elizabeth Shackleton was visited by 'my good fine old friend Mr Haworth from Clitheroe'. Shackleton had been ill all year with a foot problem, probably gout, and had been attended by three different doctors (Turner, Hall and Midgley) up to this point. Her diary goes on:

> He said he came on purpose to make me a visit, had left Mrs Haworth and Mrs Gilbert at Chatburne was to take them both home as he returned. He looked at my foot and said it was very bad ... I rejoiced to see this good man ... had 6 pounds of three sorts of powders and 6 pounds of bole .

Mr Haworth was an apothecary, and this short extract is telling for three reasons: first, because an apothecary had become a family friend, something that one might expect of a doctor but is less often seen amongst apothecaries. In a business

---

64   LRO DDb 81/39, 'Diary'.
65   RCS Mss 39, 'Letter of William Thomson', box 1, 20 March 1776; my emphasis.

where selling medicine was one arm of income (selling ingredients and making up prescriptions were the others), it clearly made good sense to be seen as a 'good fine old friend'; second, because he was obviously carrying much by way of prepared medicines with him on this ostensibly chance visit and clearly expected Shackleton to be a good customer, and third, because Shackleton *was* a good customer, and purchased remedies apparently without the direction of the doctor. In addition, of course, Haworth was engaged to make up the prescriptions of doctors. Shackleton's main doctor, Dr Turner, made over twenty professional visits during 1781. Haworth made only three visits, twice with Turner himself, but he supplied medicines on 11 separate occasions to the order of the doctors and 14 times on his own account. Thus, on 5 February, 'Mr Haworth sent julep, pills and cream of tartar with proper directions how to use them', whilst on 16 March: 'Received a letter and another bottle of rheumatism drops and a paper of bitters from Mr Haworth.' Similarly, on 21 April, 'another bottle of rheumatism drops and a letter from Mr Haworth who advises me much to take some working physick, he says will do me good', whilst on 29 April she received 'a box of working pills and a letter from Mr Haworth'.[66]

That there were ready supplies of certain medicines to be obtained from apothecaries and others, either in fixed shops or from travelling wagons, for much of the eighteenth century is confirmed in other sources. At the outset of our period, Margaret Weld's straitened circumstances, which prevented her own engagement with commercial medicine, did not stop her offering health advice. Writing to her father on 22 April 1704, she noted: 'I am sorry you have been troubled with gout since your last return to Aston. It will be very necessary to take *something* to carry it off now Easter is come.'[67] There are a number of ways to read such a passage, but one would be that there were several readily available remedies that her father might take if he chose to, testimony to a trade in drugs even at this early date. That this was the case can be seen in the efforts made by Sir Simeon to cure an unspecified chronic illness in his son. In response to various enquiries to friends and family about good doctors and apothecaries, Josiah Haddock sent him a handbill/charity note saying:

> Josiah Haddock, formerly a dispenser in Trinity College in Cambridge now a physician, chyrurgion, Apothecary and Pharmacpoian two years practice hath compounded severall wonderfull and healing remedies which are useful both in physick and in chrurgery. The said Josiah Haddock with God" blessing will endeavour if desired to heal all persons who cannot be healed elsewhere of any curable infirmity weakness or cause whatever, if not curable will endeavour if desired to give ease with the greatest safety care diligence experience and skillfullness imaginable.

Sir Simeon appended his own instructions, presumably to a servant: 'Enquire for him at the Crown Inn Newcastle-under-Lyme.'[68] Presumably he was impressed enough by a Cambridge connection to give over care of his heir to Haddock and his drugs.

---

66 Ibid.
67 BDL Weld Mss c. 13/5/12, 'Letter 22 April 1704'; my emphasis.
68 BDL Weld Mss c. 13/3/57, 'Flyer, 10 June 1706'.

The Rev. John Penrose paints a similar picture of the availability of drugs and implements, albeit that Bath is hardly representative of the rest of the country. His letter of 13 April 1766 notes: 'Your Mamma hath brought some charming gouty socks for me, and large gouty stockings, and is pleased with finding she may have at the shops here whatever she wants.'[69] Such buying opportunities extended to drugs as well. In his letter of 14 May 1766, Penrose notes:

> Having mentioned the Dearness of victuals, I must mention the cheapness of some sort of Physic; and I am credibly informed, that you Mamma bought senna enough for a penny to serve her and Fanny six or seven Times – No Laughing.[70]

One might read an implicit contrast in these two examples with their home town in Cornwall, but his letter of 8 May 1766, in which he orders 'We are very sorry Jacky's Teeth have ached. If they should ache again, he had best have recourse to Mrs Williams, and apply the same Medicine which gave him Ease', may suggest that local drug suppliers existed there too.[71] Some of the thinking that lay behind such purchases may be seen by his letter of 2 May 1766, in which he says: 'I will not have my Apothecary abused, no not in any Degree; and that, tho' no Graduate in any University, he is universally allowed to be as skillful in his Way, as an Physician in or out of the College.' Then, on 12 May he writes, deliberating whether to stay on in Bath, that his apothecary's advice 'has weight with me'.[72] Finally, when he leaves Bath on 1 June 1766, he overpays the apothecary's bill, 'desiring him to accept the Overplus as a Token of my Respect for him'.[73] Exactly similar sentiments coloured the relationship between Elizabeth Shackleton and her apothecary, as we have seen – evidence of the close bonds that might prompt middling people to periodically freeze doctors out of the drug supply picture.

Yet we should not go away with the impression that access to drugs for the middling sort in these different contexts was always stable and certain. Elizabeth Shackleton and many patients like her found that doctors did not always come when called. Nor did prescriptions and medicines arrive in the post when sent, a common complaint of William St Clare in his late eighteenth-century letters to the Whitacker family reviewed earlier. Medicines might also be damaged in the post, as we saw in the account book of Dr Loxham above. Moreover, we have already seen that for some middling families the cost of medical treatment in general could become prohibitive, notwithstanding their tendency to pay doctors late, in instalments or not at all. Even for those with the money, paying for medicine and attendance could represent significant background expenditure. Thus, between 1803 and 1811, a period when there was no serious family illness, John Bury from Manchester paid an average of

---

69   Mitchell and Penrose, *Letters from Bath*, p. 31.
70   Ibid., p. 110.
71   Ibid., p. 93.
72   Ibid., pp. 78 and 103.
73   Ibid., p. 154.

£3 per year to Dr Hardy for pills, drops, powders, plasters, blisters and advice.[74] And whilst the phenomenon of overlapping doctor/apothecary circuits and an ability for patients to consult outside the immediate locality may have made individual drug supply networks robust, issues such as the longevity of those producing drugs and generational replacement could none the less impact upon patients. The question of the longevity of drug suppliers is a key one. Only if a drug producer were in a place for an extended period of time would his product become familiar and his reputation with patients, practitioners and those who supplied ingredients be clearly visible to the community. It might even take a while for his address to become familiar for those seeking one-off doses. Generational replacement was important because the death or migration of a drug supplier might leave a large local hole in the drug supply network. In theory, market clearing should have balanced supply and demand, but even if market clearing happened, it would take time for new drug suppliers to get up and running. It is perhaps for these reasons that eighteenth-century middling people in Lancashire, Northamptonshire and elsewhere were also consumers of other sorts of medicine.

Most obviously, they were part of the market that quacks sought to conquer with their garish adverts and extraordinary claims. The subtle gradations of 'quack' and the complex relationships that existed between quacks and more regular practitioners have been well explored by Porter and are reviewed by Louise Curth in Chapter 1 of this volume.[75] In the context of this chapter, and in the particular context of the eighteenth century, the key point is that quack medicines were widely distributed through fixed outlets by the later eighteenth century. Flyers for such remedies often appear in middling family collections, and sometimes the recipe for a quack remedy gets pasted/copied into their commonplace or memorandum books. One such example from late eighteenth-century Cumbria – which, we should remember, was remarkably poorly served by doctors or apothecaries – notes:

> That the true genuine Daffy's Cordial Elixir Salutis which is only sold in Kendal by Thomas Ashburner, at his printing house in the fish market and David Harker on the Fellside, Mr Robert Wharton Joyner in Kirkland, Mr Beethom in Burton, Mr Mackrith, bookseller in Lancaster, Mr Bare in Cartmel, William Bodley Draper in Hawkshead, being found the most sovereign remedy made use of in fevers and agues ... This is to inform the public that a large and fresh parcel of that excellent Cordial, truly prepared in London, is lately come to Thomas Ashburner's printing house in the fish market in Kendal aforesaid where only tis sold by wholesale or retail ... To prevent being imposed on, carefully mind that the bottles are sealed with the above coat of arms and not with a bucks head or Lion. The price of each bottle is 2s. 6d. the large and 1s, 3d. the small bottle, with printed book of cures given gratis.[76]

---

74 MCL L4 2/5/127, 'Bills'.
75 Porter, *Quacks*.
76 Cumbria Record Office (hereafter CRO), WD Big 213, 'Advertisement'.

Of course, Daffy's Elixir is familiar to all medical historians, but the flyer is significant for this chapter in several ways. First, it is clear that there was a network of supply from businesses and private houses for this Cordial and probably for others as well. Second, there must equally have been a distribution network for elixir with the seal of a Lion or a buck's head. Third, as Porter shows, there was a national market for some quack remedies (the advertised version was *truly* brewed in London), but that they inspired local and regional copies. Finally, anyone could buy in bulk and distribute, suggesting that, in some ways at least, there was a saturation of remedies in the eighteenth century. In turn, there is other evidence of the operation of eighteenth-century quacks. Dr Samuel Solomon, a Liverpool chemist living in Gilead House, brewed and sold throughout Lancashire Cordial Balm of Gilead at 1s. 6d. per bottle, using his long, thin bottle as an advertising device.[77] The Hultin family of Lancashire preserved several quack flyers, one of which was 'Yeake's Justly Famous Pill', only to be had from Edgware Road, London, which could cure 'Deafness/noises of the head and diseases of the ear if ever so inveterate or long standing'. From the same source, Lancashire consumers could buy 'A specific tincture for the rheumatism, lumbago, sciatica, cramp, spasms and c.' and 'Persons stating their cases by letter addressed to the Hermitage as above will have the medicines forwarded with every information.' For good measure, consumers could also write for 'The celebrated Pecara Elixir', 'Restorative nerve pills' and 'Antiscorbutic Drops'.[78]

Clearly, then, the regional drug trade was complex. Doctors, apothecaries and quacks all jostled with each other for the purses of middling people. The trade was relatively unstructured and under-advertised in the eighteenth century, and whilst it is certainly true that this was the age of pills and potions, middling people in Lancashire, Northamptonshire and elsewhere appear to have been well served with a network of suppliers who delivered (for most of the time or economic life cycle) affordable basic drugs. Some of these drugs were sold on a national stage, but most were the product of a relatively robust sub-regional medical marketplace.

One fly in this ointment remains, however: the question of self-dosing. In theory at least, this issue deserves only the slightest attention in a chapter about the eighteenth-century supply and marketing of drugs. Pukes, blisters and other basic medicines were available from many outlets, as we have seen, and they could be and were administered by patients or their families. If self-dosing was more complex than this, then the other medicines administered were brewed at home from recipes kept in commonplace books. Medical historians have not, however, generally looked favourably on such books and the remedies they contained. Dorothy and Roy Porter note that because such books grew by accretion, it is difficult to pin down the authorial voice and to understand the provenance of the recipes.[79] Joan Lane notes that these medical recipes of uncertain provenance were mixed up with

77   Bolton Library ZZ 357, 'Physick in Bolton 1779'.
78   LRO DDHu 53/82/269, 'Quack bill'.
79   D. Porter and R. Porter, *In Sickness and in Health* (London, 1988), p. 268.

memoranda, sayings, accounts and stories in what she styles 'amazing catalogues'.[80] Moreover, whilst there are very good reasons why middling families might have avoided doctors in favour of their own remedies, it is often difficult to see whether the material in commonplace books was actually used.[81] Even if medical historians were more favourably disposed, there might be good reasons why commonplace books and self-dosing should be ignored in a chapter on commercial drug supply. Whilst the ingredients for these recipes might have been purchased, the medicines themselves do not ostensibly enter the marketplace and they do not have a price. They are not, in essence, commercialized.

If we think more creatively, however, this argument might be turned on its head. As the eighteenth century progressed, there were numerous avenues through which ordinary people might pick up on medical recipes. Magazines carried them, and it would surely be inconceivable that the interested consumer would not copy down a few prescriptions given to them by medical men. This was quite apart from the recipe and diagnosis books and books on herbs that were actually published in the eighteenth century. Against this sort of information backdrop, whilst many commonplace books are chaotic, some really were dedicated and structured family recipe books. Moreover, we can show that some at least of the recipes were used and refined. But can we go further and suggest that the recipes and the home-made medicines that underpinned self-dosing had some sort of market value or wider circulation, and are thus worthy of more detailed treatment in this chapter? The commonplace book of Thomas Augustus Freeman, variously of Norfolk, London, Gloucestershire and Dublin, suggests that we should look again at this source when considering the drug supply options of middling families.[82] This late eighteenth-century commonplace book carries 121 recipes for everything from flatulence and sore eyes to gangrene and fever. It is significant for five reasons. First, many of the recipes outlined in the book differ little, if at all, from those recorded by established apothecaries. Thus, for Green Sickness, Freeman's commonplace book recommends:

> Take a conserve of wormwood 24 grams, powder of steel 12 grams, ginger and winter bark of each 3 grams, simple syrup of sufficient quality. This is directed in a chlorosis or green sickness and all menstrual obstructions likewise in all decay of the constitution from chronic diseases – it is to be taken twice in a day using as much exercise as is consistent with the condition of the patient.[83]

---

80   J. Lane, 'The doctor scolds me: the diaries and correspondence of patients in eighteenth century England', in Porter, *Patients and Practitioners*, p. 241.

81   J. Barry, 'Publicity and the public good: Presenting medicine in eighteenth century Bristol', in Bynum and Porter, *Medical Fringe and Medical Orthodoxy*, pp. 29–39.

82   His book, 'A collection of choice receits compiled by Thomas Augustus Freeman and wrote by him Sunday June 20th in the year of our Lord 1779 and finished by him Sunday January 2nd 1780', can be found in RCS Mss 129a.a.3, 'Receipt book'. Whilst Amanda Vickery emphasizes the construction and maintenance of commonplace books as a female task, this is clearly not the case here; A. Vickery, *The Gentleman's Daughter* (London, 1998), p. 154.

83   Ibid., recipe 106.

Whilst we might have little idea what exactly Green Sickness was, this is exactly the same recipe as the 'strengthening powder' brewed by James Hull for Dr Loxham of Poulton at roughly the same time.[84] Moreover, in terms of the illnesses for which the cure is supposed to work, there is a resemblance to the 'large pills' that William St Clare prescribes for the Whitacker family in the late eighteenth century. In fact, some 14 of the recipes recorded by Freeman can be found in sources like apothecary recipe books and the prescriptions of eighteenth-century doctors such as St Clare or Sabine. In the sense that, if used correctly, these recipes offered the saving of money, they might be properly regarded as having a value and a place in the drug marketplace.

A second significant thing about the Freeman commonplace book is that it records recipes for quack remedies. Jones's Elixir for Numerous Disorders, Pedley's Infallible Cure for the Rheumatism, Horton's Famous American Elixir for the Rheumatism and Carlyle's Sovereign Elixir Against Decay are all detailed in this book.[85] There is nothing particularly surprising about this, except that, again, the possibility of brewing one's own quack remedy was a choice in the marketplace for drugs. In fact, the third observation about Freeman's book is that he very definitely tries out his remedies and refines them. The front page notes: 'NB. This X marked have proved effectual.' Such was his remedy for:

> heart burn, particularly good for women before and after child bearing or miscarrying. Take fine chalk, half an ounce and reduce it to a fine powder, gum arabic half an ounce in fine powder also. Mix them very well together let the patient take a small teaspoonful (not heaped) every two hours or oftner in a tablespoonful of Barley water to be continued till well.[86]

Whether a modern audience sees any medical benefit here or not, this sort of entry shows that Freeman was engaged in more than idle collecting. He was in effect subverting the market for drugs, and the tone of entries like this might suggest that the recipe was intended for a much wider audience. Such speculation is perhaps shored up by a fourth observation about Freeman's book – that very many of the recipes are sourced by the author. Cures for the falling sickness, scald head and yellow jaundice were given to him by the Rev. Moon. A remedy for the clap was given by Dr Dodds. A remedy for fits was given to Freeman by 'Mr Arthur Thompson an old gent who got it from Portugal by a jesuit thirty years since and who assures us that it is a satisfactory certain and expeditious cure'. Remedies for cancer were given by 'Mr Fogerty in London', and ague by 'Mr Lewis the Frenchman'.[87] Clearly, then, these recipes had sufficient value to warrant being passed on, and passed on

---

84   British Library, EG 386617, 'Recipe book'.

85   RCS Mss 129a.a.3, recipes 116, 37, 71 and 110.

86   Ibid., recipe 39. Porter and Porter, *In Sickness and in Health*, p. 268; also note a tendency to annotate and alter.

87   Ibid., recipes 51, 59, 85, 87, 89 and 93. See also LRO DDAr 334, 'An electuary for the slow gravel and the ulcer in the kidneys copies from the Dublin Journal, 1769'.

with assurances.[88] They had pedigree and provenance. The drugs produced at home must thus be regarded as part and parcel of the eighteenth-century market for drugs, and it is worth observing that, if anything, self-dosing becomes more common in the nineteenth century than had been the case before.[89]

A final observation about the Freeman commonplace book is the precision with which he sets of the ingredients and preparation of each medicine. Whilst confident interpretation of such precision must await more regional and chronological surveys of commonplace books, there is good reason to think that the precision was related to the development of regional and sub-regional medical marketplaces. Compare, for instance, the precision of Freeman with the much more general recipes recorded by Francis Burton in 1728, whose recipe for whooping cough consisted of 'a handful of house leek, quarter of brown sugar and boil them together until it get the consistency of a sad syrup'.[90] The precision of the later eighteenth century might be taken to suggest that families could buy exact amounts of ingredients or that they could weigh out ingredients purchased in bulk. References for increasingly exotic ingredients also suggests a ready regional market in the ingredients for self-dosing.[91]

A wide variety of other substantial commonplace collections give weight to such ideas.[92] Moreover, such conclusions make sense if one thinks about the dynamics of the regional drug trade. Thus, whilst it is true that the overlapping ambits of quacks, doctors and apothecaries meant that there were lots of drugs 'on the road' and that simple medicines could be relatively easily purchased, it is also true that neither doctors nor drugs always came when called for. Moreover, a drug trade that for much of the eighteenth century remained sub-regional must have been subject to shocks as suppliers died or moved on. Elizabeth Shackleton was certainly distressed to find in 1781 that her regular doctor, Dr Turner, had given up his surgery and was moving away. Nor should we forget that whilst the cost of individual medicines was often quite modest – in Lancashire, for instance, it cost 2s. for a Julep Cordial, 1s. for anodyne mixture, 1s. for tinctures and 2s. for Balsam – such costs might escalate worryingly in a prolonged illness. All of these pressures would have given an impetus to self-dosing, which must be regarded as adding further to the complex sub-regional drug supply networks into which many middling families found themselves plugged. What, then, was the medical and drug supply spectrum for the poor on Poor Relief?

88   Porter and Porter, *Patients Progress*, p. 104, suggest that it was socially very important to have a recipe to hand.

89   S.A. King and A. Weaver, 'Lives in many hands: The medical landscape in Lancashire, 1700–1820', *Medical History*, 45 (2000), pp. 175–200.

90   LRO DDx 151/2, 'Francis Burton's book of disbursements 1728'.

91   Porter and Porter, *In Sickness and in Health*, p. 267.

92   See, for instance, NRO Leete Collection VII/6, 'Recipe book 1796', and Wigan Record Office D/D2 EHC Volume 54, 'Langshaw commonplace books'.

Medicine for the Poor

The cost of drugs and medical interventions should, on the face of it, have been an even more pressing concern for the poor, and one guaranteed to force them to rely on self-dosing or patient resignation to their fate. Such a view would be misleading. The issue of the supply of medical treatment in general and drugs in particular to the poor (as defined by receipt of poor relief or charity) has exercised the skills of both medical and welfare historians. By common consent, the eighteenth-century Old Poor Law provided access to medicine and medical personnel at least as good as that available to the wider labouring population, and usually far better. Thus, Alannah Tomkins notes that apothecaries regularly serviced the needs of the poor in Shrewsbury parishes by the mid-eighteenth century.[93] Loudon adds gloss, suggesting that: 'The poor may sometimes have been treated with less finesse and courtesy than the paying classes but the level of payment was an incentive to high standards of care.'[94] Lane goes further. She suggests that the involvement of parishes in all aspects of medical care meant that the Old Poor Law provided 'services from the cradle to the grave'. Moreover, the New Poor Law 'was never to provide for the poorest people the comprehensive welfare service that had existed in England' under the Old Poor Law.[95] Similarly, Digby concludes that 'Both the comprehensive nature and the overall quality of the medical help given under the Old Poor Law were impressive', and she concurs with Loudon that paupers had access to medical care of equal quality to other parishioners.[96] Wear includes the poor in his generalization that by the opening decades of the nineteenth century, 'being treated by the doctor became a way of life'.[97] Doctors appear to have embraced medical contracts under the Old Poor Law with enthusiasm,[98] and even in the harshest of Poor Law counties there is evidence that overseers of the poor 'do seem to have been aware of the long term advantages of providing effective medical relief'.[99] More than this, most commentators agree that, notwithstanding intra- and inter-regional variations, what parishes were willing to pay for in terms of medical treatment expanded cumulatively across the eighteenth century. Indeed, I have argued elsewhere that whilst the proportion of total resources devoted to medical relief widely defined

---

93   A. Tomkins, 'Paupers and the infirmary in mid-eighteenth century Shrewsbury', *Medical History*, 43 (1999), pp. 214–15.

94   I. Loudon, *Medical Care and the General Practitioner 1750–1850* (Oxford, 1986), p. 231.

95   J. Lane, *A Social History of Medicine* (Longman, 2000), p. 54.

96   Digby, *Making a Medical Living*, p. 230.

97   A. Wear, 'The patient in England 1660–1800', in A. Wear (ed.), *Medicine and Society: Historical Essays* (Cambridge,1992), p. 100.

98   I. Loudon, 'Medical practitioners 1750–1850 and the period of medical reform in Britain', in Wear, *Medicine in Society*, p. 242

99   Marland, *Medicine and Society*, pp. 53–67.

might fluctuate heavily from year to year, on balance this proportion probably rose significantly between 1700 and 1800.[100]

In the context of this chapter, however, significant questions remain unanswered. How did rising expenditure translate to access to drugs? Were standards of medical care really as high as the historiography suggests? Were drugs imposed on paupers? Did paupers pay for drugs, directly or indirectly? Who supplied the drugs? We can begin to get some indication of what rising medical expenditure meant in terms of drug therapies from bills submitted by doctors to overseers. Thus, Dr Edward Swingden submitted a bill of £2 4s. 4d. to the overseers of Brington parish in Northamptonshire covering the period May 1784–February 1785. Almost the entire bill related to basic drugs, consisting of:

> A vomit for Martha Blencowe (6d.), Camomile Flowers (2d.), A Peruvian Julip (2s.), A vomit for Samuel Sutton's wife (6d.), Sudorific powders (3s.), Antimonial drops (6d.), Anaodyne Basalmic solution (2s.), Saline powders (3s.), Basalmic solution (2s.), Aperient powders (1s. 6d.), Anodyne Sudorific draught (8d.), Sudorific powders (3s.), Sudorific mixture (2s.), An astringent mixture (2s.), Anaodyne Elixir (1s. 6d.), Anaodyne mixture (2s.).[101]

This bewildering array of what looks like three basic medicines confirms a view of the eighteenth century as an age of pills and potions. What is more significant is the similarity between these treatments and those given to the middling patients of Dr Loxham of Lancashire at roughly the same time. Brington may have been unusual in the sense that the Spencer family appear to have paid Poor Relief bills out of their own pocket, but it was not alone amongst Northamptonshire parishes in paying for this sort of fairly comprehensive drug policy.[102] At Aynho on the Northamptonshire/ Oxfordshire border, the Poor Law in 1790 spent £17 3s. 6d. on medicines alone, as well as engaging three different doctors and sending two paupers to take the waters at unspecified spa towns.[103] Even in Lancashire, England's most parsimonious Poor Law county, overseers seem to have been willing to sanction not inconsiderable drug expenditure. When the overseers of Padiham examined the poor in the late eighteenth century, they found several not fit to be moved, and as well as paying out regular pensions, they sanctioned a long list of drug expenditure.[104] Between 1776 and 1800, Rusholme parish spent an average of £4 2s. directly on drugs, a very substantial bill for a population numbering at best a few hundred.[105] Similarly, Tottington parish sanctioned draughts, aperient pills, salves, infusions, plasters,

100 J. Kent and S.A. King, 'Changing patterns of poor relief in some English rural parishes circa 1650–1750', *Rural History*, 14 (2003), pp. 1–38; King, *Poverty and Welfare*.

101 NRO ZA 239/151, 'Bill'.

102 I am grateful to Elizabeth Hurren for this observation.

103 NRO uncatalogued, 'The Cartwright collection'.

104 LRO PR 2863/3/4, 'Examinations of the poor of Padiham'.

105 MCL M10/23/2/1, 'Rusholme overseer accounts'.

pukes, balsams and julep for paupers throughout the late eighteenth century.[106] Parishes in Huntingdonshire, Staffordshire and Shropshire were paying significant sums for very similar medical attendance by the mid-eighteenth century.[107]Such expenditure would seem to bear out the positive view of medical services under the Old Poor Law that dominates the historiographical literature, and suggests that the poor were also part of a complex sub-regional drug supply trade. This said, important questions remain, and these can be explored by concentrating in particular on the very rich Lancashire material.

First, then, let us address the question of drug supply. Whilst the bills of doctors contracted to pay for care of the poor might tell us what drug therapies were provided, they are surprisingly opaque over who provided drugs and how. Some doctors certainly carried drugs with them, as was the case, for instance, with doctors contracted to treat the Easington poor, who were instructed that they ought to 'bring what medicines the poor might need'.[108] We have evidence that other doctors wrote prescriptions for apothecaries to make up. Indeed, some Poor Law authorities employed both a doctor and an apothecary, availability no doubt dictating which of them attended which paupers. Such was the case with the small south Lancashire parish of Hulme, which employed two doctors and an apothecary, with the bills of the former noting 'Anodyne mixture per William Hill', the apothecary.[109] We have already seen that Dr Loxham of Poulton had a similar relationship with his apothecary in terms of supply of medicines, and this observation applies as directly to the poor as it did to middling patients. Yet by far the most common Lancashire experience seems to have been for doctors to assess a case and send medicines by post. Where we have bills to Poor Law officials from doctors employed on a casual basis to treat the Lancashire poor, there is almost always a substantial mismatch between the very infrequent attendance and the relatively frequent recording of drug supply. This suggests that medicines were sent by post to be applied either by the poor themselves or a local herbalist/apothecary, possibly the cheapest option for the contracted doctor on a fixed fee. The key point, though, is that as with middling patients, a limited supply of doctors with relatively large circuits must have meant a lot of prescriptions and medicines on the road.

The situation is made more complex if we accept that the Poor Law was only one player – and possibly not the most important – in the supply of medical care to the poor. The Poor Law did not inevitably recognize the deservingness of the sick poor, and the sick did not inevitably turn to the Poor Law as soon as they became ill. Many of 'the poor' must thus have needed to seek medical care outside the ambit of the Poor Law. Even those who were successful in establishing their entitlement may have needed to explore supplementary options given that the patients of Poor Law officials

---

106 The Poor Law collection for the parish, MCL L82, is one of the most complete in the country.

107 Kent and King, 'Changing patterns of poor relief'.

108 LRO PR 2995/1/29, 'Receipts and vouchers'.

109 MCL M10 815, 'Correspondence of overseers of the poor of Hulme'.

with illness could easily wane.[110] One option for both groups of paupers was to turn to doctors and apothecaries in their own right rather than under the auspices of the Poor Law. As both Loudon and Tomkins point out, there is ample evidence that doctors provided both consultation and drugs free of charge to the poor.[111] Similar evidence exists for Lancashire.[112] It is less often appreciated that even the very poor might seek paid medical attention. Dr Loxham of Poulton made a distinction between payments for Poor Law work and bills to four groups of poor people in his account book from the 1750s to the 1770s. Thus, some of his patients had the annotation 'poor' or 'poor only' ascribed after their name and before the treatment package and bill was noted. Others were labelled 'Very poor', and some were labelled 'Paupers'. All groups were charged for treatment, drugs and visits, on a sliding scale that placed the 'poor' and paupers (who might have Poor Law support) at the top and those labelled 'very poor' (presumably destitute but not eligible for relief) at the bottom. The numbers of any of the three groups are small, but the entries confirm that the poor were not averse to seeking medical care and drug therapy in their own right. Indeed, even those who were 'poor' appear to have received extensive drug treatments. Hence, Cuthbert Hulme of Blackpool called Loxham out on 3 August 1759 'on account of a flooding' in his wife. Loxham prescribed two does of anodyne mixture (2s.), Peruvian elixir (1s. 6d.) and a purge (2s.). It is interesting, moreover, that the debts for this medical care could be outstanding for a very considerable period, be paid in instalments, and be met partly or fully in kind. Concentrating simply on the drugs and medical care available via the Poor Law may thus give a misleading impression of the scale of the medical care network within which the poor were enmeshed. Just as importantly, small details such as the Loxham account book provide important evidence that drug therapies and medical interventions were actively sought out by the poor rather than necessarily being imposed upon them.

We can take up this theme in the context of the impact of institutional charities on the access of poor people to drug therapy. A range of studies over the last two decades has begun to highlight the complex relationship between poverty/the poor, charitable hospitals and infirmaries and the Poor Law. Some Poor Law authorities subscribed enthusiastically to voluntary hospitals, other failed to do so, and some had a chequered subscription history. There were few regional consistencies in attitude.[113] For the purposes of this chapter, what is important is that drug expenditure in such institutions was often substantial. By the early nineteenth century, the accounts of Preston dispensary, for instance, show that around 20 per cent of the budget was spent on 'drugs, surgical instruments and c.'. Such figures were also to be found

---

110 King, 'Stop this overwhelming torment'.

111 Loudon, Medical Care, p. 107; A. Tomkins 'The registers of a provincial man-midwife: Thomas Higgins of Wem 1781–1803', *Staffordshire Studies* (2000), pp. 65–148.

112 King, *A Fylde Country Practice*.

113 For the rise of the infirmary, see A. Borsay, *Medicine and Charity in Georgian Bath: A Social History of the General Infirmary* (Aldershot, 1999). On dispensaries in Lancashire towns, see J.V. Pickstone, *Health, Disease and Medicine in Lancashire 1750–1950* (Manchester, 1980), pp. 26–7.

in other regions.[114] They are almost certainly an understatement of the supply of drugs in such institutions. William Dent was working at St Thomas's hospital in the early nineteenth century. Writing to his family in Durham on the subject of his first midwifery case, he noted:

> I managed all tolerably well and the woman is doing famously now. I expect to have another [case] shortly, but the worst of it is we have to give them 5s. and find them with the medicines till they are quite well.[115]

Drugs provided by trainees must thus have added to institutional provision, and whilst some institutions excluded the sickest or the poorest through their entrance criteria, it is necessarily the case that institutions provided a further avenue for drug treatment for the sick poor.

Medical care and drugs might also be forthcoming from other charitable sources. Between 1798 and 1800, the Bolton Benevolent Society gave out £3 19s. for medicines to the sick poor. Whilst this represented a small proportion of its £151 yearly expenditure, we must recognize that four other charities were financing medical care at the same time.[116] Small sums must have added up. Moreover, it is important to recognize that medical care, and particularly the supply of drugs, was also a focus for much individual charity. Thomas Eccleston of Scarisbrick in south-west Lancashire kept a memorandum and commonplace book in the 1750s that appears to have been the basis for a much more formal catalogue of recipes to cure 'disorders that are internal forming', including fevers, rheumatism, inflammations, dropsy, scarlet fever and tumours.[117] The catalogue is significant because it gives the provenance of the cures, with many taken from Buchan, Townsend, Bigg and Ward, all publishers of diagnostic or herbal books in the eighteenth century. It is more significant because it was not a private book for Eccleston's use. Rather, 'the reader will now find some easy directions for the most common complaints that the labouring poor are most liable to – with plain and simple directions how they ought to be treated'.[118] In short, Eccleston was making up this book for his tenants and other families in the locality to use as a basis for charitable medical interventions. In south-east Lancashire, the Eckroyd family were equally involved in the provision of medical care at their door, whilst families such as the Blundell's from Crosby, near Southport, provided throughout the eighteenth century home-brewed drugs and salves, money for doctors and nursing care for the sick poor. That others were also willing to spend in order to relieve the sick poor can be seen in an entry in Dr Loxham's account book which states: '2 December 1762 Thos Cotton of

114 LRO, 'The annual accounts and report of the Preston Dispensary, 1811'.

115 RCS Mss Add 336a, 'Letter, 5ᵗʰ December 1808'.

116 Bolton Library ZZ 238/1/130/7, 'Annual Report of Bolton Benevolent Society'.

117 LRO DDSc 127/2, 'Memorandum book', and DDSc 150/2 'Book of medical recipes'.

118 LRO DDSc 150/2, 'Book of medical recipes'.

Carleton to lactis ammon [dose] for a poor man 3s. 6d'.[119] Such charitable medical care must have reinforced the strength of the sub-regional medical marketplace for the sick poor, and once again provides confirmation that they actively wanted drug interventions, rather than having them imposed by institutions or officials. The sick poor did not necessarily obtain access to better treatment or a wider range of drugs than the wider labouring population. The key point, however, is that by the later eighteenth century, the vibrant drug supply trade accessed by the middling sorts had also become a reality for other groups. Drug dissemination increased medical expectation at all levels of society.

Conclusion

Every eighteenth-century region is likely to have been littered with those who excluded themselves or who were excluded (by problems of cost, availability or circumstance) from the medical marketplace and supplies of drugs. However, this chapter has sought, using the examples of Lancashire and Northamptonshire and the experiences of the middling and poorer sorts, to paint a more positive picture. It has argued that for both the poor and middling sorts, there was a vibrant and robust sub-regional drugs trade, and one that probably became more robust and more vibrant over time. Several types of 'supplier' underpinned the trade, many of them with overlapping ambits, including apothecaries, doctors, quacks, middling and aristocratic families and institutions. Not all drugs that were supplied and consumed were paid for or had a conventional price, but their supply none the less defines the boundaries of the medical market. For the poor in particular, access to drugs must have improved remarkably over the eighteenth century. The rapid development of the voluntary hospital system from the late eighteenth century, allied with increasing self-help provision in some areas through the growth of friendly societies and burial clubs, gave some paupers very real alternatives to the Poor Law. So did the fact that medical practitioners themselves increasingly treated poor people free, or at reduced cost, from charitable or other imperatives. And of course, irregular practitioners, dispensing druggists and quacks could increasingly claim the poor and very poor amongst their customers by the opening decades of the nineteenth century.[120] This confluence of provision, allied with informal charity by middling and aristocratic families, is what Crowther has styled 'the chaotic and overlapping medical services of the time'.[121] Chaotic though these services might have been, however, it seems clear from the Lancashire examples employed here that in terms of access to drug supplies, the poor were experiencing considerable catch-up with other classes by the 1770s.

---

119 LRO DDPr 25/6, 'Account book of a doctor on the Fylde'.

120 Loudon, 'The vile race of quacks', pp. 116--17.

121 M. Crowther, 'Health care and poor relief in provincial England', in O. Grell, A. Cunningham and R. Jutte (eds), *Health Care and Poor Relief in 18th and 19th Century Northern Europe* (London, 2002), p. 206.

Of course, the experiences of middling people were not static either. Their self-dosing became more systematic and refined, and our discussion of the provenance of recipes might be read as indicating that some of the regional nuances of such self-dosing were ironed out. However, the middling sort also underpinned the extensive prescription trade for the doctors – Loxham, St Clare and Sabine – whose records have been analysed in this chapter. Indeed, their trades were so extensive that the roads must literally have been full of prescriptions and medicines. Occasionally, 'nationally available' medicines would intrude on the drugs trade, but for most places and for all of the eighteenth century, the supply of drugs to the middling sort was as much as sub-regional trade as the supply of drugs to the poor.

More work needs to be done on how the composition, pricing or dosage of drugs varied between regions, but in terms of the basic types of drugs available the age of pills and potions probably generated far fewer regional nuances in composition than in names. There were probably more regional differences in the strength/robustness of the drug trade, with communities in Cumberland or Westmorland potentially more prone to the risk of a major player dying or leaving than would have been the case in urbanizing and industrializing south Lancashire. None the less, our analysis of eighteenth-century Northamptonshire has suggested that contemporaries were able to find doctors and apothecaries in the smallest and most unlikely of places, and that many more medical men were likely to pass through than lived in a place. As Louise Curth has suggested in Chapter 1 of this volume, we have only begun to uncover the nuances of eighteenth-century drug supply.

Chapter 5

The 'Doctor's Shop': The Rise of the Chemist and Druggist in Nineteenth-Century Manufacturing Districts[1]

Hilary Marland

Introduction

During the nineteenth century, the range of medical facilities on offer in the manufacturing towns of northern England expanded considerably, through the foundation and expansion of dispensaries and infirmaries, the establishment of a formal – though far from standardized or generous – channel of medical relief through the agency of the New Poor Law after 1834, and the creation of a network of friendly societies, offering pecuniary and medical relief to their sick members.[2] In principle, the poor and labouring classes of the manufacturing districts had more access to medical treatment than they had ever had before. Those wealthy enough to pay for private medical care, meanwhile, could utilize the services of a growing body of qualified medical practitioners. Yet rich and poor alike continued to resort to a variety of alternative sources of medical assistance, either supplementing the services of regular practitioners or, for those with limited funds or eager to try a variety of healing approaches, these could form the sole means of medical relief.

Following what could be deemed as a 'golden age' of quackery in the eighteenth century, the nineteenth century saw not only the survival of traditional practitioners – folk healers, wise-women, herbalists, midwives and bone-setters – as well as the continued wellbeing of numerous itinerant quacks, but also the flourishing of new alternative therapies, including homoeopathy, mesmerism, hydropathy and medical

---

1   This article draws heavily on H. Marland, 'The Medical Activities of Mid-nineteenth-century Chemists and Druggists, with Special Reference to Wakefield and Huddersfield', *Medical History*, 31 (1987), pp. 415–39. This material is reproduced with the kind permission of the editors of *Medical History.* Copyright © The Trustee, The Wellcome Trust, reproduced with permission.

2   J.V. Pickstone, *Medicine and Industrial Society: A History of Hospital Development in Manchester and its Region, 1752–1946* (Manchester, 1985); H. Marland, *Medicine and Society in Wakefield and Huddersfield 1780–1870* (Cambridge, 1987); M.W. Flinn, 'Medical Services under the New Poor Law', in D. Fraser (ed.), *The New Poor Law in the Nineteenth Century* (London, 1976), pp. 45–66.

botany.[3] Many of these new forms of healing, particularly medical botany, were embraced enthusiastically in the northern manufacturing communities of England.[4] They were also attacked vociferously by orthodox practitioners, homoeopathy being declared by one Huddersfield doctor to be 'a species of jugglery' and 'infinitesimal nonsense', while the *Lancet* in 1849 described how 'provincial cities and towns [were] overrun ... by a vagrant pack of homoeopathists and mesmerists'.[5] Yet it was the lure of a group making no claims to promote new forms of therapy, the chemists and druggists, which would irritate and provoke orthodox medical men more than any other. By the mid-nineteenth century, chemists and druggists were the most numerous suppliers of medical aid. They were difficult to categorize and thus to target, neither fringe nor orthodox, but mere tradesmen. Their remit, in principle, was to make up the prescriptions of qualified medical men, but in practice they offered a much wider range of medical services, including over-the-counter prescribing, preparation of family recipes, and the sale of a wide range of drugs and patent remedies. By the turn of the nineteenth century, chemists and druggists were being singled out as a particular threat to orthodox practitioners, as their numbers rose and as they engaged increasingly in prescribing activities; dealing directly with the public, in many cases they cut the doctor out of medical transactions.[6]

For many regular doctors, chemists and druggists constituted the worst form of quack. It was the lure of the chemist's establishment, often referred to by client and critic – though not by the chemists themselves – as 'the doctor's shop', that was particularly provoking. Their glinting shops, packed with mysterious packages and potions and bottles of many colours, were described as Aladdin's caves which seduced and corrupted the poor:

the ignorant and uninformed have a natural tendency to seek benefits of all kinds from inferior sources. Then the easy access to the druggist's shop, vying with the gin palace in its tempting decorations, attracts those who prefer spending a few pence, to encountering the formalities and delay attendant on an application to a qualified practitioner. Then the speedy apprehension of the case by the druggist's shopman, a glance being sufficient to satisfy him both as to its nature and treatment, and his ready selection of some drug as a

3   See, for fringe practice, R. Porter, *Health for Sale: Quackery in England 1660–1850* (Manchester and New York, 1989); R. Porter, *Quacks: Fakers and Charlatans in English Medicine* (Stroud, 2000); W.F. Bynum and Roy Porter (eds), *Medical Fringe and Medical Orthodoxy, 1750–1850* (London, 1986); R. Cooter, 'Interpreting the Fringe', *Bulletin of the Society for the Social History of Medicine*, 29 (1981), pp. 33–6; R. Cooter (ed.), *Studies in the History of Alternative Medicine* (Houndmills, 1988).

4   J.V. Pickstone, 'Medical Botany (Self-help Medicine in Victorian England)', *Memoirs of the Manchester Literary and Philosophical Society*, 119 (1976–77), pp. 94–5; U. Miley and J.V. Pickstone, 'Medical Botany around 1850: American Medicine in Industrial Britain', in Cooter (ed.), *Studies in the History of Alternative Medicine*, pp. 140–54.

5   S. Knaggs, *Common Sense versus Homoeopathy* (London, 1855), p. 43; 'Homoeopathic Quackery in Huddersfield', *Lancet*, ii (1849), pp. 405–6, p. 406.

6   I. Loudon, 'The vile race of quacks with which this country is Infested', in Bynum and Porter (eds), *Medical Fringe and Medical Orthodoxy*, pp. 106–28.

certain cure for the malady of the customer, all this tells wonderfully on the ignorant of all classes. The inevitable results to the community are fearful loss of life and destruction of health.[7]

A scene in Elizabeth Gaskell's *Mary Barton*, a novel of working-class life in mid-nineteenth-century Manchester, describes how John Barton, prior to seeking a ticket for admittance to the local infirmary, turns to a druggist for assistance on behalf of a workmate stricken with typhus fever. Barton describes the case to the druggist, 'whose smooth manners seemed to have been salved over with his own spermaceti', and he 'proceeded to make up a bottle of medicine, sweet spirits of nitre, or some such innocent potion, very good for slight colds, but utterly powerless to stop, for an instance the raging fever of the poor man it was intended to relieve'. The druggist recommended that next morning they should apply for an infirmary order, and 'Barton left the shop with comfortable faith in the physic given him; for men of his class, if they believe in physic at all, believe that every description is equally efficacious.'[8]

Warnings about the dangers of the druggist resonated with accusations of their negligence and lack of care as they went about the business of earning a living, as well as despair about their attractiveness to 'the multitude'.[9] Making such accusations, however, was fraught with difficulties, given that in medical and social terms, chemists and druggists were an ambiguous group, a moving target. Whilst involved in activities which aligned them in many ways with the 'medical fringe', the middle-class and rising status of many chemists and druggists, their growing professionalism, frequent expertise, close working relationship with doctors, and in many cases, wealth and position in the communities in which they worked, made them distinct from other alternative suppliers of medical assistance. 'Druggist' embraced both the lowliest of purveyors of goods to wealthy shopkeepers and members of the local elite.

From the seventeenth century onwards, the traditional pharmaceutical practitioners, the apothecaries, had been extending their role as dispensers of drugs and turning to general medical practice. This transformation was accompanied during the late eighteenth and nineteenth centuries by pressure from the chemists and druggists, who challenged and undercut the apothecaries' dispensing trade.[10] As

---

7   PP 1844 IX (531): *Report from the Select Committee on Medical Poor Relief, 3rd Report*, Evidence of H.W. Rumsey, Esq., p. 546, Q. 9 121.

8   E. Gaskell, *Mary Barton: A Tale of Manchester Life* (first pub. 1848; Penguin edn 1970), p. 102.

9   *Report from the Select Committee on Medical Poor Relief, 3rd Report*, Evidence of H.W. Rumsey, Esq., p. 546, Q. 9 121.

10   Originally the 'drugster' or 'drugman' acted as the middleman in the passing of drugs between the importer and apothecary. During the seventeenth century, his functions were combined with those of the 'chymist', a 'dabbler in chemical medicines'. By 1700, the terms were used interchangeably in London, and by 1750, wholesale and retail druggists' shops had been established in the provinces; J.F. Kett, 'Provincial Medical Practice in England 1730–

Irvine Loudon has suggested, by the turn of the nineteenth century the ability of the apothecaries and surgeon-apothecaries to make a substantial living from the practice of pharmacy had been greatly diminished, as the number of dispensing chemists and druggists increased. The chemists and druggists dealt directly with the public, undercutting the counter trade of the apothecaries, and usurping their traditional role by dispensing for physicians. It was not unknown even for physicians to utilize the chemist's shop to give free medical advice and to prescribe, the profits from the sale of medicines being divided between the chemist and physician, effectively cutting out the apothecary.[11] The apothecaries' transition to medical practice was speeded up by the passing of the Apothecaries' Act of 1815.[12] By early in the nineteenth century, the title 'apothecary' had all but disappeared from town directories, as this group was absorbed into the category of 'surgeon', and 'surgeon-apothecary became a common label for the precursor of the general practitioner of medicine.

Chemists and druggists were one of the few medical groups to emerge during the nineteenth century who could lay claim to some form of professional standing. By mid-century they were slowly organizing and taking on some features of a profession. The formation of the Pharmaceutical Society in 1841 and the establishment of the *Pharmaceutical Journal and Transactions* in the same year, the setting up of schools and courses specializing in the education of pharmacists, and the development of uniform standards of training and examination, which became compulsory under the 1868 Pharmacy Act, were important aspects of this process. Already by 1842, the Pharmaceutical Society had 2,000 members.[13] Yet these developments did not limit the functions of the chemists and druggists to the compounding and dispensing of doctors' prescriptions or inhibit their range of medical activities.

Despite their ubiquity and the range of services they offered, chemists and druggists have received scant attention from medical historians. Those studies that have been undertaken have tended to concentrate on the growing professionalization of this group.[14] However, it is not this issue or the training of chemists and druggists

---

1815', *Journal of the History of Medicine and Allied Sciences*, 19 (1964), pp. 17–29, pp. 19–20.

11 I. Loudon, 'A Doctor's Cash Book: The Economy of General Practice in the 1830s', *Medical History*, 27 (1983), pp. 249–68, pp. 265–6. See also Loudon, 'The vile race of quacks'.

12 For more on these developments, see, for example, B. Hamilton, 'The Medical Professions in the Eighteenth Century', *Economic History Review*, 2nd series, 4 (1951), pp. 159–69; S.W.F. Holloway, 'The Apothecaries' Act, 1815: A Reinterpretation', Parts 1 and II, *Medical History* 10 (1966), pp. 107–29 and 221–36; G.E. Trease, *Pharmacy in History* (London, 1964), pp. 169–74.

13 For more detail, see Trease, *Pharmacy in History*; F.N.L. Poynter (ed.), *The Evolution of Pharmacy in Britain* (London, 1975).

14 For example, J.K. Crellin, 'The Growth of Professionalism in Nineteenth-century British Pharmacy', *Medical History*, 11 (1967), pp. 215–27, and J.K. Crellin, 'Leicester and 19th Century Provincial Pharmacy', *Pharmaceutical Journal*, 195 (1965), pp. 417–20; L.G. Matthews, *History of Pharmacy in Britain* (Edinburgh, 1962). For a new interpretation of

that will engage us here. Whilst it is generally accepted that chemists and druggists involved themselves in less orthodox activities, and that over-the-counter-prescribing and the sale of drugs directly to the public were vital components of their businesses, these functions have not been fully described and analysed.[15] This chapter will examine the medical activities of chemists and druggists, most specifically those taking them beyond their roles as medicine suppliers into the realms of medical practice. The focus will be on the northern manufacturing districts of England, with particular emphasis on the towns of Wakefield and Huddersfield.[16] The article will focus on the middle decades of the nineteenth century, taking the Apothecaries' Act of 1815 and the 1868 Pharmacy Act as rough boundaries. During the early and mid-nineteenth century, there was a remarkable increase in the numbers involved in pharmacy. This was an era of special significance for the chemists and druggists, not only because of the remarkable growth in their numbers, but also because it ushered in their independence of the apothecaries, the clause to control chemists and druggists being dropped from the Apothecaries' Act. At the end of this era, the campaign for and the passing of the Pharmacy Act had important implications for the professionalization and self-identity of the chemist.[17]

Growth and Diversification

Changes in terminology and practice were paralleled by a considerable growth in the number of chemists and druggists, stimulated by population growth, especially in urban areas. Many communities undergoing rapid urbanization saw an increase in the number of chemists' shops during the late eighteenth and early nineteenth centuries. In Sheffield, for example, the first druggist's business was recorded in 1750. By 1774, there were 3 chemists and druggists (including 1 female druggist); by 1797, 10; by 1817, 17; by 1838, 38, and by 1841, 56. By comparison, there were

---

events leading up to and the reasoning behind the formation of the Pharmaceutical Society, see S.W.F. Holloway, 'The Orthodox Fringe: The Origins of the Pharmaceutical Society of Great Britain', in Bynum and Porter (eds), *Medical Fringe and Medical Orthodoxy*, pp. 129–57.

15   Although Stuart Anderson has explored the ambiguous position of the chemist and druggist after 1920 in 'Community Pharmacy in Great Britain: Mediation at the Boundary between Professional and Lay Care 1920 to 1995', in M. Gijswijt-Hofstra, G.M. van Heteren and E.M. Tansey (eds), *Biographies of Remedies: Drugs, Medicines and Contraceptives in Dutch and Anglo-American Healing Cultures* (Amsterdam and New York, 2002), pp. 75–97.

16   See Marland, *Medicine and Society*, for the medical marketplace in nineteenth-century Wakefield and Huddersfield.

17   See Matthews, *History of Pharmacy*, and Trease, *Pharmacy in History*, and for the history of retailing, including chemists' activities, D. Alexander, *Retailing in England During the Industrial Revolution* (London, 1970); J.H. Johnson and C.C. Pooley (eds), *The Structure of Nineteenth Century Cities* (London, 1982), Part 3; M.J. Winstanley, *The Shopkeeper's World 1830–1914* (Manchester, 1983). For the background to the evolution of Boots, see S. Chapman, *Jesse Boot of Boots the Chemists: A Study in Business History* (London, 1974).

a total of 7 physicians, surgeons, and apothecaries practising in Sheffield in 1774; by 1841, the printed census returns give a figure of 87, including an unspecified number of medical students.[18] Between 1825 and 1853, the numbers of chemists and druggists in Nottingham more than doubled from 22 to 47 (while the number of qualified medical practitioners rose from 30 to 40).[19] By 1851, 114 individuals (105 businesses) were listed as chemists and druggists in the Bristol census enumerators' books, together with a similar number of qualified medical men.[20]

Wakefield, primarily a market and service centre, experienced only a steady rate of industrial growth during the nineteenth century, while Huddersfield, by contrast, was a rapidly expanding textile community, an exemplary nineteenth-century industrializing town. Both experienced urban development and population growth during the early and mid-nineteenth century – Wakefield in a less dramatic form – and the rise in the number of chemists and druggists appears to have been tied to, but not fully explained by, these processes. In 1780, there were just 2 chemists' shops in Huddersfield; by 1822, there were 5; by 1837, 9, and by 1870, 19. During the 1790s, Wakefield was served by 2 chemists, by 1822 there were 6 chemists' shops, and between 1822 and 1870, the number more than trebled to 19.[21] This increase in numbers, which was most significant in the first half of the nineteenth century, could have resulted from one of three developments, or from a combination of the three. The first possibility was that a growing number of medical practitioners abandoned their dispensing functions during this period, and turned over the making up of prescriptions to the chemists and druggists, which led to an increased volume of trade for this group. Secondly, the increase could be explained quite simply by the population growth of the two communities, which resulted in a larger market for the chemists and druggists' services. The third possibility is that the inhabitants of the

---

18   J. Austen, *Historical Notes on Old Sheffield Druggists* (Sheffield, 1961), pp. 10–12, 15, 26, 35 and 47; PP 1844 XXVII (587): Abstract of the Answers and Returns made Pursuant to Acts 3 & 4 Vic. c.99, and 4 Vic. c.7, Intitled Respectively 'An Act for Taking an Account of the Population of Great Britain', and 'An Act to Amend the Acts of the Last Session for Taking an Account of the Population'. Occupation Abstract, Part 1. Wallis's listing of eighteenth-century medics has counted at least four chemists and druggists and nine surgeons and apothecaries in Sheffield for the period around 1774; P.J. and R.V. Wallis, *Eighteenth Century Medics (Subscriptions, Licenses, Apprenticeships)* (Newcastle, 1985).

19   Trease, *Pharmacy in History*, p. 182.

20   P.S. Brown, 'The Providers of Medical Treatment in Mid-nineteenth-century Bristol', *Medical History*, 24 (1980), pp. 297–314.

21   T. Dyson, *The History of Huddersfield and District from the Earliest Times down to 1932* (Huddersfield, 1932), p. 467; *Universal British Directory of Trade and Commerce (1790–98)*; E. Baines, *History, Directory and Gazetteer of the County of York*, Vol. 1 (1822; repr. Wakefield, 1969); W. White, *History, Gazetteer, and Directory, of the West Riding of Yorkshire*, Vol. 1 (Sheffield, 1837); W. White, *General and Commercial Directory of Leeds, Huddersfield, Wakefield, Dewsbury, Bailey, Heckondwike, Holmfirth, Morley, Pudsey, and all the Parishes and Villages in and near those Populous Districts of the West Riding* (Sheffield, 1870).

two towns made growing use of the chemists' services, and thus facilitated a rise in their numbers.

Although there was an increase in the number of qualified medical men practising in Wakefield and Huddersfield during the nineteenth century, this increase did not keep pace with the growth in the number of chemists and druggists over the same period. Between 1822 and 1853, the number of qualified medical men in Wakefield increased from 18 to 26 (44 per cent). Over the same period, the number of chemists and druggists rose from 6 to 19 (217 per cent). In Huddersfield, the number of qualified medical men increased at a faster rate during the same thirty-year period, but by no means kept up with the rise in the number of chemists and druggists in the town. In 1822, there were 13 qualified medical men resident in Huddersfield. By 1853, there were 22 (an increase of 69 per cent). The number of chemists and druggists, meanwhile, increased from 5 to 16 (220 per cent), an almost identical rate of increase to that experienced in Wakefield. After *c.* 1853, the number of practising medical men in Wakefield began to fall off, from 26 in 1853 to 18 in 1870. Over the same period, the number of chemists and druggists remained steady, there being roughly nineteen in business in the town at any one time. In Huddersfield, there was also a small decline in the number of qualified medical practitioners between 1853 and 1870, from 22 to 21. In the same two decades, 5 more chemists and druggists established themselves in the town, giving a total in 1870 of 21.[22]

A nationwide survey, using information extracted from the 1841 census returns, concluded that there was one chemist and druggist in Great Britain to every two medical practitioners.[23] By the 1850s and 1860s, the proportion of chemists and druggists appears to have been even higher. In 1822, there was one chemist and druggist to every three medical practitioners in both Wakefield and Huddersfield. By 1866, the ratios were one to one.[24] The printed census returns indicate that by the mid-nineteenth century, some counties, particularly the more urbanized ones, recorded higher numbers of chemists and druggists than qualified medical practitioners. In the West Riding as a whole, 754 physicians and surgeons and 1,039 chemists and druggists were listed in the 1851 census returns; in Lancashire, there were 1,171 medical practitioners compared with 1,794 chemists and druggists; in the smaller and more rural county of Lincolnshire, the figures were 304 and 424 respectively.[25]

---

22 Baines, *History, Directory and Gazetteer of the County of York* (1822); W. White, *Directory and Gazetteer of Leeds, Bradford, Halifax, Huddersfield, Wakefield and the Whole of the Clothing Districts of Yorkshire* (1853; repr. Newton Abbot, 1969); White, *General and Commercial Directory* (1870).

23 'Unqualified Medical Practitioners', *Medical Times & Gazette*, ii (1853), p. 143.

24 Baines, *History, Directory and Gazetteer of the County of York* (1822); W. White, *Directory of Leeds, Bradford, Huddersfield, Halifax, Wakefield, Dewsbury* (Sheffield, 1866).

25 Figures cited from P. Swan, 'Medical Provision in the West Riding in 1851 and 1871' (PhD thesis, Humberside College of Higher Education, 1988), which examines the relationship between qualified medical practitioners and chemists and druggists, using data extracted from the 1851 and 1871 West Riding census enumerators' books, and 1841 to 1881 printed census returns for England. For the use of census data in assessing medical practice

The faster growth in the number of chemists and druggists compared with medical practitioners was no doubt partly offset by an increasing tendency on the part of medical men to turn over the function of dispensing to the druggist in the second half of the century. However, pharmacy passed slowly out of the hands of doctors, and, as Loudon has demonstrated, the suggestion that general practitioners should abandon pharmacy and sever their traditional links with the functions of the apothecaries was not widely implemented during the first half of the nineteenth century. For many general practitioners, the dispensing of medicines continued to provide their main source of income.[26] Up until the mid-nineteenth century, it was common practice for individuals to combine the activities of a surgeon-apothecary and druggist, or even a physician and druggist. During the first decades of the nineteenth century, for example, M. Barber of Wakefield, 'Surgeon, etc.', offered his services 'IN EVERY DEPARTMENT OF HIS PROFESSION', and also ran a chemist's shop, his late father's, in the town centre, where he dispensed his own prescriptions as well as those of other medical men. In 1823, Dr Bell (formerly of Bath and Hull) 'entered to the Premises occupied by Messrs Mitchell and Birkett, surgeon-apothecaries and druggists' and 'respectfully solicited' the continued patronage of the inhabitants of Wakefield and its vicinity.[27] During the first half of the nineteenth century, it is often difficult to determine whether individuals were medical practitioners who engaged in pharmaceutical activities, or druggists who engaged in medical practice.

By the mid-nineteenth century, individuals such as William Rowlandson of Wakefield, 'Surgeon, Chemist, etc., etc.', who, in 1842, announced in the *Wakefield Journal* that 'he has opened an Establishment for the Dispensing of Medicine, where he intends carrying on the Business of Chemist and Druggist, in all its branches', were still not untypical.[28] Several years later, however, Rowlandson abandoned the pharmaceutical side of his enterprises, or at least gave up his open shop, to concentrate on surgery and midwifery. At the end of the nineteenth century, there were still large numbers of 'dispensing doctors', and many panel doctors kept their dispensaries going until after World War II and the establishment of the National Health Service. But around the mid-nineteenth century, it appears that many regular practitioners abandoned their open shops and ceased to advertise their pharmaceutical services. The abandonment of these activities coincided closely with the passing of the 1858 Medical Act and efforts to tighten up the professional structure, to create a code of ethics and to improve the status of the medical practitioner, and it seems likely that some doctors, particularly the more status-conscious, did allow the chemist to take over the business of dispensing prescriptions.

in the region, see H. Marland and P. Swan, 'Medical Practice in the West Riding of Yorkshire from Nineteenth Century Census Data', in P. Swan and D. Foster (eds), *Essays in Regional and Local History* (Hull, 1992), pp. 73–98.

26 Loudon, 'A Doctor's Cash Book', p. 267.
27 *Wakefield Star* (5 January 1810); *Wakefield and Halifax Journal* (27 June 1823).
28 *Wakefield Journal* (6 October 1842).

However, it is inconceivable, especially when we remember that in communities such as Wakefield and Huddersfield there was one chemist to *every* medical practitioner by the 1860s, that the chemist could have survived solely on an income from this source. Of course, no chemist attempted to do this, and it seems likely that some undertook virtually no dispensing work whatsoever. Bell and Redwood even suggested that during this period, most chemists and druggists 'rarely saw a physician's prescription and therefore had little occasion for a knowledge of dispensing'.[29] (Indeed, it appears that most chemists and druggists felt that the educational standards of the Pharmaceutical Society were too high, and largely irrelevant to their functions.) During the 1830s and 1840s, a good-class family business in Highgate, London, in addition to dispensing, prescribed and sold drugs to their customers, and retailed a wide range of non-pharmaceutical goods, domestic recipes and veterinary preparations. Even a large business concern like this, which made up the prescriptions of a number of eminent London doctors, including four Presidents of the Royal College of Surgeons, was making up only an average of 350 prescriptions per annum.[30]

It can be concluded that trade with the general public was of greater importance than dealings with the medical profession for most nineteenth-century druggists. Many combined the manufacture, wholesale and retail of pharmaceutical preparations, and were involved in non-pharmaceutical activities. The sale of drugs without prescription, the ingredients of remedies, patent preparations, family medicine chests, and the chemists' own special cure-alls were staple parts of the chemists and druggists' trade during the nineteenth century. Most offered advice in addition to medicines. The increase in their numbers was probably facilitated, in part at least, by their ability to diversify and the ability to appeal to a wide range of clients.

A typical chemist's shop of the nineteenth century would, in addition to a wide range of pharmaceutical preparations, stock a selection of toilet articles, tobacco, snuff, tea, coffee, herbs, and other foodstuffs, oils, candles and dyes. In some cases, the chemist combined with his pharmaceutical enterprises the activities of a grocer, bookseller, insurance agent, tea or lead merchant. J. & W. Sanderson, druggists of Sheffield *(c.* 1794–1831), ran a large cutlers and paint and oil business as supplements to their pharmaceutical enterprises. During the second half of the nineteenth century, E.P. Hornby, a successful retail chemist and a prominent member of the Sheffield Branch of the United Society of Chemists and Druggists, launched himself into the manufacture of acids and chemicals, later establishing the Sheffield Chemical Works.[31] Early in the nineteenth century, G.B. Reinhardt of Wakefield carried on the business of 'Chymist, Druggist, Tea-Dealer and British Wine Merchant' from his town centre shop. W.P. Lockwood, chemist and druggist, made extensive use of the Wakefield

---

29   J. Bell and T. Redwood, *Historical Sketch of the Progress of Pharmacy in Great Britain* (London, 1880), p. 163.

30   A.E. Bailey, 'Early Nineteenth Century Pharmacy', *Pharmaceutical Journal*, 185 (1960), pp. 208–12.

31   Austen, *Historical Notes*, pp. 16 and 60.

press during the mid-nineteenth century for advertising purposes, promoting a wide variety of goods, including drugs, pharmaceuticals, and miscellaneous articles connected with the trade, plus a range of cosmetics, hair dyes, perfumes, candles, spices, pickles, sauces, herbs, 'Italian goods' and so on. In addition, he acted as agent to a number of insurance companies. J.R. Dore of Huddersfield sold a similar range of domestic goods, including high-quality breakfast teas, mustards, starch, furniture cream, eau-de Cologne and the 'Huddersfield Bouquet', a 'refreshing perfume', priced 1s. a bottle. He was also a supplier of Patent Paraffin Oil. Of the 19 individuals listed as a chemists and druggists in the 1853 Wakefield town directory, 13 were also in business as tea dealers.[32]

A number of individuals combined a chemist's business with other forms of medical activity. In 1854, George Henry Crowther set himself up in business in Wakefield as a chemist and dentist, before devoting himself exclusively to the practice of dentistry.[33] Other chemists and druggists branched out into medical galvanism, herbalism, phrenology or midwifery, stocked extensive ranges of surgical appliances or spa waters, or specialized in the concocting and dispensing of homoeopathic or botanic preparations, with or without advice. Thomas North Swift of Huddersfield combined the activities of a 'druggist and botanist' during the 1860s and 1870s, also acting as agent to Dr Skelton, a well-known local botanic practitioner.[34] William Dyer, Dispensing and Family Chemist of Halifax, in addition to supplying all kinds of medicine and family recipes, also traded in surgical appliances, trusses, elastic stockings and abdominal belts, and waterproof sheeting, air and waterproof cushions, enema apparatus and urinals for invalids, and acted as agent for Schweppe's Soda and Malvern Seltzer Waters.[35] John Boot, the father of Jesse Boot, was a follower of Coffinism, calling his Nottingham shop the 'British and American Botanic Establishment'. He advertised vegetable remedies, both retail and wholesale, and announced he could be consulted at his residence on Mondays, Wednesdays and Saturdays.[36] Still others combined the druggist's trade with the compounding of animal remedies and veterinary practice.

Improved opportunities for chemists and druggists to set up in trade can be seen as result of nineteenth-century population growth, especially amongst the poor and labouring classes, the groups most likely to use the services of the chemist. On top of this, there appears to have been an increased *demand* by the public for the services they offered. In Wakefield and Huddersfield, this was demonstrated by the fact that the expansion in the number of chemists and druggists greatly exceeded population growth. In 1821, there was approximately one druggist to every 2,700 inhabitants

---

32 *Wakefield Star* (20 July 1804); *Wakefield Journal* (13 December 1850); *Wakefield Express* (27 May 1854); *Huddersfield Examiner* (23 June 1860); White, *Directory and Gazetteer of Leeds, Bradford, Halifax, Huddersfield, Wakefield* (1853).

33 *Wakefield Express* (3 June 1854).

34 *Tindall's Huddersfield Directory and Year Book, for 1866.*

35 *Jones's Mercantile Directory of Halifax, Huddersfield, and Dewsbury, 1863–4* (London, 1864).

36 Chapman, *Jesse Boot*, p. 35. See also Pickstone, 'Medical Botany'.

in Huddersfield. By 1861, the ratio was one druggist to every 1,900 inhabitants. In Wakefield, the ratio rose from one druggist to every 1,800 people to one to every 840 inhabitants between 1821 and 1861.[37] Many of the villages surrounding Wakefield and Huddersfield, especially the larger ones, also had their own chemists' shops. In 1866, the village of Meltham, situated five miles from Huddersfield, had one druggist's shop for its population of 4 046. Horbury, two miles from Wakefield, with only 3,246 inhabitants, supported three druggists' shops in 1866 (1:1 082).[38] Other urban communities experienced similar trends: D. Alexander's survey of eight provincial and manufacturing towns – Manchester, Leeds, York, Norwich, Leicester, Bolton, Merthyr and Carlisle – concluded only that by 1850, there was one chemist's shop to every 1,720 inhabitants.[39]

At the same time as the ratio of chemists and druggists to the population was rising, the ratio of medical practitioners to the populations of Wakefield and Huddersfield was declining. Sigsworth and Swan have suggested that there may be an inverse relationship between the numbers of chemists and druggists and medical practitioners, with chemists predominating in urban environments during this period.[40] Their thesis, however, is not completely borne out by the Wakefield and Huddersfield survey. Wakefield, the least urbanized of the two communities, was better served by *both* medical practitioners and chemists and druggists throughout the century. Wakefield functioned as a market and service town for the region, and the town's chemists and druggists (and medical practitioners) may well have provided a service for a wider hinterland compared to Huddersfield.[41] But, as indicated above, many of the villages surrounding both towns had their own chemists' shops, and therefore did not necessarily rely on their larger neighbours for their pharmaceutical requirements. There is some indication, however, that as the number of doctors declined in both towns, chemists and druggists stepped in to fill the gap in the market. In 1821, there was one medical practitioner to every 598 people in Wakefield Township, while the ratio of chemists and druggists to the population was 1:1 794. By 1871, the ratios were 1:1 240 and 1:1 171 respectively. Over the same period, the ratio of medical practitioners to the population of Huddersfield Township declined from 1:1 022 to

---

37   Baines, *History, Directory and Gazetteer of the County of York* (1822); W. White, *Directory and Topography of the Borough of Leeds, Wakefield, Bradford, Hudderfield, etc.*, (Sheffield, 1861); Census Enumerators' Books, Wakefield and Huddersfield Townships (1861). Population figures are taken from W. Page, *The Victoria History of the Counties of England: A History of the County of York*, Vol. III (1913), p. 525.

38   White, *Directory of Leeds, Bradford, Huddersfield, Halifax, Wakefield, Dewsbury* (1866).

39   Alexander, *Retailing in England*, p. 101.

40   E.M. Sigsworth and P. Swan, 'Para-medical Provision in the West Riding', *Bulletin of the Society for the Social History of Medicine*, 29 (1981), pp. 37–9, p. 37.

41   The question of why smaller and less industrialized urban communities appear to have had more favourable doctor:patient ratios is examined in Marland, *Medicine and Society*, pp. 258–61, where it is argued that the social make-up of communities and job opportunities better explain the doctor/patient ratios than the population size of potential catchment areas.

1:1 841. Meanwhile, the ratio of chemists and druggists to the population increased from 1:2 657 to 1:1 546.[42]

Activities and Opposition

The significance of the chemists' medical activities, most particularly counter-prescribing, is confirmed by the growing concern they aroused amongst contemporaries, especially the group most threatened by these activities: doctors. Clearly, nineteenth-century doctors recognized that there was considerable potential for overlap between their own activities and those of chemists and druggists, and regarded them as serious competitors for custom. They became one of the main – though far from sole – targets for attacks upon unqualified medical practice. Criticisms of chemists and druggists tended to latch on to the theme that their activities constituted a threat to the population, because of their indiscriminate prescribing and sale of adulterated, even poisonous, articles, but the medical profession were also honest enough to stress their anxieties concerning the chemists' usurpation of the role of qualified medical men. In 1853, a leading article in the *Medical Times & Gazette* complained: 'we reflect, that already the Profession is yearly deprived – we might almost say robbed – of thousands of pounds by pharmaceutists, who prescribe over their counters or even boldly visit patients at their own homes'.[43]

Much concern was expressed in parliamentary reports about the danger of resorting to chemists and druggists in the case of illness. In 1854, Thomas Gilbert, Superintendent Registrar for Bristol, stated in his evidence to the Select Committee on Medical Relief that many children died without their parents consulting a medical practitioner because 'the difficulty of getting medical aid leads them either to doctor them according to an old Woman's directions, or to take them simply to druggists, who know nothing about the disease, and get them a little quackery'.[44] The particular danger to the public represented by 'persons who have had no professional education as druggists, and acting as oilmen, grocers, or village shopkeepers', while at the same time functioning as chemists and druggists, was stressed in the 1864 Report of the Medical Officer of the Privy Council. Whilst unacquainted with the properties of often very powerful drugs, these individuals were free to retail them directly to the public without check or control, and because of carelessness and ignorance, many serious mistakes were made, leading to illness, poisoning or death.[45] Referring to the

---

42 Census Enumerators' Books, Wakefield and Huddersfield Townships; Baines, *History, Directory and Gazetteer of the County of York* (1822); White, *General and Commercial Directory* (1870); Page, *The Victoria History*, Vol. III, p. 525.

43 'The Pharmaceutical Society and the Medical Profession', *Medical Times & Gazette*, i (1851), p. 60.

44 PP 1854 XII (348): Report from the Select Committee on Medical Relief, Q. 723, quoted in Brown, 'The Providers of Medical Treatment', p. 298.

45 PP 1864 XXVIII 1 (3 416), *Sixth Report of the Medical Officer of the Privy Council*, App. 16, pp. 743–52.

danger that chemists represented to the populations of large towns, H.W. Rumsey, in evidence to the 1844 Select Committee on Medical Poor Relief, quoted the report of Mr Dorrington of Manchester: 'It is perfectly frightful to contemplate the loss of life amongst young children and infants arising from the practice of numerous druggists in the poorer parts of the town.' Rumsey claimed that this impression was typical of his returns from forty English towns, adding that 'the great bulk of the poorer classes who cannot obtain medical relief in a legitimate way are driven to druggists and unqualified practitioners'. In Wakefield, Rumsey stated, 'probably from 4,000 to 5,000 poor resort annually to the druggists' (approximately one-third of the population). In other communities, the picture was similar. In Southampton, 'quite as many of the poor are prescribed for by druggists as by regular practitioners'. In Hull, approximately one quarter of the population were said to utilize the services of the prescribing druggist.[46]

The northern manufacturing towns were pointed to as areas where the practice of resorting to the druggist's shop had reached a peak. A leading article contained in an 1857 issue of the *Lancet*, for instance, drew attention to the problem of the unqualified practitioner (in which category the druggist was included) in the north:

> Such persons exist in numbers which would surprise those less conversant with the real state of the case than ourselves. Hanging about the suburbs of town, infesting its central parts, and acting ostensibly as druggists, these people absorb much money and destroy many lives and much health. But the north is the favoured habitat of such individuals; and more especially the manufacturing districts of Lancashire and Yorkshire.[47]

G. Wilson, a Leeds surgeon, describing the extent of unqualified practice in his district, complained in a letter to the *Lancet* in 1854, that the 'lower extreme' of a surgeon's potential practice was effectively closed to him by the prescribing druggists:

> These people sell to the working class for a few pence whatever to themselves seems fit and proper for all manner of diseases, never leaving their crowded shops, and of course living at no expense for horse, carriage, &c, while *all their receipts are in ready money.* But when the patient has spent all his ready cash, what then? Why he goes to the regular practitioner, where he gets credit for months, years, or very frequently for *ever.*[48]

For the poorer classes, the druggist served not only as a supplier of medicines and advice, but in some cases as dentist, accoucheur and surgeon. To cite Rumsey again, in Lincoln, 'the retail druggists have considerable practice among the poor, both in chronic cases and in the early stage of acute complaints; minor operations are also performed by them'. It was common practice for chemists and druggists to treat patients in the early stages of a disease, and in Brighton, for example, this

---

46 *Report from the Select Committee on Medical Poor Relief, 1844, 3rd Report*, Evidence of H.W. Rumsey, Esq., p. 546, Q. 9 121.

47 *Lancet*, ii (1857), p. 326.

48 Ibid., i (1854), p. 458.

group was said to treat the same number of persons as the hospital, dispensary and medical clubs together.[49] Rumsey suggested that, in part at least, it was the difficulties of obtaining proper medical advice that induced 'the multitude' to flock to the druggist's shop.[50] It has also been suggested that many women of the poorer classes resorted to a 'sixpenny doctor', often a druggist, during their confinements. Smith estimates that this service cost between 3s. and 7s. 6d., which could be paid in instalments, a price which remained stable throughout the nineteenth century.[51] In 1857, a *Lancet* editorial which attempted to analyse the popularity of fringe practice in the manufacturing districts explained that:

> Large towns consist almost entirely of operatives who look upon physic as a trade, – and a poor one too, – who have not the ability to form any opinion as to the proficiency of their betters in point of general education – who rather like some one of their own class – who have a strong belief in a natural gift for doctoring, and, above all, believe most fervently in cheap physic, cheap advice, and cheap visits.[52]

The practice of resorting to the fringe practitioner or the druggist's shop was not confined to the poor, however, and this made the situation yet more alarming for doctors. The middle and even upper classes shared a desire to keep doctors' bills to a minimum, a faith in the possibilities of fringe remedies, an interest in trying a variety of approaches to heal their ills, and in the practice of shopping around for medical care. Middle-class mothers were regularly accused by doctors of constantly administering medicines to their children that they had procured themselves, and chastened for not resorting to doctors when they fell ill.[53] Charles Waterton, naturalist and squire of Walton Hall, near Wakefield, exemplified an eclectic approach to medical care, relying on a variety of medical personnel and approaches when taken ill. He was an avid self-doser, regularly taking laudanum, calomel, jalep and sulphate of quinine. Waterton, something of an eccentric and medical experimenter, developed his own prescriptions, and Mr Waterton's Pills were reputedly famous throughout the neighbourhood. It is likely that the ingredients for his remedies were procured from a local chemist's shop.[54] G. Wilson, the Leeds surgeon cited above, emphasized that many of the middle class resorted first to the druggist's shop when taken ill, remarking caustically: 'Nor is the druggist system confined to the poor, for very many indeed of the middle classes go to the druggist first, and only send for the

---

49   *Report from the Select Committee on Medical Poor Relief, 1844, 3rd Report*, Evidence of H.W. Rumsey, Esq., p. 547, Q. 9 121.

50   Ibid.

51   F.B. Smith, *The People's Health 1830–1910* (London, 1979), pp. 40–41.

52   *Lancet*, ii (1857), p. 326.

53   See P. Branca, *Silent Sisterhood: Middle-class Women in the Victorian Home* (London, 1975), Chapter 6.

54   R. Aldington, *The Strange Life of Charles Waterton 17821865* (London, 1949); R.A. Irwin (ed.), *Letters of Charles Waterton, of Walton Hall, near Wakefield* (London, 1955); G. Phelps, *Squire Waterton* (Wakefield, 1976); E. Sitwell, *The English Eccentrics* (London, 1933).

surgeon when a certificate of the cause of death seems likely to be wanted for the registrar.'[55]

Both rich and poor utilized the druggist's services for the compounding of family or homely recipes. Those who could afford them kept well-stocked family medicine chests, containing well-tried remedies for common complaints. Again, local reminiscences point to the continuing popularity of self-medication, many of the remedies described using natural ingredients, including plant extracts and herbs, and rather more curious components, for example dung of cat and dragon's blood, others making use of simple medicaments obtainable from all chemists and druggists. The recipe book of James Woodhead of Netherthong, near Huddersfield, written around 1818 and containing approximately forty remedies, recommended oil of cloves for toothache, spirits of turpentine and castor oil for obstructions of the 'testines', and turmeric for liver complaints. The booklet also contained a recipe for 'female pills', composed of iron, aloes and antimony.[56] More generally, the continuing popularity of such self-help manuals as Wesley's *Primitive Physic* and Buchan's *Domestic Medicine*, and large numbers of lesser-known works, illustrates the widespread use of self-help medicine.[57] Whilst many of the self-help manuals concentrated on regimen and prevention, homely remedies frequently attempted to effect a cure.[58] Just how widespread the use of homely remedies was is demonstrated by the frequency with which chemists advertised their skills in making up such prescriptions, particularly in the local press. In 1804, for example, G.B. Reinhardt, a Wakefield druggist, promised that:

> Those families who may honor him with their Commands, may depend upon having every Article in the Medical Department, as Genuine as at the Apothecary's Hall, London; and that his most anxious Care and Attention will be exerted to the preparation of Physicians Prescriptions, and all other medical recipes.[59]

Advertisements of this nature remained common throughout the nineteenth century. In 1818, William Tee of Wakefield guaranteed accuracy in the making up of family recipes, and in 1839 G. Hackforth announced to the Wakefield public that he had

---

55 *Lancet*, i (1854), p. 458.

56 J. Woodhead, 'Netherthong, recipe book, 1818', MS, Kirklees District Archives (KC 190/1). 'Female pills' were a form of abortificient.

57 The success of William Buchan's *Domestic Medicine; or the Family Physician*, first produced in 1769, was immediate and great: 19 large editions, amounting to at least 80 000 copies, were sold in the author's lifetime alone (1729–1805). For the background to Buchan's work, see C.J. Lawrence, 'William Buchan: Medicine Laid Open', *Medical History*, 19 (1975), pp. 20–35.

58 For self-help medicine, see the essays contained in R. Porter (ed.), *Patients and Practitioners: Lay Perceptions of Medicine in Pre-industrial Society* (Cambridge, 1985), esp. G. Smith, 'Prescribing the Rules of Health: Self-help and Advice in the Late Eighteenth Century', and R. Porter, 'Laymen, Doctors and Medical Knowledge in the Eighteenth Century: The Evidence of the *Gentleman's Magazine*'.

59 *Wakefield Star* (20 July 1804).

taken additional premises in Kirkgate, which he intended to open as 'A Family Medicine Warehouse and General Drug Dispensary'. In 1855, John Handley, also of Wakefield, a member of the Pharmaceutical Society of Great Britain, promised those who would entrust him with their prescriptions and family recipes that they would be carefully compounded under his own superintendence, using the best-quality articles.[60] Compounding family remedies made up a crucial part of the chemists' business throughout the century. Judging by the way it was emphasized in their advertisements, it was possibly a far more important component of their trade than making up doctors' prescriptions.

With few restrictions on the sale of drugs, chemists, and many other retailers, were able to sell their medical wares unimpeded for much of the nineteenth century. One of the best illustrations of the involvement of chemists in the retail of drugs directly to the public was the massive over-the-counter sale of opium preparations.[61] Opium and a wide range of patent cures and infant calmatives containing opiates were easily obtainable and inexpensive, and their widespread usage, in particular their administration to young children, was a cause of great concern to the medical profession, parliament and the interested layman. Again, the practice was said to be particularly widespread in the northern manufacturing districts. Opiates were widely obtainable from chemists' shops, including the most respectable establishments, and a variety of other retail outlets. Chemists frequently made up their own preparations, and these, together with patented nostrums, were said to be sold 'by the gallon' in the manufacturing districts. George Hawksworth, a Sheffield druggist, for example, was noted during the first half of the nineteenth century for his 'Buff' or 'Hawksworth's Mixture', which was composed of rhubarb, magnesia, aromatics and opium, a favourite children's mixture.[62] In 1845, Dr Lyon Playfair described how far the practice of purchasing opium preparations had extended amongst the working classes of Lancashire. In Ashton-under-Lyne, narcotic drugs were vended by all the druggists' shops. Three druggists in one district of Manchester, 'all of acknowledged respectability', sold a total of nine gallons of laudanum weekly. A surgeon based in Wigan, who also kept a druggist's shop, certified to Playfair 'that he is in the habit of selling various preparations of opium under the forms of infants' mixture, Godfrey's cordial, paregoric elixirs, and laudanum; also, crude opium, combined with other

---

60 *Wakefield and Halifax Journal* (10 July 1818); *Wakefield Journal* (4 January 1839); *Wakefield Express* (7 April 1855).

61 See V. Berridge and G. Edwards, *Opium and the People: Opiate Use and Drug Control Policy in Nineteenth and Early Twentieth Century England* (rev. edn, London and New York, 1999; 1st pub. 1987); V. Berridge, 'Opium over the Counter in Nineteenth Century England', *Pharmacy in History*, 20 (1978), pp. 91–100; J. Ginswick (ed.), *Labour and the Poor Man in England and Wales 1849–1851*, Vol. 1 (London, 1983), pp. 47–56, 194–5. For the doping of infants with opiates, see M. Hewitt, *Wives and Mothers in Victorian Industry* (London, 1985), Chapter 10.

62 Austen, *Historical Notes*, pp. 20–21.

substances, according to popular recipes'.[63] In Wakefield and Huddersfield, vast quantities of Godfrey's Cordial, Atkinson's Infant Preservative, Peace and Steedman's Soothing Powders for Children, plus preparations of the suppliers' or customers' own creation, were sold by chemists and other retailers, in addition to crude opium and laudanum. In 1843, Dr Wright of Wakefield, honorary physician to the West Riding County Lunatic Asylum and Wakefield House of Recovery, claimed that opium preparations, notably 'soothing syrups', were prepared wholesale by most druggists in the town, 'several hundred pounds weight of these pernicious compounds' being sold annually, 'besides the stamped medicines of similar effect'.[64]

There was a vibrant market in the sale of products intended to procure abortions or, as it was often framed, to 'restore the menses', and chemists and druggists became major suppliers of abortifacients as well as birth control appliances. A wide variety of herbs and drugs were widely and cheaply available, including tansy, pennyroyal, gin and salts, iron and aloes, caraway seeds, turpentine, quinine, and later in the century, lead. Quinine, for example, was widely used as both a spermicide and to induce abortion. Chemists and druggists also acted as suppliers of a wide range of 'French' or 'female' pills, which were advertised as curing 'suppression of the menses' and 'female irregularities', preparations such as Velnos Vegetable Syrup, Widow Welch's Pills and Frampton's Pill of Health.[65] Techniques of birth control and abortion were more accessible in areas where industrial employment was available to women, and where it was possible to obtain information and remedies, typically urban, industrial areas. Frampton's Pill of Health, for example, was widely advertised throughout the West Riding during the mid-nineteenth century, claiming to remove 'all Obstructions in females'. In 1839, it was offered for sale by a long list of retailers, including England and Fell, chemists of Huddersfield, 6 Wakefield chemists and druggists, 5 Halifax chemists, and 12 Leeds chemists; presumably the actual number of stockists was very much higher.[66] Advice literature and cures for

---

63   PP 1845 XVIII (610): *Second Report of the Commissioners for Inquiring into the State of Large Towns and Populous Districts*, App., Part II, Dr L. Playfair, Report on the Sanatory Condition of the Large Towns in Lancashire, pp. 77, 62 and 65.

64   T.G. Wright MD, *A Lecture on Quack Medicines, Delivered to the Wakefield Mechanics' Institution. Feb. 20th, 1843* (London, 1843), p. 26.

65   Whilst there is little doubt that abortifacients were sold by druggists, this does not necessarily mean that they were sold with the *intention* of procuring an abortion. Hefty doses of these substances would be required to produce this effect. Nor were these preparations, particularly those containing iron, necessarily *purchased* with the intention of producing an abortion. They were frequently taken to remove 'menstrual obstructions', used in effect in a similar way to other popular nineteenth-century purgatives, while regular medical practitioners frequently used iron-based and purgative preparations for the treatment of amenorrhoea and chlorosis; see P.S. Brown 'Female Pills and the Reputation of Iron as an Abortifacient', *Medical History*, 21 (1977), pp. 291–304.

66   *Leeds Mercury* (8 June 1839). For abortion as a form of birth control in the manufacturing districts, see P. Knight, 'Women and Abortion in Victorian and Edwardian England', and A. McLaren, 'Women's Work and the Regulation of Family Size: The Question

venereal disorders were widely advertised in the local press and trade directories, and obtainable from a range of retailers, including the chemist and druggist.

During the nineteenth century, chemists and druggists made extensive use of advertising to promote sales. This coincided to a certain extent with a fall-off in the number of 'pedlar-druggists', and their replacement on the one hand by itinerant quacks and medicine vendors, and on the other by shop-keeping chemists and druggists. During the nineteenth century, the practice of individuals such as Ralph Hodgkinson of Sheffield, who kept a shop in King Street between 1775 and 1792, travelling to nearby towns and villages on market days, where he traded successfully in ancient remedies, became far less common.[67] Increased publicity for the shop-keeping druggist during the nineteenth century was largely achieved through the distribution of trade cards and via the medium of the local press. Newspaper advertisements were aimed in part at the local medical profession, guaranteeing accuracy in the compounding of prescriptions and in the quality of drugs. But the general public formed a far more important target of advertising campaigns. On setting up as a chemist and druggist in Sheffield in 1807, for example, Joshua Gillat solicited 'the favour of the public which he will endeavour always to merit by serving his friends in the best manner and on the lowest terms. Prescriptions made up with the greatest care, accuracy and neatness'.[68] When W. Clater commenced business in Wakefield in 1827, he placed the following advertisement in the *Wakefield and Halifax Journal*:

W. Clater
Chemist and Druggist
Market Place, Wakefield
Respectfully informs the *Nobility, Gentry, and Inhabitants* of Wakefield, and its Vicinity, that he has commenced Business in the above place, and has laid in an entire, fresh, and extensive Assortment of all kinds of Drugs, Chemicals, and Galenicals.[69]

In 1860, Charles Spivey of Huddersfield retired from his chemist's business, returning thanks not to the medical profession, but 'to the Inhabitants of Huddersfield and neighbourhood for their liberal support during the many years he has been amongst them'. He recommended that continued support should be given to his successor in business.[70]

Chemists and druggists employed intensive sales drives, particularly to encourage an increased turnover of patent medicines and their own special lines and preparations. Many famous brand names were first manufactured in the back

of Abortion in the Nineteenth Century', *History Workshop Journal*, 4 (1977), pp. 57–68 and 70–81.

67   M.C. Hamilton, 'The Development of Medicine in the Sheffield Region up to 1815' (MA Thesis, University of Sheffield, 1957), p. 53.

68   *Sheffield Iris* (23 February 1807), quoted in Austen, *Historical Notes*, pp. 21–2.

69   *Wakefield and Halifax Journal* (19 January 1827); my italics.

70   *Huddersfield Examiner* (28 July 1860).

rooms of chemists' shops, such as Nurse Harvey's Gripe Mixture, formulated by Arthur Oglesby, a Barnsley chemist and druggist, and Kompo, orginally known as White's Composition Essence, manufactured by a Leeds chemist and herbalist.[71] On a more local level, in 1810 R. Elliot of Huddersfield, 'Chemist and Apothecary', 'strongly recommended to the Public' a selection of his 'valuable medicines, Elliot's Restorative and Healing Tincture, Elliot's Family Cordial, The Ceylonian Powder, and Elliot's Lozenges'.[72] During the 1832 cholera epidemic, John Moss, druggist of Sheffield, sold his 'cholera pill' as a preventive. It gained a wide reputation, as did his linseed and mustard poultice for feet, and embrocation of camphor spirit for the stomach.[73] In the 1870s, William T. Bygott, dispensing chemist of Huddersfield, promised that his Toothache Elixir would cure toothache or 'tic-doloreux' in just one minute, for only 1s. 1d. or 2s. 9d. a bottle.[74] The sale of special preparations inevitably led to rivalry and imitation. In the 1873 *Huddersfield Directory*, for example, T.N. Swift advertised his own Original Swift's Specific, a 'never failing remedy' for gout, rheumatism, lumbago, sciatica, and all nervous affections, prepared only by T.N. Swift. In the same publication, R. Cuthbert, dispensing and family chemist, advertised his Flockton's Swift's Specific, also for gout, rheumatism, lumbago and so on, prepared *only* by R. Cuthbert![75]

Upon retirement or death, the chemist's and druggists's collection of prescriptions and recipes were handed over to his heirs or successors in business, as in 1832, when G.B. Reinhardt, chemist and druggist, took over the shop of his late father, situated near the old church, Wakefield. He promised that business would continue as usual in the same premises:

> whereat may be had, as usual, faithfully prepared from the Recipes of the late G.B. Reinhardt, his invaluable Medicine, BALSAM of HOREHOUND, for curing Coughs, Colds, Asthmas, Hooping Cough, Declines, and Consumptions. Also [opportunely in this particular year] his truly valuable and never failing Medicine for the Cholera Morbus, or Vomiting and Purging; and also his excellent medicines for Worms; all of which Medicines, from trial and experience, have obtained very high reputations, and can only be prepared by G.B. Reinhardt. as he is the sole possessor of his late Father's Recipes.[76]

In 1870, W.P. England & Co. transferred their large retail business to J.R. Dore, 'pharmaceutical chemist', and in so doing 'handed to him all their private formulae, receipts and copies of prescriptions, who may be fully relied on for accurately dispensing them'.[77] The technique of passing on recipes ensured not only secrecy and

---

71   A. Wright, 'Some Yorkshire Proprietaries', *Pharmaceutical Historian*, 10 (1980), pp. 6–8.

72   *Wakefield Star* (2 February 1810).

73   Austen, *Historical Notes*, pp. 27–8.

74   *Huddersfield Examiner* (1 January 1870).

75   *Huddersfield Directory and Year Book 1873* (Huddersfield, 1873).

76   *Wakefield and Halifax Journal* (16 November 1832).

77   *Huddersfield Examiner* (17 September 1870).

exclusivity, but may also have encouraged expertise, the building up of knowledge, and the preservation of tried and tested remedies.

Chemists and druggists were probably the largest suppliers of patent medicines during the nineteenth century, although they faced much competition.[78] Most stocked vast ranges. For example, during the mid-nineteenth century, W.P. England of Huddersfield and F. Cardwell of Wakefield, both well-established chemists, included Brande's Bronchial Sedative, Woolley's Pectoral Candy, Dr Locock's Pulmonic Wafers, Holloway's Ointment, and Dr Bright's Pills of Health for both sexes amongst their stock. Many chemists also claimed exclusive rights to market certain products. During the 1830s, W.P. England and Taylor & Birch of Huddersfield acted as exclusive suppliers of Concentrated Compound Decoction, prepared by Moxon & Smith, chemists of Hull.[79] In 1839 RS. Alderton of Wakefield and C. Spivey of Huddersfield were appointed sole agents for the retail of Martin Sweeting's Toothache Elixir. [80] During the same year, Mr Smith informed the afflicted of Wakefield that:

> Mrs. HAIGH has appointed him to sell her valuable Ointment, which will be found very efficacious in the following Diseases, viz.- Relief in Cancers, Abscesses, Bad Breasts, Swelling and Tumour, Wounds, Ulcers, etc. etc....The Proprietor of the above Ointment being well aware of its unrivalled efficacy, wishes it to be made generally known The Ointment may also be had at her residence, in the Little Bull Yard, Westgate, Wakefield.[81]

Chemists and druggists, however, did not enjoy anything like a complete monopoly in the retailing of medicines and patent preparations, with competition between the regulars and the fringe, but also between the various components of the fringe. The chemist and druggist faced competition from quack doctors and patent medicine vendors, unrestricted in their methods of sale by *any* attempts to enforce codes of professionalism or practice. The unqualified medical practitioner found it to his advantage to term himself a 'chemist and druggist' – by so doing, he avoided prosecution for practising without a licence. Indeed, the complaints of chemists and druggists about their fringe rivals were similar in tone to those of regular doctors concerning the competition of the unqualified. As the *Pharmaceutical Journal* grumbled in 1846:

> as the law now stands every man who has a 'doctor's shop', with coloured bottles, is a Chemist and Druggist. The itinerant quack doctors ... are, according to law, Chemists and

---

78   In a survey of the retail of patent medicines in Bath between 1744 and 1800, prior to the expansion in the number of chemists and druggists, P.S. Brown sampled 108 proprietors or manufacturers. Out of this total, half were identified – 13 dentists, 12 surgeons, 11 practitioners of physic, 11 apothecaries, 10 chemists and druggists, and two clergymen; P.S. Brown, 'Medicines Advertised in Eighteenth-century Bath Newspapers', *Medical History*, 20 (1976), pp. 152–68, p. 152.

79   *Halifax and Huddersfield Express* (2 April 1831).

80   *Wakefield Journal* (17 May 1839).

81   *Leeds Mercury* (1 June 1839).

Druggists. Although they periodically frequent the markets, they have Druggist's shops, and enjoy the same legal privileges as a Member of the Pharmaceutical Society.[82]

The public could obtain drugs and patent preparations from a variety of other retailers: stationers, newspaper proprietors, grocers, butchers, hairdressers and publicans, to name but a few. The corner shop, situated typically in the poorest areas of town, also sold drugs and patent medicines, and was much resorted to by a predominantly working-class clientele. Booksellers, stationers, printers and newspaper proprietors, with their easy access to advertising facilities, were also major suppliers of patent medicines. The Hurst family of Wakefield, for instance, booksellers, stationers, printers and proprietors of the *Wakefield and Halifax Journal*, advertised and sold a vast selection of patent remedies to their readers. Just one issue in January 1827 advertised for sale at the *Journal* office Butler's Acidulated Cayenne Lozenges, Butler's Pectoral Elixir, Perry's Essence, Solomon's Drops, Mr. Lignum's Improved Vegetable Lotion, Marshall's Universal Curate, and so on.[83] A more unlikely stockist of patent medicines was Mr Hollingshead, a Huddersfield draper, who acted as agent for the sale of John Kaye's Worsdall Pills, 'the most extensively established Family Medicine of the present day'. Worsdall's Pills were supplied in other Yorkshire towns during the 1840s by a variety of shopkeepers, booksellers, grocers, tailors, and hairdressers.[84] This large group of non-pharmaceutical medicine suppliers was seen, not surprisingly, as a major threat by chemists and druggists. However, the chemists' own lack of specialization led to difficulties in eliminating competition from other retail groups and itinerant hawkers of medicines. The *Pharmaceutical Journal* stated in 1843:

The indiscriminate sale of drugs by unqualified persons would produce much less injury to the credit and interests of the regular Druggists, if the public had the means of forming a correct estimate of the value of the articles they purchase, and of the qualifications of the parties concerned. But unfortunately in most country towns not only is every Grocer or Oilman a Druggist, but almost every Druggist is a Grocer or Oilman. The Druggist had no badge or credentials to designate his superior qualification: in fact, he is not *of necessity* more qualified than the Grocer. The blue and red bottles in the windows are common to all; and this is the criterion understood by the public as indicating what is called 'a doctor's shop'.[85]

82 *Pharmaceutical Journal & Transactions*, 5 (1845–46), p. 193, quoted in Crellin, 'The Growth of Professionalism', p. 223.

83 *Wakefield and Halifax Journal* (12 January 1827).

84 *William's Directory of the Borough of Huddersfield* (London, 1845).

85 *Pharmaceutical Journal & Transactions*, 3 (1843–44), p. 101, quoted in Crellin, 'The Growth of Professionalism', p. 222; italics in original.

Making a Living

Despite competition from other fringe groups and medicine suppliers, and indeed, the competition of the regular medical profession, chemists and druggists increased their numbers during the nineteenth century, particularly in rapidly urbanizing communities. Many were able to make decent, even excellent, livings. Towards the top end of the scale were individuals such as George Hall of Huddersfield, who during the nineteenth century ran a highly successful business from his shop in Kirkgate. In 1851, then aged 40, Hall employed two general servants and one journeyman in his shop; three apprentices were bound to him. Hall resided out of town, at Longwood House in the prosperous suburb of Fartown, where, in 1851, he farmed 28 acres, in 1861, 92 acres, apparently acquired from profits of his pharmaceutical enterprises. He employed five labourers on his land, and two domestic servants.[86] Hall was a committee member of the Huddersfield Infirmary, which he also supplied with drugs, and a member of the Town Council.

Whilst few achieved this kind of success, by the second half of the century many chemists and druggists were able to demonstrate their increased prosperity by abandoning the practice of living over the shop, choosing to reside in the new suburbs and out-townships. By 1861, half of the 18 chemists and druggists in business in Huddersfield had residences separate from their workplaces.[87] Increased employment of both domestic servants and shop assistants also points to rising prosperity. By 1851, approximately two-thirds of chemists and druggists in both Wakefield and Huddersfield employed domestic servants.[88] A further indicator of success was the trend towards the opening of branch establishments or chains in the second half of the nineteenth century. By 1884, for instance, Needham Bros., 'medical chemists', owned three shops, one in Buxton Road in the centre of Huddersfield, the others in the nearby villages of Lindley and Meltham.[89] In addition to improving their economic status, many chemists and druggists achieved a high social standing in their communities, participating in local politics and voluntary societies, individuals such as Mr William King, 'a figure well known and held in high esteem in the life of Huddersfield'. Following an apprenticeship in Hull, King came to Huddersfield in 1857, entering the business of Henry Fryer, first as assistant, then partner. After the death of Fryer, King took over his shop, with some success. King was for many years local secretary of the Pharmaceutical Society, and was active in the Infirmary and many Church societies.[90] Thomas Gissing, a Wakefield chemist and the father of the novelist George Gissing, participated in local Liberal politics and the Mechanics'

---

86   Census Enumerators' Books, Huddersfield Township, 1851 and 1861.

87   White, *Directory and Topography of the Borough of Leeds, Wakefield, Bradford, Huddersfield, etc.* (1861).

88   Census Enumerators' Books, Wakefield and Huddersfield Townships, 1851.

89   *Huddersfield Weekly Examiner* (26 July 1884).

90   *Huddersfield Weekly Chronicle* (14 November 1914). For one of the few accounts of the status of chemists and druggists, see Crellin, 'Leicester and 19th century Provincial Pharmacy'.

Institute, his special interests being botany and poetry. He also was active in the Wakefield Town Mission. Although Thomas Gissing was reputed to have 'bourgeois pretensions', when he died in 1870 his family was left in poverty, and the Westgate business sold.[91]

Chemists and druggists continued, throughout the nineteenth century, to involve themselves in a wide variety of medical activities: the sale of the ingredients of remedies, the concocting of their own prescriptions and popular recipes, the vending of patent medicines, advising and in some cases home visiting, surgical practice, dentistry and midwifery. Counter prescribing and advising, which seem to have been the most widespread non-retailing activities to be undertaken by chemists, were perhaps seen by the medical profession as the most serious infringements of the rights and prerogatives of regular practitioners. However, chemists and druggists, by virtue of their status as often highly respectable tradesmen, and because of their growing usefulness as medicine suppliers and expertise in the making up of doctors' prescriptions, were protected to some extent from the attacks of the medical profession upon fringe practices and practitioners.

Counter prescribing was very closely linked to the chemist's selling activities, and it could be argued that it was reasonable and sensible for a chemist to offer advice together with a medication, especially as a large proportion of his clientele would have been incapable of reading the instructions on a packet or medicine bottle. Also, it seems to have been *expected* that a chemist would offer advice. The poor were frequently dependent upon the advice of their local chemist, in the absence of alternative sources of medical assistance. As Jacob Bell pointed out, the chemist 'cannot avoid occasionally giving advice, without incurring the imputation of ignorance and losing the confidence of his customers ...'.[92] Moreover, chemists and druggists seem to have believed that they had a *right* to practise in this way, and it should be stressed that counter prescribing and advising were carried out by *all* chemists, whether they were members of the Pharmaceutical Society or not, and whatever their economic and social standing, although more 'respectable' chemists and druggists were far less likely to have indulged in such activities as dentistry, midwifery and home visiting. Jacob Bell, an articulate representative of the more respectable and substantial chemists and druggists, was well aware of the fact that they dispensed much advice as well as medicine. And individuals such as William Valentine Radley of Sheffield, a founder and a member of the Council of the Pharmaceutical Society of Great Britain and first secretary of the Sheffield Branch, contended that whilst no chemist had the right to call himself a 'medical man', members of the trade should be free to attend to small ailments over the counter.[93]

91   J. Halperin, *Gissing: A Life in Books* (Oxford, 1982), pp. 12–14; G. Tindall, *The Born Exile: George Gissing* (London, 1974), pp. 48–9.

92   J. Bell, *A Concise Historical Sketch of the Progress of Pharmacy in Great Britain* (London, 1843), p. 90, quoted in Brown, 'The Providers of Medical Treatment', p. 312.

93   Austen, *Historical Notes*, pp. 44–5.

Chemists and druggists responded in a timely way to changing market conditions during the nineteenth century. After 1850, purchasing power rose considerably, a result of a growth in the number of consumers and the increasing overall affluence of these consumers. The consumption of medicines, always large, was given a further boost by this development. Meanwhile, the growth in urban populations led to changes in the provision of medical care on a self-help basis. Access to herbal remedies and rural-based folk healers probably diminished, and the rising urban populace was forced to turn more frequently to retail outlets for the supply of medicines and advice. The 'retailing revolution' of the nineteenth century witnessed the emergence of wholesalers, price competition, extensive advertising, window displays, cash sales and the spread of shops, especially those catering for working-class consumers. Chemists and druggists were amongst the first retail groups to take advantage of this revolution, coming to make extensive use of newspaper advertisements for the publicizing of their services – and benefiting from a further expansion in provincial newpapers during the nineteenth century – developing modern and competitive retailing techniques, basing themselves in central locations, setting up attractive window displays, and offering customers competitive prices and special offers. Medicines and medical advice came to be seen as commodities, to be bought and bargained for, and this is perhaps best exemplified by the massive growth in the production and purchase of patent medicines during the latter decades of the nineteenth century, retailed without expertise or knowledge of the product.[94]

The pharmaceutical business came to accommodate diverse retail groups, and by the second half of the century, prosperous, well-trained and highly respectable individuals, members of the Pharmaceutical Society, could share the label 'chemist and druggist' with small-time traders and general dealers. Whilst many chemists and druggists underwent little or no training and had limited skill in their trade, entry into the higher echelons of the chemist's business demanded extensive knowledge, acquired through a long period of apprenticeship, which by the first half of the nineteenth century could cost as much as £200 for a five-year term.[95] Many trainees went on to further their pharmaceutical education while acting as assistants or managers to established druggists; others attended the specialized training courses set up after 1842 under the auspices of the Pharmaceutical Society.

---

94   The value of patent medicines sold in Great Britain rose from around £0.5 million per annum at the middle of the nineteenth century to £4 million around the turn of the century. The number of retail outlets licensed to sell patent medicines increased from 10 000 in 1865 to over 40 000 in 1905, of which approximately one third were run by qualified chemists; Chapman, *Jesse Boot*, pp. 23, 26 and 203–5.

95   Similar fees to those paid in the late eighteenth century. For example, William Lawton, chemist and druggist of Wakefield, took Jonathon Lawton (the presumed family relationship is not known) as apprentice in 1783 for two years at a fee of £21 per annum. In 1788, he took another apprentice, Joseph Fearnley, who paid a fee of £50 per annum for a four-year term; Wallis, *Eighteenth Century Medics*. For the education of chemists and druggists, see M.P. Earles, 'The Pharmacy Schools of the Nineteenth Century', in Poynter (ed.), *The Evolution of Pharmacy*, pp. 79–95.

Undoubtably, some chemists gained expertise not only in pharmacy, but also, through practical experience and informal training, in prescribing and advising. J.R. Dore of Huddersfield, for example, when opening his shop in New Street in 1860, stated, as a guarantee of his competence, that he had passed the major examinations of the Royal Pharmaceutical Society in Latin, Chemistry, Botany, Toxicology, Materia Medica and so on. He had also had many years' experience in some of the 'best establishments' in southern England. Dore vowed to gain his share of public support by close personal attention to the business, by keeping articles of only the very best kind, and by moderate charges. (He added that all poisons were kept in a distant part of the shop, thus lessening the danger of mistakes!)[96]

Already by the mid- and certainly by the late nineteenth century, many chemists and druggists could capitalize on claims of familiarity and continuity. In Wakefield and Huddersfield at least, many of the shops that were trading successfully at the end of the nineteenth century dated from the early decades of the century. A number of pharmaceutical businesses were family concerns, and these tended to be the most enduring and prosperous. For example, the Fell family of Huddersfield was involved in the druggist's trade from the 1820s onwards, when it owned two shops, run by John in King Street, and his brother, Jacob, in the Market Place. By 1851, while Jacob still had his Market Place business, Robert Fell had taken over his late father's shop in King Street. Meanwhile, Robert's brother, William, had also set up shop in the well-to-do Belgrave Terrace, where he lived with his mother, a gentlewoman and proprietress of houses. As late as 1881, Robert Fell was still in business in King Street.[97] The Fells were exceptional both in the number of family members involved in the trade – three shops were owned by them in 1851 – and in their prosperity. But it was not unusual for a business to pass through several generations during the nineteenth century.

Chemists and druggists also enjoyed the advantages of accessibility, their shops being open for long hours, with a druggist usually in attendance. Many druggists, typically those retailing in predominantly working-class areas, continued to live over their shops. With the advantages that continuity, familiarity, and accessibility brought, some achieved considerable local fame. John Gartside Elliot, a mid-century Sheffield chemist and druggist, was believed to have a great knowledge of human ailments, and even to be gifted with second sight. He gave the poor free advice and medicines, and was especially noted for his 'big pennyworths' of drugs. His shop was generally packed with customers from opening time at noon until late at night.[98] The establishment of George Hall (the prosperous individual discussed above) was 'believed in as a cure-all with a faith greater than ever Gull or Jenner commanded'

96　*Huddersfield Examiner* (28 January 1860).

97　W. White, *West Riding Yorkshire Directory* (Leeds, 1828); Census Enumerators' Books, Huddersfield Township, 1851; *Kelly's Directory of Huddersfield and Neighbourhood* (London, 1881).

98　Austen, *Historical Notes*, pp. 52–3.

by the people of Huddersfield.[99] When R.C. Walshaw became successor to George Hall, 'The People's Druggist', in the 1890s, his druggist's shop was then one of the oldest in the town. Walshaw promised to give personal attention to the preparing of medicines for small ailments 'for which the late Geo. Hall was so justly noted'.[100]

Still largely free from ethical, professional or legal restrictions, the chemist could sell what he chose to whom he chose, utilize extensive publicity, and make robust claims for his products. Whilst the middle and upper classes sought out the services of chemists and druggists on a regular basis, their largest pool of custom was made up of members of the working classes. The chemist and druggist had a wide appeal, offering a range of products, traditional herbal remedies, patent cure-alls, homoeopathic, botanic, hydropathic and allopathic remedies, sometimes specializing, but never excluding other lines from his shop. Self-medication was still attractive to many groups of society, and the chemist catered very much for this demand. Chemists and druggists also provided drugs and advice in cases where individuals may have been reluctant to seek the aid of a qualified practitioner (often with justification, in that assistance in the form required may not have been forthcoming) – for instance, in the procurement of abortions, birth control, the treatment of venereal diseases and the provision of opiates on demand.

Cost was a further factor that ensured the continuing popularity of the chemist and druggist, many of his products being available for as little as several shillings or pence, while advice was given gratis – provided, presumably, that it accompanied the sale of medicine. Meanwhile, by the mid-nineteenth century, the minimum fee generally charged for *one* visit by a general practitioner was approximately 5s. excluding medicines. More complicated courses of treatment or visits by physicians or surgeons could cost upwards of several guineas. Poor Law medical services and charitable provisions failed to expand sufficiently in many urban communities to meet the needs of the rapidly growing population, and often failed to address certain medical conditions and crises, chronic illness, minor ailments, children's disorders and a whole range of sexually related disorders and problems, all of which offered increased opportunities for the chemist and druggist. What seemed like increased provision often meant little to the poor, anxious for cheap and prompt medical assistance, without the taints of pauperism or charity; the druggist's shop provided both.

---

99   G.W. Tomlinson, *History of Huddersfield (Home Words), 1885–1887* (newspaper extracts and essays) (Huddersfield, 1887).

100   *County Borough of Huddersfield. Official handbook of Her Majesty's Diamond Jubilee Celebration, June 22nd, 1897* (Huddersfield, 1897).

Chapter 6

From 'Bespoke' to 'Off-the-Peg': Community Pharmacists and the Retailing of Medicines in Great Britain 1900–1970

Stuart Anderson

Introduction

The twentieth century witnessed an extensive transformation in the consumption and retailing of medicines in Great Britain. At first, large numbers of usually worthless, and occasionally harmful, patent medicines were advertised indiscriminately for the cure or treatment of every conceivable real and imaginary ailment. Although there were few effective drugs available for people to purchase or for doctors to prescribe, by the end of the century there were large numbers of potent and effective medicines available. The most powerful and valuable were available only on a doctor's prescription, with only medicines intended to relieve the symptoms of minor ailments available for over-the-counter sale. Yet the public's thirst for self-medication remained as strong as ever.

This chapter explores the factors that drove this transformation, and considers how and why things changed the way they did. Many factors contributed to these changes, including state recognition of the scope for harm resulting from the indiscriminate use of medicines which led to the formation of a regulatory framework to control it. New and effective therapeutic agents were developed in the twentieth century, particularly following the discovery of the anti-bacterial properties of sulphonamides in the late 1930s, which led, in turn, to the rapid development and expansion of the modern pharmaceutical industry. The introduction of the welfare state had a major impact on the consumption of medicines as well, all taking place within a rapidly changing social, political and economic context, which affected the retailing of medicines in many different ways.

There are five main sections in this chapter, beginning with an account of the regulatory framework within which medicines were supplied during the period. Medicines have always been rather more than an item of commerce, with sick people purchasing them in the hope, if not expectation, that they will make them better. But they can also be harmful when used inappropriately, and not surprisingly the state has become increasingly involved in the regulation of such substances. Initially, as we shall see, medicines were regulated under poisons legislation, but as advances were made it became necessary to invent new categories of harmful substance, such as dangerous drugs and therapeutic substances.

In practice, a wide range of legislation has had either a direct or indirect impact on the retailing of medicines. In the early part of the century, action needed to be taken against the frequently outrageous claims made for them. This included disease-specific legislation such as the Venereal Disease Act and the Cancer Act, and other legislation concerned with specific conditions such as epilepsy and consumption. These are considered in the second section of the chapter.

The third section concerns the medicines themselves, with a focus on the impact that the major drug discoveries of the twentieth century had on the retailing of medicines. The growth of the pharmaceutical industry saw a shift away from the making of 'bespoke' nostrums supplied by the local chemist to the standardization of 'off-the-peg' medicines supplied by manufacturers: it resulted in a shift in the type of medicine used, from liquid mixtures to solid-dose tablets and capsules, and it saw a shift from the use of mainly generic (non-proprietary) medicines to mainly branded (proprietary) ones.

The shift is reflected in the gradual specialization of medicine preparation, with an increasing movement from individual patients making their own home remedies, to a reliance on the local chemist making up personalized nostrums, to wholesalers making up standard preparations for issue by the chemist, and finally to dominance by manufacturers undertaking the production and promotion of branded products. This shift is illustrated in Figure 6.1.

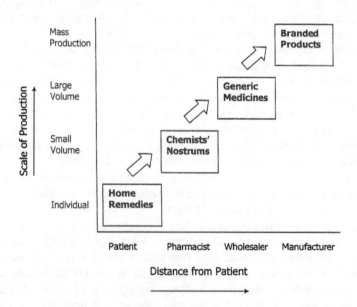

Figure 6.1   Specialization of medicine preparation.

In the fourth section, we consider the emergence of the welfare state, and review the impact this had on the pattern of medicine use. This period saw the decline of home remedies, nostrums and private prescriptions, and coincided with the rise of the prescription medicine. As we shall see, the introduction of the National Health Service (NHS) in 1948 resulted in a virtual quadrupling of the numbers of prescriptions written by doctors and presented at chemists. At the same time, the emergence of supermarkets and of specialist drug stores resulted in a further loss in market share of proprietary medicines by the chemists, who then became financially dependent on dispensing state-sponsored prescriptions.

The fifth section will briefly consider some of the social distinctions that were a common feature of the retailing of medicines both before and after introduction of the welfare state. The medicines bought and the way in which they were presented varied according to the patient's wealth and status.

Finally, the chapter will conclude by considering in what ways diverse factors such as the evolving regulatory framework, the growth of the pharmaceutical industry and the rise of the welfare state resulted in fundamental change in the retailing of medicines, and in what ways there has been continuity. It will also explore the ways in which these factors impacted on the practice and activities of retail chemists (or 'community pharmacists', as they are now called), and how they have responded to them in recent years.

The evidence brought together here is drawn from a wide range of sources. It includes archival data and contemporary publications, as well as material resulting from more recent primary research. It is also illustrated with examples taken from an oral history of community pharmacy.[1]

Regulating Substances: Defining Retail Medicines

To understand the impact of regulation on the retailing of medicines, we must first trace its origins. For most of the nineteenth century, the retailing of medicines was a largely unregulated activity, and products available for retail sale varied from harmless flavoured waters to dangerous poisons. At the time the Pharmaceutical Society of Great Britain was founded to promote the interests of the chemists and druggists in 1841, there was no control of any kind over any substance, no matter how lethal.[2] Any person could obtain quantities of even the most toxic material without

---

1   The oral history study involved recorded life story interviews with 50 retired community pharmacists. Participants practised in England, Scotland and Wales during the period 1911–95. The interviews were conducted by the author. Quotations are reproduced by permission of the interviewees. The tapes are lodged with the National Life Stories Collection of the National Sound Archive at the British Library in London as C816, *Oral History of Community Pharmacy*.

2   S.C. Anderson and V.S. Berridge, 'Drug misuse and the community pharmacist: A historical overview', in J. Sheridan and J. Strang (eds), *Drug Misuse and Community Pharmacy* (London, 2003), pp. 17–35.

constraint. There were no substances restricted to supply only on the prescription of a registered medical practitioner, no need for anyone to ask questions about the intended use of a particular poison, no need to keep records of any sale, and no penalties for inappropriate supply.

This resulted in the indiscriminate supply of a vast range of substances promoted for medicinal use by a whole host of both qualified and unqualified practitioners. The quality of what was supplied was frequently suspect, either through adulteration, inappropriate storage or defects in preparation.[3] The consequence of unconstrained supply, ready availability and low cost was indiscriminate use, with poisonous substances being used for a vast number of domestic purposes. Arsenic and strychnine were supplied in huge quantities for a wide range of agricultural and other uses, whilst many potent substances were used liberally in the preparation of medicines. There were no labelling requirements, and generally no way of knowing what a particular medicine contained.

It was in the late 1840s that public concern first emerged about the unrestricted availability of poisons. Reports from the Registrar General's Office (established in 1837) began to draw attention to the large number of deaths resulting each year from poisoning. More than a third of these resulted from the use of arsenic, with several cases of murder by arsenic poisoning being reported in newspapers during 1849, and the resulting public perception of an outbreak of secret poisoning, with chemists and druggists branded as 'traffickers'. Many solutions to the problem were proposed, including a total ban on the retail sale of arsenic, and the reporting of every sale to the nearest police station.

Both the Provincial Medical and Surgical Association (which became the British Medical Association in 1855), representing the views of the doctors, and the Pharmaceutical Society, on behalf of the chemists and druggists, took the opportunity to signal their concern to the government. In 1849, the Pharmaceutical Society found that its members were extensively involved in the sale of poisons, and its report established the Society as an authority in such sales. The two bodies put forward joint proposals to the Home Secretary, and these formed the basis of the Arsenic Act 1851. For the first time, the retail sale of a poison was to be restricted. Records of every sale had to be kept, the purchaser (who must be an adult) had to be known to the seller, and the arsenic had to be mixed with soot or indigo in order to colour it black or red. Provided these conditions were met, anyone could trade in arsenic: there was no pharmaceutical monopoly, although the Act lacked adequate provision for enforcement, and became little more than a statement of intent.

Regulating the Sale of 'Poisons'

Opium and other drugs were also on open sale and in regular use until the middle of the nineteenth century. Opium was widely prescribed by doctors for its pain-

---

3   S.W.F. Holloway, *Royal Pharmaceutical Society of Great Britain 1841 to 1991: A Political and Social History* (London, 1991).

relieving and calming properties, and was a component in a large number of proprietary medicines. Laudanum (opium tincture) was to be found in most homes as an essential standby, for use either on its own or as an ingredient of home remedies. It was commonly used as an infant soother or to keep babies quiet, and its deliberate use to produce death, either by suicide or murder, was well known. What would now be termed 'addiction' was widespread at the time, but the term had no meaning in the nineteenth century. Self-medication with potent substances was common, and no distinction was drawn between legitimate medical and illegitimate non-medical usage.[4] Inevitably, significant numbers of people became dependent on opium, fed by legitimate supplies obtained from chemists. The system of pharmaceutical regulation was concerned more with the availability of dangerous substances than with their use.

The impact of the Arsenic Act on criminal poisoning was minimal. In the late 1850s, a series of cases received a great deal of press coverage, and calls for greater control over the sale of a wide range of poisons followed. Several attempts at legislation were made, initially without success. It was not until May 1868 that a bill produced by the Pharmaceutical Society to regulate the sale of poisons was introduced in the House of Lords. An early draft of the bill had provided for the regulation of opium, but this had been withdrawn by the Society's Council following lobbying by a group of druggists who believed its regulation would have a serious impact on their trade.

An attempt to limit the supply of powerful drugs to prescription only by medical practitioners was defeated at the same time. The position of the Pharmaceutical Society was that the most effective safeguard in the supply of poisons to the public was to restrict their sale to pharmaceutical chemists, who would be able to exercise their professional judgement and responsibility. The outcome was the Pharmacy and Poisons Act 1868, which largely extended arrangements made under the Arsenic Act to a range of 20 commonly used poisons, including opium, strychnine and prussic acid.

In 1869, the Council of the Pharmaceutical Society produced a set of detailed regulations detailing how its members should keep, compound and dispense poisons.[5] This produced strong opposition from the members, with the most common complaint being that medical practitioners, with or without retail shops, would be exempt from the regulations. In effect, the protection of the public required chemists and druggists to have regulations imposed on them from above, whilst medical practitioners could be safely left to their own devices. Chemists and druggists around the country demonstrated their opposition to these proposals, and they were eventually withdrawn.

The incident demonstrated that concerted efforts by the membership could block attempts by the Pharmaceutical Society's Council to impose regulation on it. Nevertheless, under the 1868 Act, the Pharmaceutical Society was granted powers

---

4   V.S. Berridge, *Opium and the People* (London, 1999).
5   Holloway, *Royal Pharmaceutical Society*, p. 251.

to deem a substance a 'poison', to decide which substances should be available for sale by anyone, and who should be allowed to become both authorized (chemists and druggists) and listed (agricultural and horticultural suppliers) sellers of poisons.

The 'Professionalization' of Retail Medicines

Developments over the decades that followed were to confirm and consolidate this arrangement. Sales of proprietary medicines increased spectacularly with the rise in working-class buying power, nearly tenfold over the fifty years between 1855 and 1905, whilst the population barely doubled. Medicine license duty, required for the retail sale of medicines, was reduced in 1875, leading to an increase in the number of vendors from about 13,000 in 1874 to 20,000 ten years later.[6] Some of the proprietary medicines available contained dangerous concentrations of powerful drugs, such as morphine, strychnine and aconite. Only a small number was labelled 'poison' as required by law, and none actually listed the ingredients on the bottle.

During the 1880s, attempts were made to bring proprietary medicines under professional control. But the doctors and the chemists and druggists had different objectives. The doctors wanted medicines containing poisons to be available only on prescription, whilst the chemists and druggists were more concerned with preventing unqualified persons from selling them.[7] The number of deaths resulting from chlorodyne (which contained morphine and chloroform) led to a campaign against all proprietary medicines by the *British Medical Journal*, whilst a number of legal cases led to the sale of all proprietary medicines containing scheduled poisons being restricted to registered chemists. The Pharmaceutical Society vigorously prosecuted any unqualified dealer who attempted to sell them.

The medical profession viewed the rise of pharmaceutical regulation of dangerous substances with alarm, particularly after their attempts to restrict the availability of poisons to prescription only had failed. Their campaign against patent medicines, and hence restriction of self-medication, was driven by self-interest, with general practitioners resisting attempts by their own College of Physicians to restrict doctors' involvement in retail trading. An amendment to the Pharmacy and Poisons Act 1868 made it possible for registered medical practitioners to also register as chemists and druggists.

The Pharmacy Act 1908 gave pharmacists further responsibilities in relation to the control of poisons, requiring that the purchaser of opiates should be known to the seller, and that an entry be made in the Poisons Register. However, it placed no control over the manufacture or possession of narcotics, with both opium and cocaine being freely available in unregulated quantities without prescription. The Pharmaceutical Society was given the task of policing the Act, although the only real protection against abuse was the professional discretion of the chemist. Such control was largely ineffective, however, as a conscientious chemist might limit sales to

---

6   Ibid., p. 245.
7   Ibid., p. 246.

one bottle per customer, but the customer was always free to obtain further supplies elsewhere.[8]

The medical campaign against patent medicines continued, with articles attacking the 'widespread system of home-drugging' which resulted from the ready availability of opiates in proprietary medicines. In 1909, the BMA published a book, *Secret Remedies: What They Cost and What they Contain*, followed in 1912 by *More Secret Remedies: What They Cost and What they Contain*, to educate the public about the true nature of proprietary medicines. These contained the results of analyses of several hundred patent medicines. They demonstrated that almost all contained nothing but innocuous ingredients worth a fraction of a penny, despite the usually great claims made for them and the glowing testimonials which were offered in their support. Many thousands of copies were sold, and the issue received extensive publicity, both locally and nationally.

Manufacturers who had not already done so began to tone down their claims. After 1900, those whose remedies once contained opium began to drop it from their formulae. *Liquifruta medica* was guaranteed to be 'free of poison, laudanum, copper solution, cocaine, morphia, chloral, calomel, paregoric, narcotics or preservative'. Expensive products making outrageous claims began to disappear from the market. The system of pharmaceutical regulation began to be reinforced by informed consumer choice.[9]

The Creation of 'Dangerous Drugs'

In the early part of the twentieth century, different types of medicine began to be regulated in different ways. It was international developments that eventually led to radical change in the system of control of addictive substances. At the instigation of the United States government, a series of conferences was held, culminating in the International Opium Convention that was signed at The Hague in 1912. This committed the signatories to restricting the trade and consumption of addictive drugs to 'medical and legitimate uses', and to regulate all preparations containing more than 0.2 per cent of morphine or more than 0.1 per cent of either heroin or cocaine.

Throughout the nineteenth century, it was the Privy Council Office (as the central government department of state with overall responsibility for legislation) that had overall responsibility for the control of medicines and poisons, including opiates. The beginning of the First World War brought the Home Office (as the British government department responsible for law and order in England and Wales) into the key government role in relation to the control of harmful substances. This saw the advent of a harsher system of control. In Britain, the efficiency of the army became

---

8   Ibid., p. 254.
9   Ibid., p. 249.

a key issue, as rumours grew about the rapid spread of the apparently 'recreational' use of cocaine amongst soldiers.[10]

Domestic control was quickly arranged by including it in regulations under the Defence of the Realm Act (DORA 40B), a catch-all Act which served as cover for a wide variety of wartime regulation. An Order made in May 1916 prohibited the sale or supply of cocaine and other drugs to any member of the forces unless ordered by a doctor on a written prescription, dated and signed, and marked 'not to be repeated'. It was quickly extended to the civilian population by an order-in-council. For the first time in Great Britain, a number of drugs became available only with a doctor's prescription. The supremacy of pharmaceutical control had been challenged by a system of medical regulation.

The issue of drugs and the army had in fact arisen early in 1916, not because of illicit cocaine sales, but through infringements of the Pharmacy Acts by two London stores. In February 1916, Harrods and Savory and Moore had both been fined for selling morphine and cocaine without complying with the restrictions concerned. The drugs had been sold in the form of gelatine lamels, consisting of small packets of drugs in a handy case, which had been advertised by Savory and Moore in *The Times* as a 'useful present for friends at the front'. Both firms were prosecuted by the Pharmaceutical Society.[11]

With the end of the war, signatories were obliged to honour their commitment to the Hague Convention. In Britain, this formed the basis of the Dangerous Drugs Act 1920. The Act extended the DORA 40B regulations to a wider range of narcotics, including medicinal opium and morphine. It prohibited the import of opium prepared for smoking, and the import, export and manufacture of raw opium, cocaine, heroin and morphine except under licence. In addition, the manufacture, sale, possession and distribution of preparations containing more than 0.2 per cent of morphine, or more than 0.1 per cent of either cocaine or heroin was strictly regulated. The sale of drugs regulated in this way was restricted to medical practitioners and to pharmacists acting on a doctor's written prescription. The sale of narcotic drugs was to be recorded in books open to inspection by the police.

There was little opposition to the Dangerous Drugs Bill, and it passed into law with virtually no controversy. But its impact on both the medical and pharmaceutical professions was significant. Passage of the Act marked the beginning of the displacement of a pharmaceutical system of regulation of this category of retail medicine by a medical system of control through the writing of prescriptions. When regulations under the Act appeared, the Pharmaceutical Society's Council took exception to them, since they made an important class of drugs dependent on a doctor's prescription. They sought to reinstate the freedom of the chemist to sell

10 V.S. Berridge, *Opium and the People: Opiate Use and Drug Control Policy in Nineteenth and Early Twentieth Century England* (London, 1998).

11 S.C. Anderson and V.S. Berridge, 'Opium in Twentieth Century Britain: Pharmacists, Regulation and the People', *Addiction*, 95 (2000), pp. 1 and 2–6.

drugs to persons known to them or introduced by a known person. The government was unsympathetic, and the Act remained unchanged.

The Extension of Regulation

The development of a number of potent medicines, including the barbiturates and digitalis, in the 1930s necessitated some rethinking of poisons legislation. The result was the Pharmacy and Poisons Act 1933. This contained a Fourth Schedule which listed five poisons which could only be sold to the public in accordance with a prescription given by a doctor, dentist or veterinary surgeon.[12] The creation of this Schedule represented a major increase in the medical profession's control of the supply of drugs to the general public.

Despite the introduction of the medically controlled prescription-based system in 1920, and the creation of Schedule Four to the Pharmacy and Poisons Act 1933, there remained some leeway for pharmaceutical regulation. The 1920 Dangerous Drugs Act had lowered the limits below which products containing morphine, cocaine or heroin could be supplied without prescription. The impact of these changes was, not surprisingly, different for over-the-counter medicines than it was for prescription medicines. Manufacturers of patent medicines, for over-the-counter sale, significantly lowered the morphine content of their preparations in order to stay outside the prescription-only limit.

Despite specific legislation that outlawed the supply by retail of medicines for specific conditions such as cancer and venereal disease (see below), there remained concerns about the content of many medicines sold by retail and the claims being made for them. The Food and Drugs Act 1938 made it illegal for a person to sell a drug labelled in such a way that it falsely described the drug, or that was in any way calculated to mislead as to the nature, substance or quality of the drug.[13] It also became an offence to publish an advertisement that did so. However, the value of this safeguard was seriously undermined by the fact that manufacturers of proprietary medicines were still not required to disclose their composition, provided the appropriate medicine stamp was fixed to each bottle or packet. This practice was to end only with passage of the Pharmacy and Medicines Act 1941.

By the 1920s, there existed a number of substances for medicinal use that were neither poisons nor dangerous drugs, both of which were chemical substances that could be analysed. The first Therapeutic Substances Act, passed in 1925, did not challenge the public's right of access to these new medicines; it simply regulated by licence the manufacture, but not the sale, of a limited number of products, the purity or potency of which could not be adequately controlled by chemical means.[14] Such products included vaccines, sera, toxins, antigens and insulin. It was not considered necessary at first to restrict the retail sale or supply of these substances, but the

---

12   Holloway, *Royal Pharmaceutical Society*, p. 395.
13   Ibid., p. 396.
14   J.R. Dale and G.E. Appelbe, *Pharmacy Law and Ethics*, 3rd edn (London, 1983).

introduction of penicillin and other antibiotics towards the end of the Second World War meant that regulation of their manufacture and sale had to be addressed.

The Penicillin Act 1947, and later the Therapeutic Substances (Prevention of Misuse) Act 1953, both recognised that antibiotics were substances 'capable of causing danger to the health of the community if used without proper safeguards'. These permitted their supply to the public only by medical practitioners, or from pharmacies on the authority of a doctor's prescription. Both Acts were replaced by the Therapeutic Substances Act 1956, which brought the control of both the manufacture and the supply of therapeutic substances under a single statute.

Only with passage of the Medicines Act 1968 did this patchwork of legislation concerning the regulation of medicines finally come to an end. Medicines were no longer to be controlled under poisons legislation, and categories such as therapeutic substances ceased to exist. Only with the Medicines Act, together with the repeal of all the previous ones, was legislation concerning the retailing of medicines finally brought within a single coherent framework.

Restricting Retail Medicines: The Regulation of Claims

Whilst legislation during the second half of the nineteenth century and the first half of the twentieth began to define categories of harmful substances (as poisons, therapeutic substances, dangerous drugs and so on) there were other strands of legislation which were designed to regulate some of the more outrageous claims being made for proprietary medicines. Indeed, the range of medicines which could be sold by retail, and the conditions for which they could be advertised, continued to diminish during the first half of the twentieth century. At the start of the century, medicines could be advertised with claims to cure any condition, whether real or imaginary. But by the middle of the century, the claims that could be made for them were strictly regulated. In this section, we consider how legislation led to the gradual attrition of many categories of proprietary medicine.

One of the largest such categories was that euphemistically referred to as 'female medicines'. Abortion had first been made punishable by law under the Offences Against the Person Act 1861. It carried the threat of life imprisonment for both the mother and the abortionist until the passage of the Abortion Act 1967.[15] Despite this, there existed a healthy trade in items promising the return of 'regularity' to women.

By the end of the nineteenth century, quacks and abortionists were using new advertising media to peddle wares purportedly designed to respond to the demand.[16] Such products were typically given very small advertisements in newspapers, often of only a few lines, with the word 'ladies' in large letters to catch the eye.[17] A large

---

15   A.S. Williams, *Women and Childbirth in the Twentieth Century: A History of the National Birthday Trust Fund 1928–93* (Stroud, 1997).

16   A. McLaren, *A History of Contraception: From Antiquity to the Present Day* (Oxford, 1992), p. 191.

17   *More Secret Remedies*, p. 184.

number of such remedies were the subject of more or less veiled recommendations that they could be used to cut short an unwelcome pregnancy. Great ingenuity went into describing the claims for these products, taking great care not to suggest that they could be used to procure abortion. Dumas Paris Pills were typical. They were described as follows:

> The *Paris Pill* is in reality a carefully selected combination of the most powerful drugs known to medical and botanical sciences, whereby a maximum certainty of producing the desired effect is absolutely assured, the explanation of this remarkable result being as follows: If any specific drug contained in the Paris Pill be not actively suitable for a particular female organisation, there are other active ingredients present, which, from their varied and searching nature, are in every way calculated to at once grapple with and overcome the most obstinate case. In the face, therefore, of such a remedy as here described, it can be well understood that there need be no fear of a failure of effect.[18]

Other products included Nurse Powell's Corrective Pills, Mrs Lydia Pinkham's Vegetable Compound, Towle's Pennyroyal and Steel Pills, Dr Davis's Famous Female Pill's, Jefferson Dodd's Corrective and many more. Together, these constituted a massive business, and the total advertising spend was colossal. At the 1897 trial in Exeter of one Luisa Fenn, who sold abortifacients under the business name of 'Madame Douglas', it was revealed that she had spent some £600 on advertising in the course of just six months. This was about twelve times the yearly wage of the typical working man.[19] Before purchasing such pills, most women would probably have first tried hot baths, gin and strenuous walks, amongst other methods.

A wide range of substances claiming to produce the desired effect was sold. Lead in the form of diachylon pills were consumed in large quantities in England. Phosphorus taken from match heads was used for the same purpose. In cities, patent medicines that were 'guaranteed to cure irregularity of the monthly period' began to edge out traditional remedies.[20] However, these were themselves invariably based on traditional emmenagogues (substances able to cause abortion) such as aloes, iron, savin, ergot of rye, rue, tansy, quinine and pennyroyal. Douching and injections were also used.[21]

For the pharmacist, the sale of emmenagogues provided a small but nevertheless worthwhile business opportunity. A number of products could be sold legitimately for this purpose, including slippery elm bark and pennyroyal. By the 1930s there was considerable unease in official circles about the ready availability of such products. The Joint Committee of Midwifery set up an abortion inquiry in 1937. Its interim report made seven recommendations, which included one 'that the supply of slippery elm bark and essential oils of penny royal and parsley be restricted', and another

---

18   Ibid., p. 187.

19   *The Chemist and Druggist* (26 June 1897), p. 1004.

20   H. Marland, *Medical Society in Wakefield and Huddersfield 1780–1870* (Cambridge, 1987), pp. 240–41.

21   E. Shorter, *A History of Women's Bodies* (New York, 1982), pp. 177–224.

'that the advertising of abortifacients be prohibited'. In the event, the Joint Council of Midwifery inquiry into abortion came to nothing, and the situation carried on much as before.[22]

Retail chemists were an obvious port of call for desperate women. Many received requests for items which might be used to aid in the procurement of an abortion. The problem for the chemists was that many of the products concerned had a perfectly legitimate and innocent alternative use. Such was the case with slippery elm bark, which had an entirely legitimate use as a health food. But the advice to members of the pharmacy profession from its professional body was perfectly clear: 'If it is suspected, even on the most slender of evidence, that the purchaser requires a particular substance for this purpose [that is, to bring about the miscarriage of any woman] then the only possible action on the part of the seller is the refusal of the sale.'[23] This advice was accompanied by detailed instructions about the form in which particular substances might be sold.

A woman would rarely request such an item on her own behalf. The messenger was sometimes a man, frequently a child, and occasionally an older woman. In some areas, requests for such items would be surprisingly common. Brian Hebert recalls working in a pharmacy in Portsmouth in the 1930s:

> Slippery elm was the requested item, and of course we followed the Pharmaceutical Society's instructions of breaking it up into, I think it was described as less than two inch lengths then, but certainly short lengths. You break it all up, and sell it to the child. It was always a child who would come in for it. And, er, sure enough, within two minutes the child would be back and say 'mummy says have you got the bigger pieces?' and that was commonplace, quite commonplace. And then penny royal pills, and all the rest of it, were asked for.[24]

Venereal Diseases

At the turn of the century, there was no restriction on the advertising of products claiming to provide a cure for venereal diseases. A wide range of proprietary products was available, with most containing lead or mercury compounds. Burgess's Lion Ointment referred to venereal diseases directly. It was claimed that '*Burgess's Lion Ointment and Pills* have deservedly become the popular remedies for curing all diseases of the skin [including] tumours, fistulas, shingles, venereal sores.'[25] The principal ingredient was lead oleate, blended with resin, wax and fatty ingredients. A product called Mergandol was recommended by its producers as an antisyphilitic

---

22   Williams, *Women and Childbirth in the Twentieth Century*, p. 123.

23   Pharmaceutical Society of Great Britain, *Statement upon Matters of Professional Conduct* (London, 1941).

24   B. Hebert, interview recorded 1 September 1995, *Oral History of Community Pharmacy* (1995), C816/23, 1B: pp. 365–81.

25   *Secret Remedies*, p. 181.

for both intramuscular injection and for external application. Its principal ingredient was mercury perchloride.[26] In addition, *Secret Remedies* contained a number of preparations which might suggest to the gullible that they offered a cure for venereal diseases. Rino Curative Ointment, for example, contained a number of impressive-sounding ingredients, but none that would actually help.

The first serious attempt to limit the public's right of self-medication for such conditions came in the form of the Venereal Diseases Act 1917. This had been a wartime measure aimed at maintaining the health and efficiency of the armed forces. The Act restricted the treatment of venereal disease to qualified medical practitioners. It also forbade anyone from making 'by advertisement or other public notice, a claim to give advice on, prescribe for or treat such diseases'. One of the main aims of the Act was to prevent the sale of proprietary medicines, and chemists' counter prescribing, for venereal diseases.[27]

For retail chemists, the Act presented a dilemma. Trade in such products was not insignificant, and they knew that at least some of the products they supplied did some good. The advice given to them by their professional body was a masterpiece in balancing the demands of trade, professionalism and the law: should a person ask for a particular preparation by name only, that person could be supplied legally. But if the person inquired as to its efficacy for the treatment of some form of venereal disease, any discussion on the merits or otherwise of the preparation immediately rendered the supply illegal. The supply had now introduced a 'knowledge' possessed by the supplier.[28] Similarly, supply was forbidden when the prospective purchaser asked 'for something (not known to himself) good for the treatment' of the disease. The only action possible under these circumstances was to refer the person to a medical practitioner or to a local clinic, thus forgoing a sale.

There were nevertheless other ways in which chemists could benefit financially from venereal diseases. In reality, there was still a whole range of products available for sale from pharmacies for their treatment. A chemist working in Liverpool in the 1930s recalls that: 'we sold a large volume of contraceptives, but we also sold a lot of gonorrhoea bags. There was a lot of VD around then. It was a gauze bag which fitted over the penis. We sold them the bags and then referred them to hospital.'[29] Before penicillin, the main treatments of VD were arsenical products such as Salvarsan (arsphenamine). However, these were only available on prescription. But other products could be sold. A chemist who worked in London in the late 1930s recalls that: 'we had cases of people coming in saying "I've got crab? What have you got

---

26 *More Secret Remedies*, p. 239.

27 Holloway, *Royal Pharmaceutical Society*, p. 396.

28 S.C. Anderson, 'The Most Important Place in the History of British Birth Control: Community Pharmacy and Sexual Health in Twentieth Century Britain', *The Pharmaceutical Journal*, 266 (2001), pp. 23–9.

29 V. Hammond, interview recorded 10 July 1995, *Oral History of Community Pharmacy* (1995), C816/11, 1B: pp. 351–8.

for it?" Usually we would supply benzoyl benzoate.'[30] And another chemist working in Liverpool in the late 1940s recalls that: 'we saw a certain amount of VD. We did a steady trade in mercury ointment, which was sold in three-inch tins. No prescription was necessary.'[31]

Cancer

At the beginning of the twentieth century, a large number of products claimed to offer a cure for cancer. *Secret Remedies* in 1909 and *More Secret Remedies* in 1912 gave detailed accounts of the many quack remedies available for cancer at that time. It found that they had little or nothing in common. Some were liquids for internal use. One was found to contain no more than diluted and slightly impure alcohol. Another was a blue fluid containing mainly terebine and methylene blue. A third was a brown, syrupy liquid consisting mainly of wood tar.[32]

Other remedies for cancer were intended for external use. The first was a plaster mass of resin and soap containing lead oleate as the active ingredient. The second was an ointment of Dutch origin containing ammonium alum and zinc sulphate, together with sodium sulphate. A third preparation was an ointment containing copper oleate and aluminium oleate in a lard and resin base. There was a bottle of lotion available which was labelled 'cures cancerous or malignant sores', followed by a list of other diseases, and the statement that it was suitable for 'even cases that have been under the treatment of doctors and at infirmaries for years'. On analysis, it was found to contain zinc sulphate, phenol and glycerine.[33]

And so the list went on. Sometimes the range of ailments these products claimed to cure was so wide that they were effectively cure-alls. Many included the cure of cancer amongst many other claims. Examples include Burgess' Lion Ointment ('cures tumours'), Crimson Cross Special Ointment ('for the treatment of cancers and tumours') and Wallace's Specific Remedy Number 2 (could be used for 'growing ulcers such as cancer and ovarian dropsy'). Most of the containers bore Inland Revenue stamps, which exempted them from declaring their contents. Such products were mainly advertised in newspapers, although some were sold on market stalls and other temporary premises, and some were given further legitimacy by being sold through retail chemists.

In fact, the advertising and sale of such products continued throughout the inter-war years. It was only with the passage of the Cancer Act in 1939 that this practice was ended. Essentially, the Act placed a duty on local councils to provide adequate facilities for the treatment of people with cancer, and dealt with the prohibition of

30   A. Sheridan, interview recorded 4 July 1995, *Oral History* (1995), C816/09, 1B: pp. 320–28.

31   W. Adlington, interview recorded 21 October 1995, *Oral History* (1995), C816/40, 3A: pp. 89–94.

32   *Secret Remedies*.

33   *More Secret Remedies*.

advertisements. As a result of the Act, it became an offence for anyone to 'take part in the publication of an advertisement referring to any article, or articles of any description, in terms which were calculated to lead to the use of that article or articles of that description in the treatment of cancer', or to 'offer to treat any person for, or to prescribe any remedy for, or to give advice in connection with the treatment of cancer'.[34]

With the passage of the Cancer Act, the legitimate retail trade in all such products ceased. 'Advertisement' was deemed to include 'any notice, circular, label, wrapper, or other document, and any announcement made orally or by any means of producing or transmitting sounds'. 'Publication of the advertisement' was deemed to extend to all those involved not only in the manufacture, production or importation of the article or articles in question, but also those selling it offering it for sale. There was little scope for working round the Act, and the manufacturers of such products turned their attention elsewhere.

Chronic Diseases

Although the Cancer Act effectively put an end to the claims about curing cancer, there was nothing to stop the equally outrageous claims still being made about curing a wide range of other conditions. Nevertheless, efforts to do so continued throughout the period between the wars, and eventually resulted in more extensive legislation.

The Pharmacy and Medicines Act 1941 represents a watershed in the retail sale of medicines in Great Britain. It was the outcome of several years of effort to institute some measure of control over the advertising and sale of proprietary medicines. The Act abolished medicine stamp duty with effect from 2 September 1941, and required for the first time full disclosure on the label of the active ingredients in all proprietary medicines. It prohibited the advertisement to the public of any article in terms that were calculated to lead to its use in the treatment of certain stated diseases: Bright's disease, cataract, diabetes, epilepsy or fits, glaucoma, locomotor ataxy, paralysis and tuberculosis. Medicines intended for the treatment of any of these conditions could from now on only be advertised to the medical profession.

The Pharmacy and Medicines Act also restricted the distribution channels of medicines. Their retail sale was now restricted to a range of individuals who could be held to account. These were 'registered medical practitioners and registered dentists; authorised sellers of poisons; and persons who had served a regular apprenticeship in pharmacy and who, at the time of passing of the Act, were conducting on their own account a business comprising the retail sale of drugs'.[35] Such persons were permitted to sell medicines only from a shop (not from a market stall), and sales had to be under the personal control of the person concerned. However, the sale of

---

34 H.W. Fowler, *Aids to Forensic Pharmacy*, 5th edn (London, 1960), p. 140.
35 Holloway, *Royal Pharmaceutical Society*, p. 396.

vegetable drugs, natural and artificial mineral waters and proprietary medicines was not normally restricted to authorized persons.[36]

But there was no end to the inventiveness of the manufacturers of proprietary medicines. In the 1930s, there was a fashion for combining non-human organs in 'pluriglandular' tonics for the treatment of conditions supposed to result from general glandular insufficiency. Pluriglandular preparations for the treatment of sterility could be bought from pharmacies without a doctor's prescription. Fertilinets were advertised for use in female disorders, menstrual and climacteric disturbances and frigidity. Pregnantol was available to combat barrenness and miscarriage, influence the natural events of fertilization, regulate the course of pregnancy, and ensure healthy offspring.[37] A range of hormone beauty baths, bust development glands, gland tablets for male and female impotence were sold under the brand name Juvigold. And so it went on.

More Secret Remedies in 1912 identified a number of products, usually euphemistically referred to as 'tonics' or 'restoratives', that were targeted at sexual weakness. Gordon's Vital Sexualine Restorative was typical. Its advertisement referred to 'interesting and instructive remarks to young and middle-aged men on how to preserve strength and retain the powers'.[38] The medicine itself was a tonic containing metallic hypophosphites. It is clear that such products were advertised and sold through retail chemists.

In 1941, the Pharmaceutical Society found it necessary to include in its Statement Upon Matters of Professional Conduct an instruction to the effect that 'advertisements of medicines should not be issued to the public referring to sexual weakness'. By 1953, this had been extended to other areas, and had been elaborated to indicate what the appropriate response of the pharmacist should be. The Statement then read: 'no material should be displayed which makes a reference to sexual weakness, premature aging or loss of virility, or any reference to complaints of a sexual nature in terms which lack the reticence proper to the subject'.[39] By the 1950s, professional regulation had an important part to play in supplementing statutory regulation.

This section has demonstrated that retail chemists played an important part in the supply of medicines for a wide range of serious illnesses, in addition to minor ailments. Collectively, they often represented an important part of the chemists business. In the first half of the twentieth century, as much as half of the average chemist's income came from the sale of proprietary and non-proprietary medicines. Only with the introduction of the NHS in 1948 did the dispensing of prescriptions come to dominate both the work and income of the chemist. The shifting pattern of reliance by the chemist on the retailing of medicines during the course of the century is illustrated in Figure 6.2.

---

36 Ibid., p. 397.

37 *Chemist and Druggist Yearbook* (London, 1939), p. 72.

38 *More Secret Remedies*, p. 54.

39 Pharmaceutical Society of Great Britain, *Statement upon Matters of Professional Conduct* (London, 1953).

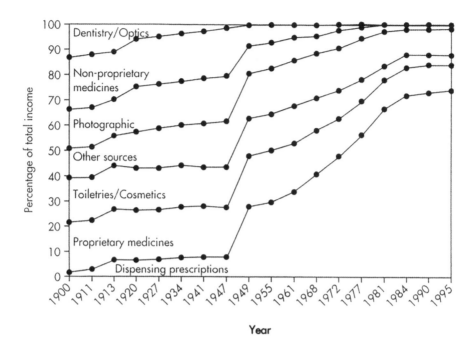

Figure 6.2   Sources of income of retail chemists 1900–2000.

The Nature of Retail Medicines

The regulation of substances led to the definition of medicinal substances according to how dangerous they were: the regulation of claims aimed to protect the public from the outrageous claims of charlatans, and to direct them to more appropriate courses of action, such as seeing a doctor. But the range of medicines available to the public during the first half of the twentieth century constituted a wide spectrum, which provided no clues as to either the danger involved or the extent of the benefit claimed. The range extended from the sale of individual ingredients for the preparation of home remedies on the one hand to proprietary medicines manufactured to exacting standards on the other. In between was every conceivable option. This section considers how the retail sale of the three main categories of retail medicines – home remedies, chemists' nostrums and proprietary medicines – waxed and waned during the twentieth century.

Home Remedies

At the beginning of the twentieth century, it was still common for families to rely heavily on home remedies made to their own formulae for a whole range of minor, and sometimes not so minor, ailments. People would present scraps of paper to the local chemist asking for a few pennies' worth of particular ingredients. These were the home remedies, the secret formulas handed down from one generation to the next, usually written on a scrap of paper, and taken to the chemist to be made up. The chemist would see many similar formulae, differing slightly in the relative quantities of ingredients. Sometimes people would take in recipes for home remedies and ask the chemist to make it up for them. Alan Kendall undertook his apprenticeship in a retail chemist's shop in Shipley, Yorkshire, in 1938. He recalls that:

> A lot of home recipes were brought in. In the winter time, the main one was three penny worth of chlorodyne, and three penny worth of liquorice. [This was] mixed together and made up in an eight ounce bottle. This was more or less Mist. Tuss. Nig. [black cough mixture] wasn't it? And then there would be variations on that. Things like 'All Fours', which was a combination of honeyseed oil, with tincture of opium, I believe, and peppermint oil, and possibly another of the aromatic oils. Paregoric [camphorated tincture of opium] often went with people asking for linseed as well, a mixture of … they used to boil their own linseed up to make a mucilage from it, and then mix that with either paregoric or liquorice, or sometimes chlorodyne.[40]

The trade in home remedies clearly altered with the seasons, and the items requested were not always for medicinal purposes, as Alan Kendall recalls:

> Christmas time was the worst time of the year for these sort of things, because several times a day people would come in with their own pet recipe for ginger wine essence, which always had a slight variation on the amount of tincture of capsicum in it; also some strong tincture of ginger and citric acid, and then some would want raspberry flavouring, and others would want lemon flavouring, and others would want orange flavouring. It was the bane of our lives as apprentices, because we always had to do this sort of thing, you see.[41]

Part of the seasonal variation was due to differences in the occurrence of particular minor ailments, such as coughs and colds. Alan Kendall continues:

> I can't remember what was needed during the summer months on these recipes, but everybody had their own pet remedy for colic. Colic was tincture of rhubarb and syrup of ginger, I think it was, which they used to take. Sweet nitre was also a popular thing [sprit ether net.] which we used to sell in winter time, because of people with a cold-a

---

40   A. Kendall, interview recorded 5 December 1995, *Oral History* (1995), C816/48, 1B: pp. 78–92.

41   Ibid., pp. 119–31.

heavy cold-and they used to want to sweat it out, and so would take the sweet nitre in a hot drink.[42]

People used a wide range of home remedies, and some of the formulae were treated with great secrecy. They were often handed down from one generation to another, occasionally even skipping a generation. Often, the variation from a standard theme was quite minor, with perhaps something omitted to reduce the cost, or something extra added in order to change the colour or taste. Home remedies remained popular until introduction of the NHS in 1948, when medicines became free for everyone.

Nostrums: The Chemists' Secret Remedies

At the beginning of the twentieth century, the core of the chemist's business was counter prescribing. This involved the recommendation and sale of a particular medicinal product to a customer. Legally, the chemist was forbidden from making a diagnosis by examination of the patient. But there were few products the chemist could not sell. A number of poisons were controlled under the Pharmacy and Poisons Act 1868, but even here, all that was necessary was to label the medicine with the name and address of the vendor, and to record details of the ingredients and the name of the customer in a prescription book.

For those without secret family recipes, and those who could not be bothered with the effort of making their own medicines, there were always the nostrums. These were medicines prepared by the local chemist to his own formula, and were invariably labelled as 'the mixture' or 'the tonic'. Nostrums were usually supplied in response to requests such as 'Have you got something for my cough?' or 'Have you got something for my indigestion?' and so on. The patients thought they were getting something made up exclusively for them, and it was usually sold for a few pennies.

Whatever the patient was going to receive, it was always a good idea to keep them waiting. Jack Maskew undertook his apprenticeship with Banners Pure Drug Company in Liverpool in 1943:

> They would get mist. morph et ipecac., mist. ammon. chlor. et morph. – various of the standard national formulary preparations, you see. You didn't keep them ready made up. They were ready there to pour out, and put a label on, and you'd write on it. You wouldn't bring out anything straight away, because the mere fact that you kept them waiting 5 minutes proved that you were making something up specially for them, see, for which they were very pleased and grateful, and you'd go out and charge them one shilling, something like that.[43]

In reality, the chemist would have large containers of popular medicines like cough mixtures and tonics made up ready in the dispensary. They would usually be made to

---

42 Ibid., pp. 132–45.
43 J. Maskew, interview recorded 20 October 1995, *Oral History* (1995), C816/39, 2A: pp. 69–84.

a standard national formula, perhaps with a minor 'secret' ingredient, often no more that a particular flavour or colour, to distinguish theirs from their neighbour's. In time, many of these were packed and labelled ready for sale. Very often, there would be a whole series of own formula remedies: 'Smith's Cough Mixture', 'Smith's Cold Remedy', 'Smith's Tonic' and so on. People with fairly minor complaints would go to the pharmacy in the hope of getting relief for a few pennies. Jack Maskew continues:

> They'd come in and say 'I've got a bad cough. Can you give me something for it?' I would ask what type of cough it was. Was it tight or loose, that sort of thing. You'd say 'Just hang on a minute.' Then I'd make something up for them. We didn't keep proprietary cough mixtures. We would supply our own from a stock bottle. We had our own standard bottle for coughs. It was called 'Black Magic'. There were also other house nostrums with names like 'Black Lightning', 'Banners Tonic' and 'Strawson's Tonic Mixture'. A lot of them still went under Strawson's name [the shop had previously been owned by Strawson's]. Whatever the patient was going to receive it was always a good idea to keep them waiting.[44]

Although people would request those items which were heavily advertised, such as the Beecham range of products, it was actually much more common for the public to put their faith in the advice and expertise of the local chemist. For minor complaints, and sometimes more serious ones, they would present their symptoms at the pharmacy. John Cave undertook his apprenticeship at a shop in Guildford, Surrey, in 1936. He recalls:

> Patients seldom asked for a named preparation, unless it was Andrews Liver Salts, Beecham's Pills, or something like that. They would come in and say 'I want something for my cough', and nine times out of ten we would make then up something special, because it did them a lot more good than if they bought something off the counter, or so they thought.[45]

Such nostrums continued well into the 1960s, and only finally disappeared with the implementation in 1973 of regulations under the Medicines Act 1968, which effectively prevented small-scale manufacture of medicines in community pharmacies. Geoffrey Knowles managed his own pharmacy in Hoylake on the Wirral, until he retired in 1984. He remembers that:

> I continued to make a few nostrums until I retired. But new regulations had been brought in following the Medicines Act [1968], which made it more difficult. There were regulations about how you must label them: they had to be labelled in the dispensing manner rather than the commercial manner ... and you were not allowed to keep any stock in hand. The

---

44 J. Maskew, interview recorded 20 October 1995, *Oral History* (1995), C816/39, 2B: pp. 134–48.

45 J. Cave, interview recorded 6 July 1995, *Oral History* (1995), C816/10, 1B: pp. 178–94.

Pharmaceutical Society inspector rapped my knuckles once or twice because he saw a little stock waiting to be issued.[46]

Although nostrums remained popular with the public, particularly with older people, until well into the 1970s, their place had largely been taken by heavily advertised branded products, the proprietary medicines. A significant shift in the public's preference occurred in the early 1950s, with the growth in advertising, and particularly the arrival of television. Proprietary medicines were amongst the first consumer products to be advertised on television. Christine Homan undertook her apprenticeship with Boots the Chemists in Lambeth, South London. She recalls that:

> Initially people came in asking for something for a cough, or whatever. The trend towards asking for branded products by name came towards the end of my two years with Boots [in 1954]. Gilbert Harding [a TV personality] was advertising Macleans Indigestion Tablets on television. It started a trend for asking for named brands. People came in and started asking for 'Gilbert Harding Tablets'. Prior to that people were not really aware of brand names.[47]

To the retail chemist, the sale of all medicines, whether raw materials, made-up mixtures or proprietary medicines, was useful trade. But the differing forms were not equally profitable: for made-up medicines, he charged a shilling or so for making something with ingredients which usually cost him a fraction of a penny; on proprietary medicines, he had to settle for whatever profit margin he could squeeze out of his supplier. And the retail chemist was not the only source of medicines available to the public. There was a bewildering range of outlets for medicines. Quack remedies were still very much in evidence, and these were available from hawkers and street traders as well as by replying to the many advertisements that appeared in local and national newspapers, magazines and pamphlets.

Proprietary Medicines

The largest category of medicines available for retail sale, certainly in terms of turnover, was the proprietary medicines. These included well-known products such as Beecham's Pills, Andrews Liver Salts and Carters Little Liver Pills. They were extensively advertised direct to the consumer on everything from railway hoardings to newspapers, and were promoted through sponsorship and celebrity endorsement. As we have seen, the period of rapid expansion was during the second half of the nineteenth century, with sales rising from £600,000 in 1860 to £5 million in 1914.[48]

---

46 G. Knowles, interview recorded 17 October 17 1995, *Oral History* (1995), C816/36, 2A: pp. 290–96.

47 C. Homan, interview recorded 24 November 1995, *Oral History* (1995), C816/46, 2A: pp. 76–92.

48 Holloway, *Royal Pharmaceutical Society*, p. 308.

The range of outlets from which they were available also expanded. To the grocers, market stalls and chemists' shops were added department stores and multiple drug stores.

Multiple drug stores in Britain owe their origins to an important legal case that was decided in 1880. During the 1870s, a number of limited companies, including the Civil Service Co-operative Society and leading department stores such as Harrods, had started selling drugs and medicines.[49] The Pharmaceutical Society held the view that the maintenance of professional standards required that individual pharmacists retain ownership and control of every pharmacy. They believed that the Pharmacy Act 1868 gave them that protection. Following the case of *The Pharmaceutical Society* v. *The London Provincial Supply Association*, they found that it did not. A final decision by the House of Lords allowed companies to carry on the business of chemist and druggist, and many did so. The first was Jesse Boot. Within three years of the ruling, Boot had opened ten branches.[50] By 1890, three other companies had more than ten branches: Taylors in Leeds, Warhursts in Liverpool and Timothy Whites in Portsmouth. By 1900, Boot had opened over one hundred branches, and there were already a large number of other multiple chemists' companies in existence.[51]

From their beginnings, the multiples and department stores followed a strategy of selling drugs and proprietary medicines at reduced prices. Jesse Boot built his business on cut-price offers. The opportunity for bulk purchase gave the company chemists enormous commercial advantage. The biggest manufacturers such as Holloway's offered profit margins of 14.5 per cent on orders of over £5, but only 5 per cent for the normal orders of the retail chemist. The largest chains negotiated even more favourable terms.[52] Widespread cost-cutting was a disaster for the small independent-proprietor chemists, and they soon got together to fight back. At the instigation of a London chemist by the name of William Glyn-Jones, who later went on to become Secretary and Registrar of the Pharmaceutical Society, a Proprietary Articles Trade Association (PATA) was formed in 1896, 'to unite the interests of manufacturers, wholesalers and retailers'.

The objective of the PATA was resale price maintenance for proprietary medicines. Wholesalers agreed to withhold supplies of listed articles from retailers found to be cutting prices. It started with a list of 16 articles; by 1897 there were 142 on the list, and in 1924 there were over 2 000. Resale price maintenance was firmly established following its acceptance by the company chemists in 1900. Its success was due to the groundwork carried out by the Pharmaceutical Society. Chemists and druggists were by far the most strongly organized of the retail trades.[53] This was the result of the

---

49   Ibid, p. 274.

50   S. Chapman, *Jesse Boot of Boots the Chemists: A Study in Business History* (London, 1974).

51   Holloway, *Royal Pharmaceutical Society*, p. 278.

52   Ibid., p. 310.

53   Ibid., p. 318.

fact that entry to it was firmly regulated by the twin mechanisms of training through apprenticeship and statutory registration only following successful completion of the Society's examinations.

The establishment of resale price maintenance was good news for the independent-proprietor pharmacist, whose profitability was secured, but bad news for the patient, who no longer had access to reduced-price proprietary medicines. For some, the cost of proprietary medicines was still high. If the price of the real thing could not be reduced, one solution was to produce imitations of the advertised product, and to sell them at a lower price. For example, a formulary in use in a chemist's shop in Birkenshaw, West Yorkshire, between 1885 and 1927 includes a formula for an 'Imitation Phosferine'.[54] Phosferine was a popular nerve tonic in the early part of the twentieth century produced by Beecham's.

A number of products were known by names that were often assumed to be proprietary names but actually were not, and could therefore be produced and sold very cheaply. These included Golden Eye Ointment, Epsom Salts and Friar's Balsam. But as the twentieth century unfolded, the market for proprietary medicines became more focused. Mergers and takeovers amongst manufacturers led to heavier promotion of fewer brands. Many familiar products disappeared, although some, like Beecham's Pills, survived until the end of the twentieth century.[55]

From Bespoke to Off-the-Peg

It was not only the range of medicines available to the public that underwent substantial change during the course of the twentieth century: so did the dosage forms in which they were presented. These changes resulted largely from the emergence of a research-based pharmaceutical industry. The consequences of this were far-reaching, leading to the therapeutic revolution of the 1950s and 1960s during which large numbers of new therapeutic substances were developed. But they included a dramatic shift from medicines being extemporaneously prepared in the dispensary by the pharmacist ('bespoke medicines') to their being made in factories by pharmaceutical manufacturers and supplied in a ready-for-use form to the chemist ('off-the-peg medicines'). This in turn led to a shift in dosage form, from an emphasis on liquid-dose medicines (draughts and mixtures) to an emphasis on solid-dose forms (tablets and capsules). Finally, research on medicines was accompanied by research on better methods of delivering them, and a range of innovative dosage forms was developed.

At the start of the twentieth century, nearly all the medicines supplied from chemists were made up individually. There were a few proprietary medicines available (Beecham's and Holloway's Pills and so on), but the nostrums, home

---

54   W.E. Court, 'The Formulary of a West Yorkshire Pharmacy 1885 to 1927', *Pharmaceutical Historian*, 27(1) (1997), pp. 2–9.

55   S.C. Anderson and P. Homan, 'Best for Me, Best for You: A History of Beecham's Pills 1842 to 1998', *The Pharmaceutical Journal*, 269 (2002), pp. 921–4.

remedies and prescription items were all made up individually. For the chemist of the time, there was an art to making an elegant product: this was known as *secundum artem* (Latin for 'to make favourably with skill'), and as much attention was paid to the finish and the wrapping as to the making of the medicine itself.

Machinery to mass-produce medicines were developed in the later decades of the nineteenth century. Mass-production was central to the businesses of Holloway and Beecham, which would not have been possible without it. But at that time there were few effective drugs that could be provided in this way. Those that could included aspirin tablets, digoxin and later phenobarbitone. It was only following the mass-marketing of the sulphonamides in the late 1930s that the possibility of mass-producing large numbers of effective drugs became a reality.

The shift from bespoke to off-the-peg medicines occurred over a number of decades, and underwent a number of distinct phases in its development. Pharmaceutical wholesalers had been in existence for many years, providing chemists with their pharmaceutical needs, from raw materials to containers, labels and equipment. Slowly they began to provide some of the standard medicines in a ready-made-up form, usually in large Winchester bottles. These usually relieved the chemist's apprentice of the chore of making up fresh stock bottles on a daily basis.

By the 1950s and 1960s, wholesalers had developed more compact products. These were the liquid concentrates, from which chemists would make up their own stock bottles, or else dilute prior to dispensing. Later, they supplied the mixed powders for a wide range of mixtures, which again all the chemist had to do was to make up with water. By the 1970s, the number of prescriptions for liquid medicines had greatly declined, and the vast majority of drugs being prescribed were then available as solid-dose medicines for oral use, mainly tablets and capsules.

From Liquid to Solid-dose

The shift from bespoke to off-the-peg was also accompanied by a shift in the form of medicine supplied, from liquid to solid-dosage form. Although ingredients for the preparation of home remedies were often solid, despite including liquids such as aromatic oils and tinctures, the preparations made in the pharmacy were invariably liquids, either multi-dose mixtures or single-dose draughts. Proprietary medicines, on the other hand, were often in solid-dose form, such as Beecham's Pills and Andrews Liver Salts.

As new drugs were developed and promoted to the medical profession, the great majority were presented in solid-dose form, mainly tablets and capsules. These had distinct advantages over liquid forms: the unit dose was accurate and unambiguous, and could be manufactured to exacting standards; they were a much more compact form than mixtures and therefore required less storage space, and they were stable for a much longer period than liquid medicines.

But these changes did not happen overnight. The trend started in the late 1920s, and was not really complete until the 1980s. The prescription books kept by retail chemists provide a rich source of the data needed for plotting this trend. The proportion of all prescriptions written accounted for by a particular dosage form can be calculated for each of a number of sample years.

Figure 6.3 illustrates this trend for one shop in south London over the years 1900–2000. It demonstrates graphically the fact that in 1900, over 60 per cent of all prescriptions written were for oral liquids (mainly mixtures), and that just over 10 per cent were solid-dose forms (mainly pills and cachets). By 1980, this pattern had been completely reversed: 70 per cent of all items dispensed were in solid-dose form (mainly tablets and capsules), whilst only 7 per cent were supplied as oral liquids (mainly elixirs and syrups). Very few of the remaining products needed to be made up extemporaneously. The days of the bespoke medicine were all but over.

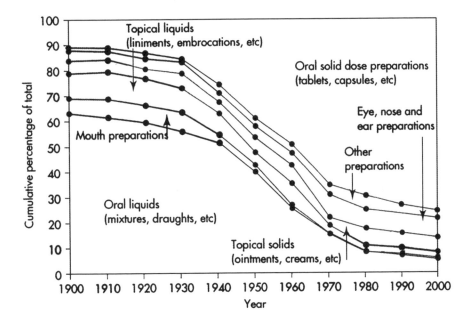

Figure 6.3   Principal dosage forms 1900–2000.

The Retailing of Medicines and the Welfare State

Medicines have always been rather different from other commodities, in that the need for them is universal, and at the same time people would prefer not to need them. Whilst the rich have always been able to call on the services of the doctor and to obtain whatever medicines were considered appropriate, and the middle and working classes have been able to purchase nostrums or patent medicines, the options available to the very poor have been few indeed. Inevitably, they often relied on folk remedies made from plant materials collected locally.

During the reign of Queen Victoria, one source of medicines for the poor was through welfare. State provision for the destitute was originally based on the Poor Law 1834. Its aim was not so much to relieve poverty, but to deter the poor from applying for relief, by forcing working men onto the labour market. At this it was very successful. By 1900, around 30 per cent of the population lived in poverty, but less than 3 per cent were in receipt of Poor Relief. Those who were in a position to do so made provision for themselves by relying on mutual help. A number of organizations emerged to meet this demand. By mid-Victorian times, mutual help Friendly Societies had become major providers of social security. People who shared a religious belief, occupation or area of residence would help each other in times of misfortune by the creation of a common fund. This generally provided security against poverty through illness, or the expense of a funeral.

Even in 1815, around 8.5 per cent of the population belonged to a Friendly Society of some kind. But the movement grew rapidly, and by 1900 there were nearly 24 000 Friendly Societies and branches, with nearly 4.5 million members. This was about half the adult population of Great Britain at the time. An additional million or so received benefits through membership of a trade union. For a contribution of usually 4–8d. (about 1 or 2 per cent of a weekly wage), members received sick pay, death benefit and medical care, which included access to a doctor under contract to the society, and the cost of any medicines prescribed.

The impact of these initial attempts at welfare on the retailing of medicines was negligible. Friendly Societies were anxious to keep the costs of any medicines supplied to a minimum. Some established their own formularies of standard preparations, mainly those that appeared in national reference works such as the British Pharmacopoeia. Local authorities began to do likewise in relation to those medicines to be supplied under Poor Law provisions. But the key factor was that doctors were given a fixed rate per capita which included the cost of any medicine, so there was always an incentive for doctors to prescribe low-cost medicines since they could pocket any saving made.

Retailing Medicines and the National Health Insurance Act 1911

The election of a Liberal government in Britain in 1905 led to a steady stream of reforms covering a wide range of public services. Concerns for the considerable number of people who were still not covered by any health insurance scheme were raised by a number of campaigners. The task of reforming health insurance fell to David Lloyd George. He realized that any new system could not be supported from taxation alone, and that it would require contributions from the beneficiaries. Since this would then be in competition with the Friendly Societies, he decided to bring them into the programme by asking them to administer it to those sections of the working class so far excluded from insurance.

The new role of the Friendly Societies was to include administration of both medical and pharmaceutical services. When Lloyd George presented his bill to Parliament in May 1911, he announced that the societies would arrange with chemists for the supply of medicines and appliances under the scheme. He said that he had 'no doubt that they would make as advantageous terms with the chemists as they had in the past with the doctors'. But the Friendly Societies had other ideas. Their plan was to establish their own dispensaries in all the large towns. One of the biggest proposed to set up a central drug store and branch dispensaries, to be controlled and administered by themselves. They began to canvass support for the setting up of a factory for the preparation of galenicals, drugs, chemicals and sick room requisites, which would then be distributed to depots around the country.

But the Pharmaceutical Society objected, claiming that the proposals would deprive qualified chemists of some 14 million customers per year. 'The effect on pharmacists will be disastrous,' declared the *Pharmaceutical Journal*. It argued that the existing network of chemist shops should be used, rather than the creation of new establishments.[56] The objections of the pharmacists prevailed. When the Act was finally passed, it incorporated most of their demands. It was a contributory scheme, involving contributions from employees, employers, and government. It did not apply to workers' dependants, but its provisions included general medical services and the supply of medicines. 'The first thing that I think should be done', said Lloyd George, 'is to separate the drugs from the doctors.'[57] He was anxious that there should be no inducement for underpaid doctors to skimp on drugs. The experience of provision both under the Poor Law and by Friendly Societies was that whenever doctors received an inclusive fee for attendance and medicines, the temptation to use cheap drugs was not easily resisted.

The impact of health insurance on the practice of community pharmacy was considerable. The *Pharmaceutical Journal* records that the first prescription under the new Act was dispensed at 8.40 a.m. on 15 January 1913.[58] The numbers of prescriptions presented caught the chemists completely by surprise. Within a year, the numbers were more than three times what they had been previously. Numbers rose from below 15 million to over 50 million per year. Many pharmacies did not have the basic equipment or the right ingredients to meet the demand. The number of prescriptions written by doctors and presented at chemists during the period 1900–2000 is shown in Figure 6.4.

The influx of prescriptions varied according to the social class composition of the area. In a prosperous area of west London, the year's takings from National Insurance dispensing was only £25 11s. 1d., representing less than 1 per cent of turnover. In depressed Rotherhithe, on the other hand, the takings were £616 9s. 8d., representing nearly 60 per cent of turnover.[59] Pharmacies in densely populated working-class areas, which had previously dispensed only one or two prescriptions per week, were now receiving several hundred per week.

---

56   Ibid., 85 (1911), pp. 706–7.

57   Ibid., 88 (1912), p. 717.

58   J. Anderson Stewart, 'Jubilee of the National Insurance Act', *The Pharmaceutical Journal*, 189 (1962), pp. 33–5.

59   Holloway, *Royal Pharmaceutical Society*, p. 340.

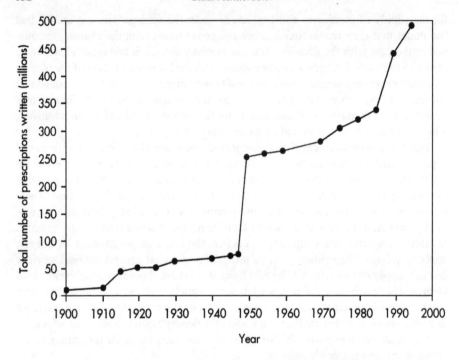

Figure 6.4   Number of prescriptions written by doctors 1900–2000.

Dispensing such large numbers of prescriptions was not without its drawbacks. Pharmacists had to price their own prescriptions. They had to be on the panel of each area for which they dispensed prescriptions, so those in London were often on the lists of numerous insurance committees. Copies of many prescriptions had to be entered in the prescription book to satisfy poisons legislation. And virtually all dispensing was extemporaneous, with each medicine being made up individually. The dispensing fee for a bottle of mixture was 2d., the highest fee being 6d. for a dispensed plaster. The chemist was paid this plus 150 per cent of the cost of the ingredients.

When the National Health Insurance (NHI) scheme was introduced, chemists did not hesitate to serve under it. It was felt that the scheme might help chemists in working-class areas by providing them with a useful supplement to their income, and also offered them an opportunity to practise their dispensing skills. The scheme was important to retail pharmacy in two ways: first, in the recognition it gave to the principle that dispensing should be limited to pharmacists, and second, in the volume of business it brought to pharmacies.[60] But it also laid the foundations for future contractual arrangements between the pharmacy profession and the government. It enabled companies as well as individual proprietors to contract to provide dispensing

---

60   Ibid., p. 341.

services, it rejected the idea of a salaried service for the dispensing of prescriptions, and it established a contract based on unit of service rather than per capita. All these elements were to be retained in the negotiations leading to introduction of the NHS in 1948.

For community pharmacy, the period between the two world wars was one of relative stability. The number of prescriptions written by doctors rose steadily rather than dramatically, from around 50 million per year in 1920 to around 70 million a year in 1940. This level of prescribing provoked a discussion in government about over-prescribing by doctors, but for the typical pharmacist, the dispensing of prescriptions written by panel doctors remained a relatively minor activity. Much of the population remained uncovered by insurance, and retail chemists continued to spend much of their time on traditional duties, such as making and supplying nostrums (something for a cold or for indigestion) and selling patent medicines. There was still a brisk trade in the sale of ingredients for domestic remedies. Pharmacists provided free diagnosis, free advice, and cheaper medicines than the doctor.

By 1937, practically all chemists' shops in Britain were in the insurance scheme. There were about 13 000 of them in England and Wales, and a further 1 800 in Scotland. The nature of the contract slowly evolved, and by 1937 chemists were paid on the basis of the cost of the ingredients, calculated according to a standard price list, together with a dispensing fee regulated according to the nature of the article dispensed. There was also a useful trade in the dispensing of private prescriptions. However, in England and Wales most doctors continued to do this themselves, with only about 20 per cent finding their way to pharmacies. In Scotland, about 90 per cent of doctors wrote prescriptions for their private patients to take to the chemist's shop.[61]

Retailing Medicines and the National Health Service Act 1946

For the Pharmaceutical Society, plans for a National Health Service were much less contentious than had been the plans for the National Insurance Scheme forty years earlier. It was seen largely in terms of an extension of the existing scheme to the whole population. The new service was to be free to all at the point of delivery. It was divided into three distinct parts: the hospitals, managed by regional hospital boards; primary care, as provided by GPs and dentists, who retained considerable independence in the management of their practices, and the auxiliary services, such as ambulances, maternal and infant welfare and home helps, which were left in the hands of local authorities.[62]

One innovation in the NHS Act was the proposal for health centres. These would be places where several doctors would practise together, along with other health

---

61   *Report of the Working Party on Differences in Dispensing Practice between England and Wales and Scotland* (London, 1948), paras 34 and 35.

62   C. Webster, *The Health Services Since the War, Volume I: Problems of Health Care, The National Health Service before 1957* (London, 1988).

professionals, including nurses and pharmacists. In the early stages of planning, the pharmacists' major concern was the extent to which the proposed new health centres would employ salaried pharmacists, and hence compete with private chemist contractors. Early planning documents referred to patients being able to 'obtain their supplies on the prescription of their doctor, either from shops OR other premises of a pharmacist, or from any health centre where dispensing services are provided'.[63]

The Pharmaceutical Society and the National Pharmaceutical Union, representing the independent-proprietor pharmacists, were assured by the government that health centres would be limited to a few carefully controlled experiments, and that the question of including pharmaceutical services in them would only arise on new housing estates. Since there were more than enough chemists' shops to go round, pharmacy services did not figure prominently in early health centre planning. In the event, the policy faltered, and by 1963 there were only 18 purpose-built health centres in England and Wales.[64]

For most chemist contractors, the new NHS was simply an enlarged National Insurance Scheme. It was finally implemented on 5 July 1948. Negotiations on the terms of remuneration for chemist contractors ran to the very last minute. The new terms were largely an updated version of the NHI scales. The chemist was paid for each prescription dispensed, with payments being made in accordance with a Drug Tariff. There were four elements to the chemists' remuneration. The chemist received the wholesale cost of the appliance or ingredients, an on-cost allowance of 33.3 per cent, to cover all overhead expenses, an average dispensing fee of 1s., with higher rates for special services, and a container allowance of 2½d. per prescription. The last was a new payment compensating the chemist for supplying a container for the medicine. Under the NHI scheme, patients had either brought in their own container or had paid a deposit. By 1948, some 16 800 chemists in Britain had contracted to supply medicines and appliances under the National Health Service.[65]

The impact of implementation of the NHS on community pharmacists was dramatic and immediate. Large numbers of prescriptions written by doctors were presented at pharmacies. Within a year, the numbers had almost quadrupled, from around 70 million a year to around to over 250 million. The reasons for this were many. First, with the inclusion of the entire population in the service, the numbers visiting doctors more than doubled. Second, many doctors had continued to undertake their own dispensing under the National Health Insurance scheme, often employing dispensers for this activity. Under the NHS, there were fewer incentives for them to do so, except those in rural areas where patients did not have ready access to a pharmacy. Many of these dispensers were women, and with the coming of the NHS, many became the new breed of receptionists. The shift in the proportion of prescriptions written by doctors but dispensed by themselves or pharmacists is illustrated in Figure 6.5.

---

63 Holloway, *Royal Pharmaceutical Society*, p. 342.
64 Ibid., p. 343.
65 Ibid., p. 345.

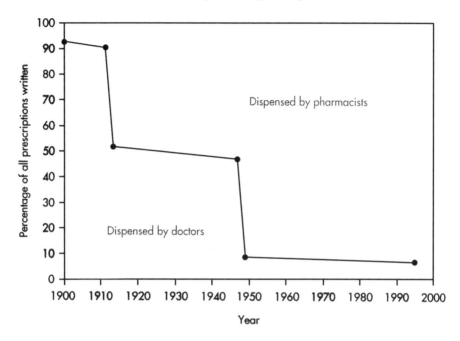

Figure 6.5   Proportion of prescriptions dispensed by doctors and pharmacists 1900–2000.

The new arrangements took some time to settle down. As in 1913, there were problems with the system for pricing prescriptions. The pricing bureaux were understaffed and completely unable to cope with the enormous increase in workload. It was not until 1954 that all the arrears were cleared. Evidence of profligate and over-prescribing was widespread, with stories of large quantities of cotton wool being prescribed to help families keep warm, and large volumes of tonics and foodstuffs also being prescribed. A prescription charge of 1s. per prescription was introduced in 1951, and this rose to 1s. per item a year later.

But there were other factors contributing to the large number of prescription items. Since the service was free to all, and there was no charge for medicines, there was little incentive for those who could afford to do so to continue to see doctors privately and to pay further for their medicines. Those pharmacists who had a substantial business in the dispensing of private prescriptions before the NHS found that this business greatly diminished afterwards. Home remedies remained popular until the introduction of the NHS, but once people could obtain any medicine, for however minor a complaint, on prescription from their general medical practitioner, there was no longer any incentive in spending even a few pennies on the ingredients required for a home remedy. The same was true of the nostrums made up individually by the chemist. The concept of the make-it-yourself home remedy effectively died with the introduction of the NHS.

Likewise, the sale of proprietary medicines for the treatment of minor complaints like coughs and indigestion dropped significantly after introduction of the NHS, as people realized they could get any medicine free on prescription from their general medical practitioner. But the dip was short-lived, as people realized it was usually easier and quicker to purchase a proprietary medicine than to queue up at the doctor's for a prescription. Other factors helped the sale of proprietary medicines to pick up again in the early 1950s. The introduction of prescription charges meant that it might again be cheaper to buy something yourself rather than to get a prescription from the doctor. The arrival of television advertising brought powerful messages about proprietary medicines into the homes of many. And increasing prosperity meant that increasing numbers of people were able to resort to branded products rather than home remedies for a wide range of conditions, from headache to hangover.

The Retailing of Medicines and Social Class

Throughout the first half of the twentieth century, there remained clear distinctions in both access to and use of retail medicines according to social class. The upper classes tended to call out the family doctor for even the most trivial of complaints. The result was usually a prescription, to be dispensed by the doctor or a local chemist. The huge growth in the use of patent medicines in the second half of the nineteenth century coincided with the growth of the middle classes, although patent medicines were also popular with the large working class having a regular wage. Reliance on home remedies using a few pennies' worth of ingredients from the chemist was largely the province of the poor.

Both doctors and pharmacists played their part in maintaining social distinctions. In the pharmacy, distinctions were made in both the finishing and wrapping of medicines based on social class. Pharmacies were to be found in most communities, from those serving the poorest inner cities to those offering exclusive services to the rich. There was therefore a great diversity of practice. Some high-class pharmacies would have nothing to do with National Insurance (or Panel) prescriptions. One retired pharmacist recalled a manager in a smart area of London who would disdainfully re-direct patients to a 'more appropriate chemist's' further down the street.[66] But most pharmacies had a mixed business in which private and Panel prescriptions were equally welcome, and although some pharmacists recall that all patients were treated in the same way, others have indicated that clear distinctions were made between them. In many places, social class divisions were as apparent during a visit to the chemist's as anywhere else.

To begin with, the prescriptions themselves were conspicuously different. Most Panel (that is, National Health Insurance) prescriptions were for standard mixtures that would be readily available off the shelf. Private prescriptions were often personalized in some way, perhaps by the addition of an extra ingredient or maybe

---

66   C. Howitt, interview recorded 24 November 1995, *Oral History of Community Pharmacy* (1995), C816/46, 2A: pp. 76–92.

by a small change in their proportion: as a result, they invariably required individual dispensing. But the majority of prescriptions for both private and Panel patients were for mixtures of one sort or another. Private prescriptions were generally much more elaborate, often written in flowing, ornate handwriting, and of course, always in Latin, which served as a 'secret code' between the doctor and the chemist.[67]

Some of the distinctions made seem to have more to do with raising the cost of the ingredients than with impressing the patient. Thus, one pharmacist recalls the prescriptions of a doctor whose panel patients had their mixtures made up in *aqua fontana* (tap water), whilst his private patients had the same mixture made up in *aqua distillata* (distilled water).[68] Greater scope existed for underlining social divisions in the prescribing and dispensing of solid-dose preparations such as pills (small spheres of mixed medicaments). These could be coated in a variety of ways, and usually the nature of the coating reflected the social standing, or at least the wealth, of the patient. Panel patients would invariably receive the basic pill with a simple varnish finish. More well-to-do patients would receive pills finished in silver, whilst the social elite would receive theirs finished in gold. But the elite were not always defined in terms of wealth: one pharmacist recalls that in a certain cathedral city, the gold-finished pills were reserved for the canon and the bishop.[69]

Lifestyle Drugs and Designer Labels

Labels for medicine bottles also provided an opportunity for social distinction. At least one chemist's shop possessed two types of label with exactly the same wording for the same preparation. One was printed in plain type without borders for Panel patients, the other was printed in exuberant copperplate lettering with ornate borders for the private patients. Wrapping and sealing the bottles were also occasions for emphasizing social status. Private patients would have their bottles immaculately wrapped in white demi paper and sealed with red sealing wax. The prescriptions of Panel patients were most usually left unwrapped, although in some places a paper bag was used. Another pharmacist recalls that in one shop where he worked in Bristol, the medicines of private patients were wrapped in white demi, whilst those of Panel patients were wrapped in green parcel paper. When complete, the wrapped bottles would be placed conspicuously on an open shelf in the front of the dispensary, white bottles to the left, green bottles to the right, so that it was always clear to any other customers who happened to be in the shop at the time just where the prescription had come from.[70]

---

67 R. Howarth, interview recorded 6 October 1995, *Oral History* (1995), C816/32, 2A: pp. 289–308.

68 J. Bearman, interview recorded 17 May 1995, *Oral History* (1995), C816/02, 2B: pp. 132–48.

69 W. Adlington, interview recorded 21 October 1995, *Oral History* (1995), C816/40, 1B: pp. 165–77.

70 M. Howitt, interview recorded 24 November 1995, *Oral History* (1995), C816/43, 2A: pp. 287–99.

Sometimes social distinctions extended to the way in which patients were addressed when collecting their medicine. One retired pharmacist from Northampton remembers the instructions he was given as an apprentice about what he should tell the patient. If a liquid medicine was to be handed out to a Panel patient, he should tell the patient to 'take one tablespoonful three times a day, and one at night'. But if he was giving the same medicine out to a private patient, he should say 'take one tablespoonful three times a day, and one on retiring'.[71]

Waiting for prescriptions also differentiated between social classes. In at least one chemist's shop in London, where the bulk of the business involved dispensing prescriptions, separate waiting rooms were provided for Panel and private patients.[72] Priority was often given to the dispensing of private prescriptions, which often took longer because of the need to make them up specially, and the details had to be entered in the prescription book. Very often, of course, the person waiting to collect the prescription was a servant or messenger, although in some places the doctor would come to the chemist's in person in the morning, after his rounds. He would collect the dispensed medicines later in the day, and deliver them to his private patients during his evening round.

There was also considerable social status associated with whether the chemist stocked a particular item or had to get it in specially. John Savage, a retired pharmacist in York, remembers a particularly smug private patient who one evening presented a prescription with a Harley Street (London) address, immaculately written in Latin. The patient had just returned from seeing the doctor that day. The prescription was for some tablets which were relatively new, but which nevertheless by that time were to be found on the shelves of every pharmacy, as they were available to any patient. The last line of the prescription contained a number of Latin words which were unfamiliar to either the chemist or his apprentice, and it took them some minutes to work it out. Eventually, they were successful. It read: 'take three days to obtain'.[73] Three days later, a very satisfied private patient collected his tablets from the chemist!

Today, those social distinctions have largely died out. However, remnants remain in the existence of a small number of high-class pharmacies catering to a rich clientele demanding a personal service for both the dispensing of private prescriptions and the sale of proprietary medicines. Thankfully, the retailing of medicines remains mercifully free of designer labels.

---

71   B. Trasler, interview recorded 8 August 1995, *Oral History* (1995), C816/03, 2B: pp. 107–25.

72   G. Portlock, interview recorded 24 November 1995, *Oral History* (1995), C816/24, 1A: pp. 267–91.

73   J. Savage, interview recorded 13 September 1995, Oral History (1995), C816/27, 2A: pp. 156–72.

Conclusion

The over-riding theme of this chapter has been change: at no time has the retailing of medicines undergone a greater transformation than during the first half of the twentieth century. Yet there have also been important elements of continuity, both of supply and demand. There has been no diminution in the public's thirst for medicines, for everything from the relief of minor symptoms to the cure of life-threatening diseases. The arrival of effective drugs to deal with the major killers of previous generations, such as tuberculosis, and the establishment of immunization campaigns to eradicate infectious diseases such as smallpox and polio, have radically altered public perceptions about what medicines can do. There are now unrealistic expectations that new drugs can be rapidly developed for any situation, from AIDS to SARS.

These shifts in public expectations have included an increasing focus on what have come to be termed 'lifestyle' drugs. Examples include drugs for regulating and encouraging fertility, such as the contraceptive pill and in vitro fertilization therapy. There are drugs such as Viagra to overcome impotence, drugs to help people lose weight, and drugs to reduce their cholesterol levels where dietary measures alone have not been sufficient. Yet despite such advances, the public's appetite for unconventional remedies, their wish to believe the claims of the most bizarre of complementary practitioners, remains as undiminished as ever. Here perhaps is continuity with previous generations, who were so ready to believe the claims of any hawker peddling quack remedies. The human desire to take medicines knows no bounds. Yet at the same time, the public's thirst for information about how medicines work and how to take them has never been greater. And one of the principal sources of that information and advise is the retail chemist.

So the changes that have occurred in the retailing of medicines during the twentieth century are perhaps more superficial than might at first appear. They are about what medicines are available, and about who makes and supplies them. As we have seen, the thirty-year period 1930–60 witnessed the transfer of responsibility for the making of medicines, initially from the family to the chemist, and later from the chemist to the manufacturer. It also saw the depersonalization of the medicinal product, with the chemist no longer making something 'specially for them'. Ironically, recent drug developments mean that the future is perhaps once again with personalized medicines, this time based on the genetic makeup of the patient.

The changes have also concerned where medicines can be sold. During the period, the number of outlets for over-the-counter medicines increased greatly, such that they are now to be found on the shelves of every supermarket. By 1995, the value of the over-the-counter medicine market in the United Kingdom, through both pharmacy and grocery sales, was over £1.25 billion. This shift has been aided by recent changes in drug regulation that have facilitated a shift of an increasing number of drugs from prescription-only to pharmacy-sale categories, and ultimately to a general sales list.

The importance of the development of the welfare state on the retailing of medicines, and particularly on the practice of retail pharmacy, in Great Britain cannot be overstated. The National Insurance Act 1911, and to a lesser extent the National Health Insurance Act 1948, had an impact on both which continues to define their nature in the twenty-first century. Had the views of the Friendly Societies prevailed rather than those of the pharmacists, the retailing of medicines would look very different today than how it actually is. Eventually, of course, the chemists welcomed the changes with open arms. The new prescriptions produced a substantial increase in turnover for most pharmacies. The terms of remuneration were, by modern standards, extremely generous, and many pharmacists became very prosperous as a result.

The costs of the drugs themselves became a major concern of the Ministry of Health, and remains so today. A wide range of options have been considered in an attempt to control it.[74] Before the NHS, very few branded products were prescribed by doctors. Their typical prescription was for a standard mixture to a formula appearing in a national pharmaceutical reference. In the 1930s, the proportion of branded products began to rise as first the sulphonamides and later other antibiotics began to appear. Unfortunately for the government, the introduction of the NHS coincided with the therapeutic revolution, with large numbers of effective but branded drugs becoming available. The proportion of branded products prescribed rose rapidly, and by 1957 they accounted for half of all prescriptions. By the late 1970s, the proportion exceeded 80 per cent, and it was only in the 1980s that efforts to persuade doctors to prescribe cheaper generic drugs began to have an effect. The relative proportion of branded and generic drugs prescribed by doctors during the course of the twentieth century is illustrated in Figure 6.6.

It was the pharmacy profession's response to the changed circumstances following introduction of the NHS in 1948 that were to shape the relationship between it and the state for the rest of the century. The additional workload created by the rise in prescription numbers needed to be accommodated. Many pharmacists took the opportunity to expand the dispensary, usually at the back of the shop, at the expense of general shop space nearer the front. In 1948, a high proportion of prescriptions were still prepared extemporaneously one at a time, and most were in the form of mixtures or syrups. For most pharmacists, this was an opportunity to practise the skills that they had learned in their apprenticeship, and they were usually more than happy to spend their working days preparing prescriptions in the dispensary at the back of the shop.

For community pharmacy in Britain, the contingency arrangements made in the wake of introduction of the NHS became normalized. During the 1950s and 1960s, the community pharmacist had all but disappeared from the public's awareness.[75]

---

74   C. Webster, *The Health Services Since the War, Volume II: Government and Health Care, The National Health Service 1958 to 1979* (London, 1996), pp. 143–4.

75   S.C. Anderson, 'Community pharmacy in Great Britain: Mediation at the boundary between professional and lay care 1920 to 1995', in M. Gijswijt-Hofstra, G.M. Van Heteren

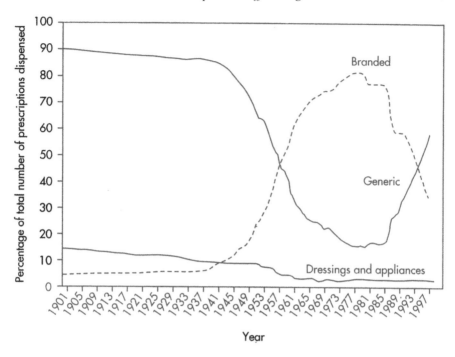

Figure 6.6   Prescriptions for branded and generic drugs 1900–2000.

Public esteem for the chemist was at an all-time low. The issue was brought to a head at the British Pharmaceutical Conference in 1981. In what has become a very famous address, the then Minister of Health, Dr Gerard Vaughan, announced to the conference that 'one knew there was a future for hospital pharmacists, one knew there was a future for industrial pharmacists, but one was not sure that one knew the future for the general practice pharmacist'.[76] The pharmacy profession had made two serious errors of judgement: it had failed to monitor and recognize the impact of changes in its practice, particularly its impact on the public, and it had failed to convince the government of its continuing relevance and contribution to the health of the nation.

The minister's statement was a watershed in the history of pharmacy in the twentieth century in Great Britain. It led directly to the 'Ask your pharmacist' campaign from the National Pharmaceutical Association, which first appeared in women's magazines in 1982. Discussions between the pharmacy profession and the government led to agreement that there should be an independent committee

and E.M. Tansey (eds), *Biographies of Remedies: Drugs, Medicines and Contraceptives in Dutch and Anglo-American Healing Cultures* (Amsterdam, 2002), pp. 75–97.

76   'What Future for General Practice Pharmacists?', *The Pharmaceutical Journal*, 227 (1981), pp. 300–301.

of inquiry set up 'to consider the present and future structure of the practice of pharmacy in its several branches, and its potential contribution to health care, and to review the education and training of pharmacists accordingly'. This culminated in the publication of the Nuffield Report on Pharmacy in 1986.[77] Developments since then have been aimed at extending the range of services provided by the community pharmacist to areas beyond the traditional dispensing role. These so-called extended roles can be seen as a return to the 'traditional' role of the community pharmacist before the introduction of the welfare state, and an attempt to draw the pharmacist out of the dispensary and back into contact with the public.

We can conclude, therefore, that during the twentieth century the changing nature of the medicines and the ways in which they were retailed were inextricably linked to the role of the retail chemist. The role of the chemist was transformed alongside the transformation in the retailing of medicines. The chemist changed from being the maker and supplier of medicines to the supplier of manufactured medicines with information about their use. The twenty-first century already shows the signs of providing equally radical change.

---

77 *Pharmacy: A Report to the Nuffield Foundation* (London, 1986).

Chapter 7

'A Cascade of Medicine': The Marketing and Consumption of Prescription Drugs in the UK 1948–2000

Judy Slinn

Introduction

In a speech addressed to Labour Party MPs in the autumn of 1949, Aneurin Bevan, then Minister of Health, introduced a term which attracted considerable attention at the time. It has continued to be widely quoted since then and, in fact, provides the title of this chapter. A year after the inauguration of the National Health Service (NHS), Bevan said: 'I shudder to think of the ceaseless cascade of medicine which is pouring down British throats at the present time.'[1] No doubt he had in mind the very rapid rise in the number of prescriptions issued. In June 1948, before the NHS began, chemists dispensed 6.8 million prescriptions, a figure which had doubled by September that year, following the start of the NHS, to 13.6 million.[2] During the first full year's operation of the NHS, 121 million prescriptions were issued, more than had been anticipated, and the figure continued to rise, as we shall see. In retrospect, this has been seen as a sign of a large and unmet need, and many doctors were shocked both by the number of cases of long-standing chronic illness as well as of serious illness which emerged following the introduction of the NHS.[3] As one GP recalled:

> Particularly at the beginning there was a great pent up demand wave ... You suddenly realized there was a lot more of illness about of a minor or even major nature than was hitherto thought.[4]

However, these figures were also instrumental in creating a widely held belief – at least in the official mind - that the British people were heavy consumers of medicine, a view that, repackaged in different ways, was to be reiterated by many British

---

1   P. Hollis, *Jennie Lee: A Life* (Oxford, 1998), p.164.
2   C. Webster, *The National Health Service* (Oxford, 1998).
3   M. Drury, 'The General Practitioner and Professional Organizations', in I. Loudon, J. Horder and C. Webster (eds), *General Practice under the National Health Service 1948–1997* (London, 1998).
4   I. Tait and S. Graham-Jones, 'General Practice, its Patients and the Public', in Loudon, Horder and Webster (eds), *General Practice under the National Health Service*.

politicians of all party hues over the next forty years, colouring the debates about the marketing and consumption of prescription drugs in the UK.

Prescription Drugs

The complex nature of the transaction through which prescribed drugs reach the consumer has played a large part in defining and structuring the marketing of prescription medicine since the introduction of the NHS. One description of the transaction (written by a business journalist) highlights the contrast with the markets for consumer products:

> Selling drugs, however, is a complicated task, and one shot through with contradictions. One is that the people who consume the product, the patients, are different from the people who select it, the doctors. Then there is another group of people who pay for it – sometimes the patient, sometimes the government, sometimes an employer, sometimes an insurer. Another is the relationship between the customer and the company. In most capitalist enterprises, marketing people are meant to find out what the customer wants, and get the production people to make it. In drugs it is the other way round. The researchers find out what the customer needs and then the marketing people go out and make sure they take it.[5]

These three significant aspects of the transaction have been instrumental in determining the way marketing developed during much of the period covered in this chapter. The first of these is that that the consumer – the patient – does not choose the product. Until the 1980s or later, few patients had any detailed knowledge, nor was there much available in the public domain, about prescription drugs. Moreover, freedom to prescribe was strenuously defended as a *sine qua non* of their professionalism by the medical practitioners' professional body, the British Medical Association (BMA). The second feature is that, depending on the health care system, the consumer of the medicine – the patient – pays either nothing or a small proportion of the price, and is generally unaware of the actual cost of the drug.

In Britain, prescriptions were free for patients in the early years of the NHS, with the cost of medicines being paid for by the government out of general taxation. Although the flat-rate charge for prescriptions, first imposed in 1951, has been changed a number of times since then, at the same time the proportion of the population entitled to exemption from the charge – broadly speaking composed of the young, those over 60 (women) and 65 (men) and those with chronic conditions – has also increased, so a good deal of the cost of the nation's drugs bill is still paid by the government out of taxation.

Finally, the third aspect of the transaction is that until the 1980s, it seems that few medical practitioners, who were also the prescribers, were aware of the prices charged for drugs, despite the many attempts made by successive governments to

---

5   M. Lynn, *The Billion-dollar Battle: Merck v Glaxo* (London, 1991), pp. 127–8.

secure economy in prescribing.[6] Even when doctors were made aware of the price, however, their freedom to prescribe the medicine they considered to be the most effective meant that price was not a factor of the first importance.

The Post-war Context

In the late 1940s, several closely linked factors combined to create a radical change in the market for prescription drugs: namely, the introduction of the NHS, the rising tide of expectations about the ability of medical science to cure illness, and the introduction of newly discovered and developed drugs. The first and most obvious of these was the introduction of the NHS, increasing at a stroke the size of the market. Before the Second World War, the National Health Insurance (NHI) scheme, established in 1911 for men in work (at that time it applied to some 12 million) covered somewhere between a quarter and a third of the population, for basic medical care.[7] For most people, this involved a consultation, possibly a sick note where necessary, and a bottle of medicine. According to the recollections of GPs, the NHI scheme cemented the relationship between consultation and prescription:

> Prescribing has always played an important part in the relationship between general practitioners and their patients. In the early nineteenth century the apothecary could charge for his medicines but not for his opinion. [One GP] remarked: 'This goes back to the old tie-up between their consultation and the bottle of medicine, and the 3/6d that was charged[for both]. They went together, so that when the NHS started, people expected a prescription.[8]

The NHI scheme did not cover the dependants of those insured, so large numbers of women and children, along with the elderly and the unemployed, were denied access to medical consultation and diagnosis and prescription medicine because they could not afford to pay for it. They were obliged to resort to traditional remedies, and where they could afford them, the over-the-counter (OTC), generic medicines available in pharmacies and the highly advertised patent medicines, such as Beecham's Pills, which had been consumed in large quantities since the nineteenth century and continued to find a market alongside prescription medicine. However, the contrast between before and after the NHS is well illustrated by the figures for medical expenditure as a whole: in 1930, only 16 per cent of medical expenditure per head in Britain was publicly funded, but by 1950 the figure had become some 82 per cent per head [9]

---

6   W.D. Reekie, *The Economics of the Pharmaceutical Industry* (London, 1975).

7   A. Digby and N. Bosanquet, 'Doctors and patients in an era of national health insurance and private practice 1913–38', *Economic History* Review, 41(1) (1988), pp. 74–94.

8   Tait and Graham-Jones, 'General Practice, its Patients and the Public'.

9   C. Webster, 'Medicine and the Welfare State 1930–1970', in R. Cooter and J. Pickstone (eds), *Medicine in the Twentieth Century* (Amsterdam, 2000).

In 1948, British pharmaceutical companies therefore anticipated a considerable increase in the market for their products. In France, following the end of the war, the introduction of a national health scheme, which did not cover all the population, had led to a 30 per cent increase in the demand for drugs, the British company May & Baker was told by its parent company, Rhone Poulenc.[10] In the USA, even without a national health scheme, there was:

> ... a widespread expectation in the industry that there existed a vast potential market for new pharmaceutical products, and that catering to this market, however costly, would prove to be highly profitable.[11]

Consumers/patients also had high expectations. These were fuelled firstly, of course, by the availability of medical care and free prescription medicine, but also by a growing consciousness of the importance of good health and a belief that people had a right to expect good health.[12] The realization that better health could be achieved and that problems which had been untreatable could now be treated successfully came as a result of the discovery and development of new drugs in the period now known as the 'therapeutic revolution', stretching from the late 1930s to around 1960. In this, the most significant early milestone was the development of penicillin during the Second World War.

The Development of Penicillin

The story of the development of penicillin is too well known to require retelling here, but its significance can hardly be exaggerated, eclipsing as it did all previously introduced prescription drugs. As the most recently published popular account of the drug's development notes:

> Until the middle of the twentieth century, mothers routinely died from infections following childbirth; children were killed by diarrhoea, scarlet fever, measles, and tonsillitis ... Soldiers most commonly died not from war injuries but from resulting infections such as septicaemia and gangrene. Away from the battlefield, boils, abscesses and carbuncles were common portals for life-threatening illness; the smallest cut could lead to a fatal infection.[13]

Penicillin conquered infection, and stories of its use and success – miracle cures – were headline news in the press, both during the war, when most of the available

---

10   J. Slinn, *A History of May & Baker* (Cambridge, 1984).

11   D.C. Mowery and N. Rosenberg, *Paths of Innovation: Technological Change in 20th Century America* (Cambridge, 1998).

12   J. Pickstone, 'Production, community and consumption: The political economy of twentieth century medicine', in Cooter and Pickstone (eds), *Medicine in the Twentieth Century*.

13   E. Lax, *The Mould on Dr. Florey's Coat* (London, 2004), p. 3.

supplies of the drug went to the battlefields, and in the immediate aftermath when supplies became readily available for civilian use.

The development of the deep fermentation process for producing penicillin in the USA during the war enabled the drug to be manufactured on a large scale after the war across the world, including in Britain. Glaxo, for example, was licensed by Merck to use their deep fermentation process, and between 1946 and 1956, Glaxo paid Merck around £0.5 million in royalties for the transfer of the technology. Over the same period, the company also paid Merck a further and similar sum for the right to manufacture streptomycin (see below).[14] However, by the early 1950s production of penicillin proliferated to such an extent across the world that the drug became effectively a commodity and prices fell accordingly. Penicillin became the single most important prescription pharmaceutical not only in Europe, but also in the USA, where at that time its sales accounted for 10 per cent of the industry's total turnover.[15]

The happy conjunction of the introduction of drugs which could cure infection – penicillin first, followed by other antibiotics introduced in the 1950s, which were effective against a variety of infections – and the NHS is highlighted in one GP's recollections:

> The NHS enabled you to prescribe drugs which the patient would never previously have been able to afford to buy. There is nothing worse than standing on Thursday night at the foot of the kid's bed and knowing the kid needed penicillin and knowing damn well there was no money to buy it. But the day after the NHS, you could prescribe as many bottles of penicillin as you liked. That made all the difference to doctoring.[16]

Significant as its sales, if not its profits, were, penicillin is perhaps even more important in terms of its effect on practitioners and patients in fostering the belief that infection was vanquished and that medical science would continue to find new drugs, providing better health for everyone. As Pickstone has noted:

> The very success of medicine in apparently removing the scourge of infectious disease, meant that the postwar generation assumed a right to be healthy. In most of the West, the economy was buoyant, unemployment low and consumer expectations high.[17]

The Therapeutic Revolution

Until the late 1930s, doctors had very few specific medicines, or 'magic bullets', to cure diseases. Research by organic chemists had led to the discovery of analgesics

---

14 R. Davenport-Hines and J. Slinn, *Glaxo: A History to 1962* (Cambridge, 1992).

15 J. Goodman, 'Pharmaceutical Industry', in Cooter and Pickstone (eds), *Medicine in the Twentieth Century*.

16 Tait and Graham-Jones, 'General Practice, its Patients and the Public'.

17 Pickstone, 'Production, community and consumption'.

such as aspirin in the late nineteenth century, followed by the arsenical drugs, effective against the venereal disease syphilis, in the years before the First World War. There were some significant advances in anaesthetics in the inter-war years, whilst the discovery of vitamins and hormones, among the latter particularly insulin, led to the development of new therapies. In 1938, May & Baker introduced to the market its new sulphonamide drug, sulphapyridine, discovered and developed the previous year; M & B 693 offered for the first time a cure for bacterial pneumonia. It was followed by the development and introduction of other sulphonamide drugs by several companies. During the war, the most significant development was, of course, penicillin, discussed above, and then, through the immediate post-war years and the 1950s, the rate of discovery, development and introduction of new products accelerated remarkably.

The change was indicated in Glaxo's memorandum of evidence to the Guillebaud Committee in 1953:

> We market approximately 50 pharmaceutical products, of which about 20 were sold before the war. … The tempo of development in the pharmaceutical industry in the last generation, and particularly perhaps in the last twelve to fifteen years, has been remarkably rapid. With the growth of chemotherapy and with the increase in the knowledge of physiology and pharmacology that makes possible the experimental evolution of drugs, immense new fields of research have been opened.[18]

The discovery and introduction of penicillin sparked off a search for more anti-infective drugs, and was rewarded with the antibiotics. The first broad-spectrum antibiotic was streptomycin, which was found to be effective against tuberculosis. It was patented by Merck in 1948, and was made available on licence to other manufacturers in the USA and in Europe through the Rutgers Research Foundation.[19] There followed in the early 1950s a spate of discoveries of antibiotics by US firms; these included Lederle's aureomycin, Parke Davis's chloromycetin, and Pfizer's terramycin and tetracycline, each of which was patented by the company discovering and introducing it. However, these corporations decided not to license other companies to manufacture and sell the antibiotics, thus ensuring that they would obtain and retain monopolistic profits during the lifetime of the patent. Other new drugs of the 1950s and the early 1960s included those based on cortisone, the psychoactive drugs for treating problems of the central nervous system, new treatments for cardiovascular problems, including the first beta-blockers, and the introduction of the oral contraceptive pill.

All of these were patented by whichever company discovered and developed the new drug, reinforcing what now became the dominant paradigm of the pharmaceutical industry, one which has proved remarkably enduring through the second half of the twentieth century. It reads thus: for the industry's corporations,

---

18   NA: MH 137/227.

19   R. Landau, B. Achilladelis and A. Scriabine (eds), *Pharmaceutical Innovation* (Philadelphia, PA, 1999).

research and development led to innovation and the introduction of new products; patenting the discoveries enabled the innovating company to enjoy monopolistic profits (for a time), which in turn financed more research and development, leading, it was anticipated, to more new products.[20] An implicit and highly significant element in the paradigm, however, is the need for highly skilled and extensive marketing to ensure that a new drug penetrates as many markets as possible across the world. This was highlighted and succinctly encapsulated by Sir David Jack, formerly head of Glaxo's Research and Development, in his evidence to a Parliamentary Select Committee:

> The outcome of its research programme determines the potential of a company, its development and marketing activities determine its performance within that potential.[21]

In other words, no matter how innovative a drug is, it will not find its own way to success in the marketplace, and as the industry found in the second half of the twentieth century, skilful development and marketing could more than compensate for a lack of complete originality in a product. The success of Glaxo's Zantac in the 1980s, it is generally recognized, owed more to successful marketing than to originality (see below). Glaxo's historian has argued that lessons learned from the company's failure in the 1970s with its cardiovascular drug Trandate played a part in enabling its success with Zantac. Mistakes in the marketing of Trandate included a failure to focus on the right influential prescribers, an inability to make the drug's advantages transparent, and a complex dosing regime – all these in a highly competitive sub-market with a number of already well-established competitors, and one where the company had no previous experience or reputation.[22]

Marketing Drugs: Origins and Early Development

Late twentieth-century consumerism has encouraged the development of complex definitions of marketing, but for our purposes at this stage, a simpler definition of marketing as the process of promoting and selling will serve. The creation of modern sales management in the sense of a managed sales force, systematized and standardized, has been claimed as an American phenomenon.[23] It took place in the USA in the decades around the turn of the nineteenth and twentieth centuries, as mass-manufacturing methods developed in a number of industries and the companies employing them sought to penetrate mass markets for their products.

---

20 R. Ballance, J. Pogany and H. Forstner, *The World's Pharmaceutical Industries* (Aldershot, 1992).

21 D. Jack, 'Research and Development in the Pharmaceutical Industry', *Science in Parliament,* 41(9) (1992), p. 4.

22 E. Jones, *The Business of Medicine* (London, 2001), p. 254.

23 W. Friedman, *Birth of a Salesman* (Harvard University Press, 2004), Introduction, pp. 4–13.

Amongst them were the US pharmaceutical companies, small by comparison with their twentieth-century successors, but already moving into mass-manufacturing.[24] In Europe, the large chemical companies of Germany, then world leaders in the innovation of chemical drugs, were also aware of the need for extensive and skilful marketing, as Carl Duisberg, Chairman of Bayer, noted in 1913. Having described the company's activities in creating a new 'synthetic remedy' in terms recognizable throughout the twentieth century, he concluded:

> And, finally, it is the calculating salesman's turn; he must bring in enough to cover all the expenses of the innumerable expenses of the innumerable experiments that have been made, if the new drug, which has swallowed so much money, is to survive and prosper.[25]

However, in Britain at that time, the companies that made up the pharmaceutical industry were small or medium-sized. Some had incorporated their businesses, some were still partnerships, and many of them were family-owned or influenced and managed. Most of their business was the extraction and/or purification of the vegetable and mineral materials which were used for the then prevalent galenical remedies, although there was some basic chemical manufacture. Their products were distributed to wholesalers, pharmacies and medical practitioners, with a fairly large proportion being exported, particularly to the countries of the British Empire. In the home market, they might employ a few 'travellers', as they were known in Britain at that time, but the businesses tended to rely as much on regular advertising in the trade press, word of mouth, reputation and recommendation, particularly in their local area, while overseas they relied predominantly on agents.

This was a far cry from the US 'detailman', then emerging in his full glory across the Atlantic – the sales representative whose principal, although not exclusive, focus was the medical practitioner who would prescribe the drug. It was the firm of Burroughs Wellcome, established in London by two American pharmacists, which was the first to use the 'detailing concept' in Britain, soon after the establishment of the company in 1880. It was as the survivor of the two founders and its guiding influence for some forty years, that Henry Wellcome has been given the credit for many of the marketing initiatives made by the firm. Significant amongst these was the litigation on which he embarked in 1903, to defend the firm's trademark, Tabloid, registered in 1884.[26] In the course of this, a good deal of useful publicity was generated, and the action was successful, fixing the link between Tabloid and Wellcome inextricably in the mind of the public. The first US company to establish a subsidiary branch and subsequently manufacturing operations in Britain was Parke Davis (Burroughs Wellcome did it in reverse – two Americans established a British company which some decades later set up a branch in the USA). Parke Davis opened its London branch, which looked after the parent company's business in Europe and

24   J. Liebenau, *Medical Science and Medical Industry* (London, 1987).

25   J. Liebenau, 'Industrial research and development in pharmaceutical firms in the early twentieth century', *Business History*, 26(3) (1984), pp. 327–46.

26   G. Macdonald, *In Pursuit of Excellence* (London, 1980).

a large part of the rest of the world outside North America, in 1891, and by 1907 the company was employing 27 salesmen in Britain.[27]

In the inter-war years, the largest sales force in the British industry was probably that of Glaxo, although the company at that time only had a small pharmaceutical business. Glaxo representatives, who were required to be qualified pharmacists, marketed the full range of Glaxo products, by far the largest proportion of which was at that time babyfood, through their visits to welfare clinics and nursing homes as well as to medical practitioners – GPs and hospitals – and to pharmacists. The 'home representatives', as they were known, numbered more than 40 in 1939, each provided, if they required it, with a company car and already enjoying what came to be an institution, the annual conference of salesmen.[28]

Rebuilding Marketing Capacity Post-war

The sales forces of most, if not all, British pharmaceutical companies were depleted during the war as salesmen, like others, left for active service in the armed forces or elsewhere. In any case, pharmaceutical supplies, like almost everything else, came under government control so that there was little scope for marketing activity, and indeed little to market, during the war. In the years immediately after the end of the war, therefore, the companies urgently needed to recruit new salesmen. There were new entrants to the industry too, requiring to build up or augment their sales forces. One of these was Imperial Chemical Industries (ICI), which through the manufacture of the much-needed anti-malarials and involvement with penicillin had entered the industry during the war, establishing its Pharmaceutical Division in 1944.

Another newcomer was Abbott Laboratories, subsidiary of the American company of that name, based in Chicago since 1888. The parent company's research programme during the inter-war years – when, like most of the US pharmaceutical companies, it had considerably extended its R&D capabilities – had led to the discovery and development of Pentothal, an anaesthetic compound with the twin advantages of acting swiftly and allowing fast recovery. These attributes made it an ideal anaesthetic for battlefields, and in 1937, mindful of the prospects of war in Europe, and in that event, the likely difficulties in transporting supplies across the Atlantic, Abbott established a small factory in Perivale, west London, principally to manufacture Pentothal to ensure that supplies of the drug would be available.

At the end of the war, Abbott Laboratories UK, having fulfilled its *raison d'être*, prepared to expand its operations. At that time it had only two sales representatives in the country, one in London and one in Bournemouth. The company therefore started to recruit salesmen in 1945, gradually building up a force – mainly former pharmacists or those qualified in pharmacy – which could cover all regions. Like other companies at that time, representatives faced considerable transport problems,

---

27 T. Deeson, *Parke Davis in Britain: The First Hundred Years* (London, 1995).
28 Jones, *The Business of Medicine*, pp. 244–6.

since petrol rationing, introduced in 1940, was not removed until May 1950. Abbott's first purchase of a car in the post-war years took place in the autumn of 1951.[29]

Abbott's marketing development illustrates well the growth of a relatively small company at this time, and a similar pattern may well be found at other companies in Britain at that time, seeking to expand their operations. However, Abbott had the advantage of being the subsidiary company of a large American corporation and the fruit of its extensive R&D programme in its portfolio of products to sell, as well as the benefit of its extensive marketing experience. Abbott's first advertising manager joined the company in 1950, and a sales manager was appointed in that year. Training courses were established for the now larger sales force, as more salesmen were recruited and the very large areas initially looked after by the representatives broken down into smaller ones. In 1949, the company had moved its manufacturing operations to a larger factory in Jarrow, enabling it to widen its portfolio and increase its output. In the mid-1950s, the sales force was doubled and a new structure put in place with an extra tier of management – regional sales managers. This clearly evidenced an anticipation that the company and the market would continue to grow[30]

Consumption, Costs and Prices in the 1950s

The number of prescriptions continued to rise, from 204 million in 1949/50 to 227 million in 1950/51, while total expenditure on pharmaceuticals by the NHS increased from £32 million to £35 million in those years. In 1951/52, the cost of the drugs bill rose to £45 million, although the number of prescriptions issued was a more stable 220 million. In fact, the total number of prescriptions peaked in 1955/56 at 228.5 million, dropping back to 203.2 million in 1958/59, although the cost of the drugs bill reached £70 million in the mid-1950s and continued to rise steadily to £100 million in 1961. Whilst the number of prescriptions per form also fell from 1.7 in the mid-1950s to 1.5 by the end of the decade, the average cost per prescription continued to rise through the decade. In 1953/54, the average cost per prescription was 4s. 1d., but by 1956/57 it was nearly 5s. 3d. and in 1958/9 it reached 6s. 6d.[31]

It was these figures which focused government attention on drug consumption in the 1950s, although the focus became more narrowly directed to cost and price. Two committees were appointed by the government in the 1950s to examine the cost of drugs to the NHS: the Guillebaud Committee, which reported in 1956, and the Hinchcliffe Committee, which reported in 1959. Both came to the conclusion, deeply unwelcome to the government of the day and even more so to the Treasury, that the cost of the drugs bill had risen and was continuing to rise because of the

---

29 J. Slinn, *Pharmaceutical and Health Care: A History of Abbott Laboratories in the UK* (Cambridge, 1999).

30 Ibid.

31 NA, MH 137/152, 137/156: Reekie, *The Economics of the Pharmaceutical Industry*, pp. 15–18.

number of new drugs which were coming on the market. The Treasury view since the start of the NHS had been that demand could be reduced by the imposition of charges. As one civil servant noted in 1949: 'There is no doubt that many people are demanding drugs … which they would go without or buy at the chemist if the National Health Service were not free.'[32] That argument had rather less force by the mid-1950s, when even after the prescription charge had been increased in 1956, the number of prescriptions continued to rise.

Because of the indirect nature of the transaction by which prescription drugs were supplied, discussed at the beginning of this chapter, over-consumption of drugs, if indeed it existed at all, was almost impossible to identify. The Ministry of Health had some mechanisms for identifying and tackling wasteful, irregular and excessive prescribing. The monitoring of what was described as 'irregular prescribing', which included doctors prescribing for people who were not their patients, was delegated to the Executive Councils; 140 of these administered the services provided by GPs at the local level. Investigations into excessive prescribing were the responsibility of a Prescribing Investigation Unit, set up in 1950 at the Ministry of Health. GPs whose prescribing costs were found to be 'substantially' above the average prevailing in their area could expect this issue to be raised by the Regional Medical Officer, by letter or in person.[33] On excessive prescribing, the evidence remains unclear, since most of the government files on this remain closed, but the BMA was always quick to defend its members' right to prescribe, and to oppose what it regarded as interference with that right, enshrined in the NHS Act. Individual doctors, too, could be very defensive, as some pharmacists found, of what they saw as an attempt to usurp their right to prescribe.[34]

Wasteful prescribing was equally difficult, the Ministry found, to identify and control. Although agreement was reached between the Ministry, the industry and the medical profession in the early 1950s that some drugs considered to have little or no therapeutic value would no longer be prescribed, it was difficult to achieve more, the Ministry felt, without an approved list, and that was opposed by both the medical profession and the industry.[35] The opposition successfully contested the introduction of any kind of list for some forty years (see below).

The attempts that were made in the 1950s to control or reduce consumption were half-hearted to say the least. The Guillebaud Committee noted the connection between consultation and prescription discussed above and made a rather weak recommendation suggesting that further efforts should be made to educate doctors

---

32 NA, T227/734.

33 NA:MH 137/152.

34 S. Anderson, 'Community pharmacy in Great Britain', in M. Gijswijt-Hofstra, G.M. Van Heteren and E.M. Tansey (eds), *Biographies of Remedies* (Rodopi, 2002).

35 J. Slinn, 'Regulating the cost and consumption of prescription pharmaceuticals in the UK 1948–1967', *Business History*, 47(3) (2005), pp. 352–66.

to be more careful in their prescribing of expensive drugs as well as in the quantities they prescribed – and to educate patients out of the 'bottle of medicine habit'.[36]

However, this was largely ignored, and the government, convinced that the drugs bill was too high, pushed ahead with attempts to control prices. It may be noted here that the view to which successive governments clung – that the drugs bill was too large – has been contested, and not only by those opposing the principle of price control. The argument was made and evidenced that the British, by comparison with other European nationalities, were not particularly voracious consumers of prescription medicine.[37]

After some three years of negotiations with the industry's representative and powerful body the Association of the British Pharmaceutical Industry (ABPI), the government accepted the scheme devised by the ABPI to regulate prices. The Voluntary Price Regulation Scheme (VPRS) was intended to establish prices that were 'fair and reasonable', a definition which remains the basis of the system today. In its early years, the VPRS was a disappointment to the government, its estimated savings being less than had been anticipated. The scheme itself was re-negotiated in 1960, 1964 and 1969 and at various times since then; it has been known since 1978 as the Pharmaceutical Prices Regulation Scheme (PPRS). As the subsidiary companies in Britain owned by US and European corporations became a party to the scheme, it came to be seen as at least a safeguard against excessively high pricing.[38] The details of the VPRS and the PPRS have been discussed elsewhere and at length as both the principle and detail of price regulation continue to generate debate.[39] The view of successive governments has continued to be, as encapsulated by an official at the Ministry of Health in 1960:

> Partly because of lack of 'consumer resistance', partly because a number of important products are protected by patents from competition, it has never been thought safe to rely on normal market factors to regulate prices of proprietary drugs supplied under the NHS through family doctors.

In the context of the marketing and consumption of pharmaceuticals, the significance is that price cannot be used as a marketing tool as simply as it can with other consumer products in other industries. The price controls exercised through what are effectively profit controls in Britain have played a part in this, but as was noted in the early 1960s in the USA, the patenting of significant new discoveries also contributed significantly:

> On the basis of experience in the corticosteroids, tranquillisers and antibiotic markets … genuine price competition among ethical drugs is effectively prevented, for the most

---

36 Ibid.

37 M.H. Cooper, *Prices and Profits in the Pharmaceutical Industry* (Oxford, 1966).

38 Ibid.

39 Reekie, *The Economics of the Pharmaceutical Industry*; W.D. Reekie, *Prescribing the Price of Pharmaceuticals* (IEA Health and Welfare Unit, 1995); D.G. Green, et al., 1997.

part, by the existence of product patent privileges. Patent or patent application holders may exercise restrictions on output, and the resulting high levels of prices used to finance selling campaigns which contribute to the otherwise serious imperfections of market information and make it impossible for small sellers of generic name products to obtain any significant share of the retail prescription market.[40]

Marketing in the 1950s and 1960s

The selling of prescription drugs – new, reformulated and old – used a variety of promotion methods, all directed at the medical profession. These included advertising in medical journals, direct mailshots, sometimes accompanied by samples, to members of the profession, and increasingly in the 1950s, the holding of meetings and symposia to inform doctors, particularly about new drugs. However, the method considered by the pharmaceutical manufacturers to be the most important – and the one which took the largest part of the marketing budget – was the use of the sales representative, making individual and personal calls on doctors, both in hospitals and in general practice, and on pharmacies. So how did the representatives divide their time? In the case of one British pharmaceutical company, it has been noted:

> By the late 1960s, Glaxo's UK representatives sold a bewildering variety of products; dried milk powder, Farex, vitamins, vaccines, antibiotics, corticosteroids and even veterinary medicines. Although all had qualified in pharmacy and received regular in-house training, it was difficult for them to promote such a broad portfolio. Typically they would spend the early part of the morning calling at GPs' surgeries, usually without an appointment, and in an era before large group practices, were often able to build up trusted personal contacts. Later in the day they visited retail chemists, hospital staff including pharmacists, and called at maternity and child welfare clinics … When pharmaceutical products were to be launched, the representatives paid particular attention to hospital consultants.

The relative success Glaxo enjoyed with its dermatological product Betnovate, launched in 1963, has been attributed to the decision to target its marketing promotion on hospital consultants; by contrast, its pricing policy for the corticosteroid cream was unfortunate, since it chose to price it at a lower level than the then market leader, and three years later, under pressure from the Ministry of Health, reduced the price still further.[41] The significance the companies gave to the influence over prescribing held by consultants has been noted elsewhere; at Abbott Laboratories UK, the sales representatives whose areas contained Harley Street in London and senior hospital consultants elsewhere were ranked as the most important in the 1950s.[42]

Marketing was expensive; when Glaxo measured itself against a number of the largest US pharmaceutical corporations in the mid-1950s, the company noted that

---

40 Jones, *The Business of Medicine*, p. 237.
41 Ibid.
42 Slinn, *Pharmaceutical and Health Care*.

its own marketing expenses were running at nearly 18 per cent of its turnover. This was, however, considerably less than its US competitors were already spending. Among them, Smith Kline & French, at 23 per cent, was the nearest to Glaxo; after that, in an ascending scale, both Merck and Pfizer were spending around 27 per cent of turnover, Parke Davis 31 per cent, and Abbott 33 per cent.[43]

The US was, of course, geographically a large country, and its pharmaceutical market the largest in the world. British companies discovering and launching new drugs at this time wanted to access that large market, but without sales forces there, the only way they could do so was through licensing agreements with US corporations. Their sales forces grew very rapidly in the post-war period:

> ... the pharmaceutical representative as a familiar fixture in the physician's office resulted from the dynamic reorganization of the industry immediately after World War II. ... The 1940s and 50s were a pivotal period for the prescription drug industry, as novel and efficacious medicines began to pump out of a suddenly vibrant research pipeline. ... Between 1939 and 1959 sales of pharmaceuticals increased from US$300 million to US$ 2.3 billion; by 1959 the nationwide corps of detail men had grown from 2000 at the end of the 1920s to more than 15,000 nationwide.

Therefore, when the Beecham Group's research laboratories discovered its first significant prescription drugs, the semi-synthetic penicillins, in the late 1950s, Beecham made an agreement with Bristol-Myers which gave that corporation an exclusive licence to sell the Beecham drugs in the USA and in the rest of the world outside the British Commonwealth in return for a royalty payment and technical help in establishing a fermentation plant.[44] Other such marketing arrangements led to ICI's first beta-blocker, propanolol, being licensed in the USA to Ayerst.[45] Boots' ibuprofen, a non-steroidal anti-inflammatory, introduced in 1969, was marketed in the USA by Upjohn, a company with which Boots had a long-standing agreement.

A brief account of the marketing by Glaxo of the antibiotic griseofulvin illustrates the need for licensing in the USA and the significant role of the publicity and promotion to members of the medical profession both before and contemporaneously with the launch of the drug.

Griseofulvin was identified by ICI in the early 1950s as effective in controlling fungi in plants, but it appeared at that time to have little potential for commercial exploitation. However, a few years later, both ICI and Glaxo began experimental work on the drug, and as the potential for using it in animals and humans began to emerge, the two companies agreed in 1957 to share the patents. Favourable reports of the effectiveness of Grisovin, as Glaxo named its version of the antibiotic, in clinical trials in the USA run by Dr Harvey Blank, an eminent Professor of Dermatology,

---

43   Davenport-Hines and Slinn, *Glaxo: A History*, p. 169.

44   H.G. Lazell, *From Pills to Penicillin: The Beecham Story* (London, 1975).

45   A.A. Daemmrich, *Pharmacopolitics: Drug Regulation in the United States and Germany* (Chapel Hill, NC, 2004).

forced the pace, and Glaxo moved quickly to set up licensing arrangements in the USA and in Europe.

In the USA, Johnson & Johnson and Schering were the chosen licensees who secured approval for the product from the US regulatory authority, the FDA, in 1959 and publicized and promoted it at the American Medical Association in the spring of that year. In October that year, Johnson & Johnson funded an International Symposium at the University of Miami. The market for dermatology products was and remained small, but at least in part due to these early promotion efforts, Grisovin captured a large share of it.[46]

Whilst British companies were forced at this time into licensing products for sale in the USA, in the 1950s many of the US corporations had or were establishing subsidiary companies in countries overseas, usually with their own sales forces, too. A number of US corporations came to set up operations in Britain (as did the German and Swiss companies), some establishing themselves from scratch, as did Pfizer, while others such as Merck, Sharp & Dohme, for example, acquired one of the smaller British companies as a base on which to build. In 1956, Smith, Kline & French Laboratories of Philadelphia bought for £1 million the company known as A.J. White Ltd, Menley & James Laboratories, which had been its manufacturing agents and distributors since 1928.

SK&F soon built up its marketing sales force and claimed to be one of the earliest employers of female sales representatives, with its recruitment of two women to the sales force in the early 1960s.[47] Parke Davis, the US company whose early establishment in Britain has been noted, was, according to its historian, at the peak of its success in the early 1960s. It was employing at that time 80 representatives to promote not only its major prescription medicine, the antibiotic Chloromycetin, but also veterinary products and a large range of OTC medicines.[48] The 1960s were the heyday of the all-purpose salesman with a large portfolio of products. In the 1970s and the 1980s, the pharmaceutical companies increasingly created specialist marketing forces, to reflect their own focus on prescription medicines.

In contrast to SKF, Glaxo did not appoint its first female representative until 1973.[49] The arrival of the US companies did undoubtedly stimulate greater competition in the UK market as well as elsewhere, and perhaps British firms learned at closer quarters about American methods of promotion. Not all of these were wholly admirable, as investigations in the USA itself in the 1960s revealed. In 1963, Merck introduced the anti-inflammatory drug Indocin for the treatment of arthritis. A US senate inquiry into drug promotion in 1968 found that the company had promoted it for treating types of arthritis other than the four for which it had been proved to be effective;

46 Davenport-Hines and Slinn, *Glaxo: A History.*
47 L. Finucane, *SK & F: From Camberwell to Welwyn Garden City 1956–1989* (Welwyn, 1989).
48 Deeson, *Parke Davis in Britain.*
49 Jones, *The Business of Medicine*, p. 246.

instructions given to Merck sales representatives included a damaging document stating:

> It is obvious that Indocin will work in that whole host of crocks and cruds which every general practitioner, internist and orthopoedic surgeon sees every day in his practice ... Tell 'em again, and again, and again ... Tell 'em until they are sold and stay sold.[50]

How far such practices obtained in Britain in the mid-1960s is unclear. Late in 1968, the British retail and pharmaceutical company Boots received approval from the Dunlop Committee (the Committee on the Safety of Medicines – see below) to market ibuprofen, named Brufen, the result of a lengthy R&D search for an alternative to aspirin as a treatment for rheumatic diseases. At a major sales conference in December that year, the representatives were informed of the sales campaign in which they would participate.

The sales briefing given to the representatives has a period feel about it today, but was probably not untypical of the approach in general use at that time. Brufen, the conference was told, was a new product offering very significant advantages over other drugs. It could be sold on its merits. They were also told of:

> ... the importance of the first three weeks in deciding the rate of 'take-off' of a new drug. During these three weeks the hundred best GP prescribers had to be seen and also the most influential consultants. Advance appointments must be made to coincide wherever possible. Stockists and stock levels must be closely watched. ... the importance of making a planned approach to each hospital, seeing influential doctors at all levels and linking up with the pharmacist and local chemists. They should all receive a full detail on Brufen. Detailing should be framed to stress Brufen's superiority over the drugs known to be used at present but there was no need to 'knock the opposition' ... Brufen must be sold on its benefits to the patient.

The sales and marketing campaign planned was likened to a battle, and the strategy set out as a battle plan to the representatives. Each would have a Brufen portfolio, grey in colour, produced as a 'Brufen Bible':

> Whilst working it should be kept in the car (but not left open on the seat!) and used for checking up on technical data etc. and for revision of technical and sales platforms. It must be read and used.[51]

In 1958, the ABPI produced its first code of marketing practice for the industry, intended to ensure that the information proffered by sales representatives was accurate and not misleading.[52] This has been revised at regular intervals since then.

Later, the ABPI also introduced examinations for pharmaceutical company sales representatives.

---

50 Lynn, *The Billion-dollar Battle*, p. 96.
51 Boots archives, Ludwigshafen, 0196/128.
52 Reekie, *The Economics of the Pharmaceutical Industry*.

Meanwhile, another government committee, this time under the chairmanship of Lord Sainsbury, was appointed in 1965 to investigate the industry's relationship with the NHS, more particularly to explore whether prescription medicines were too expensive and whether the pharmaceutical companies were making excessive profits.[53] Following its investigations, the Committee's report was critical of some marketing practices employed by the industry.

The Findings of Sainsbury

The Sainsbury Committee report began by noting that in the pharmaceutical industry, prices, profits, research and sales promotion were all 'closely entwined', each having a 'profound influence' on the others. Because of this, Sainsbury provides us with a useful window on promotion and marketing practices at that time. The committee's analysis of NHS prescriptions in 1965 found that 49 per cent of the drugs prescribed were of American origin, 14 per cent Swiss, 10 per cent other European and 27 per cent British. Sainsbury found that the British companies spent 12 per cent of turnover on sales promotion, whilst the US companies spent 15 per cent, the Swiss 13 per cent and other Europeans 18 per cent. Nearly 70 per cent of sales of NHS products in the British market were patented, branded drugs, and another 20 per cent were branded, unpatented drugs.

In this context, the Committee moved on to explore marketing practices. Competition, it noted, 'is centred almost entirely on the various forms of sales promotion designed to inform, persuade or "remind" doctors of the merits of the products offered'.

The evidence submitted to Sainsbury revealed that most companies spent 45–50 per cent of their promotion expenditure on the sales representatives. The companies were eager to explain that this served a useful purpose, but Sainsbury was unconvinced:

> We were told that the function of the representative was not to sell products but to inform doctors about them. The industry stresses the importance of the representative as a two-way channel of information, the representative informs the doctor about medicines and the new methods of treatment and gathers information about the use of medicine in practice which he reports back to his company.

The main recommendations made by the Sainsbury Committee for tighter control of pricing through the industry supplying the government with more information on costs did not find favour in any quarter, and the changes made following the report were small. We may, however, surmise that the information on marketing costs now in the public domain led the companies to be careful in expenditure, and over the next decade there were more attempts by government to persuade them to reduce promotion costs. By the time Sainsbury reported, however, new moves to

---

53   Sainsbury Committee Report, Cmnd 3410, 1967.

regulate the safety of prescription medicines were being introduced which, over the next decade or so, introduced new elements into the development and marketing of drugs.

Safety Regulation

The discovery in 1960–61 that use of the drug thalidomide by pregnant women was linked to the birth of children with malformed limbs and bodies led to a demand for more regulation of safety trials before drugs were launched on the market in Europe, in Britain and in the USA, although the drug had not been widely used in America as it had not been licensed by the FDA. In Britain there was already in existence a working party looking at toxicity issues, but the thalidomide cases led to the formation of the Committee on the Safety of Medicines and the evolution of a system of regulation which would ensure – in so far as it was possible to do so – that any new drug had been through extensive clinical trials designed to establish that it was effective and free of major side effects.[54]

In the USA, this led, it has been suggested, to a 'drug lag' in the 1970s as the FDA tightened its procedures and demanded more information, a lengthening of the period of time before a drug could be marketed.[55] In Europe and in Britain, whilst there was no perceptible 'drug lag', inevitably the time between discovery and launch of new drugs lengthened, and this in turn reduced the amount of time left before patent expiry, the time when the company wanted to obtain maximum financial returns. It also increased the costs of discovery and development. Pharmaceutical companies had to develop new capabilities in designing and documenting clinical trials to achieve licensing as early as possible in patent life and use promotion methods to secure worldwide penetration of markets.

Marketing and Consumption in the 1970s and 1980s

Through the 1970s, consumption of prescription medicine, as measured by the number of prescriptions, continued to rise steadily but not spectacularly. In 1970, the total number of prescriptions issued was 306 million, in 1980 it was 374 million; by 1985 it was 393 million. In terms of the number of prescriptions per head of population, from 5.5 in 1970, the figure rose to 6.2 in 1975, 6.6 in 1980, and just under 7 in 1985. The total cost of pharmaceuticals to the NHS continued to rise, but as a proportion of NHS expenditure it fell between 1965 and 1980; in 1965, pharmaceutical expenditure represented some 11 per cent of NHS spending, in 1970

---

54   E.M. Tansey and L.A. Reynolds (eds), *The Committee on Safety of Drugs*, Wellcome Witness Seminar Proceeding, Vol. I (London, 1997).

55   Daemmrich, *Pharmacopolitics.*

it was 10 per cent, and in 1975, 8.5 per cent. By 1980 it was rising again, up to 9.4 per cent, and by 1985 it had reached 10 per cent again.[56]

One study in the mid-1970s suggested that companies continued to spend some 14 or 15 per cent of sales on promotional expenditure, with almost a half of that going on the sales force. The 'informing function' continued to be significant, and the meetings for medical practitioners were attracting larger numbers by 1974 than they had in 1969.[57] Glaxo's historian has noted that in the 1970s, the company's marketing efforts shifted away 'from repeated calls by representatives towards promotional meetings of invited audiences. Special conferences were organized targeting particular disorders and their specialist physicians, so that a carefully prepared message could be delivered to key decision makers.'[58] Often these were followed by specialist publications. At the same time, the company reorganized its sales force, creating separate divisions for babyfood, veterinary and human products.

There is some evidence to suggest that in the wake of thalidomide, medical practitioners were becoming more wary about the information supplied by the industry. A survey carried out in 1975 by the *Journal of the Royal College of General Practitioners* found that most GPs were only inclined to prescribe a new drug on the basis of information from a commercially sponsored source in a few low-risk therapeutic classes, for example mild analgesics and cough medicines. In therapeutic classes considered to be higher-risk, such as drugs for cardiovascular problems and those for treating disorders of the central nervous system, they required other information from a more neutral source. GPs were more inclined to follow hospital consultants in prescribing new higher-risk drugs, and this was reflected in the companies focusing their representatives on calling on those they identified as 'influential prescribers'.[59]

The industry as a whole struggled with a slowing down in the rate of introduction of new drugs in the 1970s. In this situation, pharmaceutical companies often reformulated and/or searched for new uses for drugs which had been in their portfolio for some time. Abbott Laboratories, for example, had launched the antibiotic erythromycin in the late 1950s, and it evidenced considerable longevity. By the early 1980s, the company was selling 18 different formulations of the drug across the world; the discovery in the late 1970s that it was effective against the bacteria causing Legionnaire's Disease, gave a further boost to sales, and in 1988 sales of erythromycin represented 9 per cent of the company's worldwide sales [60]

56   Loudon, Horder and Webster (eds), *General Practice under the National Health Service*, p. 302.

57   S. St. P. Slatter, *Competition and Marketing Strategies in the Pharmaceutical Industry* (London, 1977).

58   Jones, *The Business of Medicine*, p. 248.

59   Slatter, *Competition and Marketing Strategies in the Pharmaceutical Industry.*

60   Slinn, *Pharmaceutical and Health.*

There were, however, some significant new products in this period. One of these was the discovery by James Black and his team at the British laboratories of Smith Kline & French of the histamine-2 receptor antagonist cimetidine, for the treatment of ulcer disease. Launched as Tagamet late in 1976, in its first year sales in Britain alone reached £10 million. It was launched at a symposium at the Royal College of Physicians, followed by a press conference at Millbank Tower, and apparently unusually at that time, a film was made about its development.[61] By 1981, Tagamet was achieving sales of nearly $300 million in the USA.[62]

In the late 1970s, Glaxo's researchers had also been working on that area which was a rapidly growing market and discovered ranitidine, which it named Zantac. Launched in 1981 in Britain and in Italy, Zantac had two advantages over Tagamet: it was administered in two rather than four doses a day, and it had fewer side effects and drug interaction problems. The use that Glaxo made of these in marketing Zantac, in a campaign that is widely recognized as an almost textbook success case, achieved sales and profits for Glaxo which took the company from a medium-sized British pharmaceutical company into the top ranks of international pharmaceutical corporations.

Glaxo decided to market Zantac, 'not as a Tagamet monopoly breaker but as a major evolutionary advance in the treatment of peptic ulcer and other acid-aggravated disorders'.[63] This was unusual for a second product, as was the decision to go for a premium price. As sales grew rapidly in 1981–82 in Italy and the UK, followed by elsewhere in the world, Glaxo made its plans to launch Zantac in the USA. In 1977–78, Glaxo had bought a foothold in the USA through its purchase of a fairly small US company, Meyer Laboratories. Its small sales force of 150 detailmen had been expanded, but was too small to market Zantac across the USA.

The Swiss company Roche, on the other hand, had a US sales force of 700, and with the patents on its commercially successful (albeit much criticized) drugs Valium and Librium running out, was looking for products to market. An agreement was reached under which Glaxo and Roche would co-market and sell Zantac under the Glaxo name; the return to Roche was '40 per cent of sales revenue on a rising scale over five years'.[64] Zantac was launched in the USA in July 1983, and by 1986 the USA was the largest single market for the drug, and its total sales reached $1 billion, the first drug to do so.[65]

According to one account, the marketing and promotion techniques used by Glaxo, ranging from educational symposia to consumer awareness bulletins, as well as new formulations and extended therapies such as maintenance, not only gained for the company a larger share of the market but also successfully expanded the

---

61   Finucane, *SK & F*.

62   R. Wright, 'How Zantac became the best-selling drug in history', *Journal of Health Care Marketing* (Winter, 1996), pp. 24–9.

63   Jones, *The Business of Medicine*, p. 253.

64   Ibid, p. 392.

65   Wright, 'How Zantac became the best-selling drug in history'.

market for H2-blockers, enabling the company to sell more.[66] Since the late 1980s, the $1 billion drug has become, if not a commonplace yet, certainly no longer an isolated event. In 1988, Merck achieved sales of that order with Vasotec, a drug which reduces high blood pressure and relieves congestive heart failure.[67] Meanwhile, the development of the biotechnology industry offered new opportunities to the pharmaceutical industry.

The Development of Biotechnology

Discoveries in bioscience in the 1970s, particularly those of recombinant DNA (rDNA) and monoclonal antibodies, led the way to the creation of what is known as the biotechnology industry. The first biotech company in the world, Genentech, was established in the USA in 1976; its first success was to produce the human growth hormone somatostatin from bacteria, and it went on to use rDNA technology to make human insulin. Between the mid-1970s and the mid-1980s, more than 300 small to medium-sized research-intensive biotech companies were formed in the USA.[68] Most were funded in their early years by venture capital, and some were able to proceed successfully to a flotation on the stock exchange. By the early 1980s, a number of proteins with therapeutic value had been cloned into a variety of micro-organisms, and large-scale production was under way.

Development of a biotech industry in Europe was slower, but took off in the 1980s. In Britain, the Spinks Report of 1980 highlighted the significant contribution to the economy and national competitiveness that the growth of science-based industries could make, and a number of initiatives directed to the creation of a biotech industry followed. There were other European-wide initiatives to promote the formation and development of biotech companies in the 1980s.

What most biotech companies found, however, was that from discovery to development was a long and expensive process; moreover, there was the hurdle of meeting the requirements of the national regulatory authorities, the FDA in the USA, and the MCA in Britain. The pharmaceutical companies had found that dealing with the regulatory authorities required expertise and experience; by 1980 it reckoned that from the initial synthesis of a drug to FDA approval took on average eight years. When approval was obtained, there was the question of marketing and distribution, a further very expensive process, as we have seen. Whilst some pharmaceutical companies started to use biotechnology knowledge and techniques in their own R&D laboratories,[69] they also watched the development of the biotech industry with interest and were ready to step in with alliances and agreements, proffering further

66   Ibid.
67   Lynn, *The Billion-dollar Battle.*
68   A. Gambardella, *Science and Innovation: The US Pharmaceutical Industry during the 1980's* (Cambridge, 1995).
69   L. Galambos and J. Sturchio, 'Pharmaceutical Firms and Transition to Biotechnology: A Study in Strategic Innovation', Business History Review, 22 (1998), pp. 250–78.

much-needed funding for biotech companies in exchange for products to enhance their sometimes lack-lustre pipelines.

The last two decades of the twentieth century, then, saw the growth of a network of collaborative agreements of all kinds between the major pharmaceutical companies and the biotech companies; many of these gave milestone and royalty payments to the biotech company, while the pharmaceutical company would develop and market compounds discovered by biotech.[70] National boundaries and interests disappeared in the complex web of collaborative agreements that was created and by and large still exists today. By no means untypical was the British biotech company Celltech, established (with government backing at the time) in 1980. In the mid-1990s, it had a network of major collaborations with three US companies Schering-Plough, American Home Products and Merck, with the German company Bayer, and the British company Zeneca.[71] As Jurgens Drew of the Swiss company Roche, which was by then a majority shareholder in Genentech, said in 1993:

> No single company has the in-house capability to accomplish all these facets of drug discovery alone. It will be necessary for the pharmaceutical company wishing to develop drugs from the Human Genome Project to form alliances with many partners – in both biotechnology and academia – to carry out the process as efficiently and effectively as possible.[72]

Reconstruction and Consolidation in the Industry

By the mid- to late 1980s, governments across the world were becoming concerned at the rising costs of health care. In Britain, despite the introduction in 1985 of a black list of drugs – that is, those which were not to be prescribed – the cost of the drugs bill to the NHS started to rise more sharply. The cost of pharmaceutical services as a proportion of total NHS spending rose to 10.3 per cent in 1990 and 11.2 per cent in 1995; the total number of NHS prescriptions reached 444.6 million in 1990, rising to 520.7 million in 1994.[73] New drugs were expensive as the cost of developing them rose, and in Britain, as elsewhere, a larger proportion of the population were older people, with more chronic illnesses requiring therapeutic treatment. In the interests of economy, the government also exhorted doctors to prescribe and pharmacists to supply generic drugs – that is, those no longer protected by patent. Whilst most of the companies cited in this chapter as illustrations continued to produce generic versions of their drugs after patent expiry, relying on brand name loyalty to maintain

---

70 Gambardella, *Science and Innovation*.

71 McNamara et al., 2000.

72 M. Sharp and J. Senker, 'European Biotechnology: Learning and Catching Up', in A. Gambardella and F. Malerba (eds), *The Organization of Economic Innovation in Europe* (Cambridge, 1999).

73 Loudon, Horder and Webster (eds), *General Practice under the National Health Service*, p. 305.

market share even if profitability declined, there also developed companies which specialized in the manufacture of generics.

Pressure to reduce costs was one of the significant factors in a process that started in the 1980s of larger pharmaceutical companies being created by merger and acquisition. Smith Kline Beckman's merger with the Beecham Group in the late 1980s exemplified both the trend to consolidation and its increasingly cross-border nature. In 1995, Glaxo acquired Wellcome; in 1999, Zeneca (de-merged from ICI in 1993) merged with the Swedish company Astra. In Europe, Rhone Poulenc merged its pharmaceutical interests with those of Hoechst to create the Franco-German Aventis (recently acquired by or 'merged' with Sanofi). The merger of Smith Kline Beecham and Glaxo Wellcome in 2000 created, briefly, the largest company in the world, GlaxoSmithKline (GSK), but it was soon overtaken later that year by the merger of Pfizer and Warner Lambert. The merger that followed, between the already greatly enlarged Pfizer and the American Swedish combination of Pharmacia Upjohn, created the largest pharmaceutical corporation in the world.

The need to achieve critical mass, both in R&D and increasingly in marketing, also drove other reconstructions, including some involving smaller players in the industry, such as the acquisition of Boots' pharmaceutical interests in 1995 by the German company BASF, which then, some five years later, sold its pharmaceutical business to Abbott Laboratories. The merger of the two US companies Bristol-Myers and Squibb (BMS) in 1989 meant that the merged company had, in the early 1990s, a sales force numbering 2 000 to promote Capoten, a new cardiovascular drug. Merck had developed a competing drug, and had a sales force of 700 to market it.[74] In 2001, AstraZeneca launched Nexium, the company's new ulcer drug, deploying 2 700 detailmen to do so in the USA.[75] Despite all this large – and undoubtedly very expensive – activity, until the turn of the century no single company had a very large market share, because of the fragmentation of the market into different therapeutic classes, although the industry was increasingly dominated by a group of very large companies.

In the 1970s, it was noted that any company seeking to maintain a presence in the industry and promote its branded products required a sales force of representatives of a certain minimum size, however large or small the company's turnover; in 1970 Roche, with sales of £9 million, fielded 66 sales representatives in Britain, while Berk, with sales of £2–3 million, deployed 58–65 sales representatives.[76] Thirty years later, the small and medium-sized companies in the industry can no longer afford a sales and marketing operation on the scale employed by the large and dominating corporations of the industry.

---

74 Lynn, *The Billion-dollar Battle*.
75 F. Guerrera, 'Pursuit of the pill prescribers', *Financial Times* (26 April 2001).
76 Slatter, *Competition and Marketing Strategies in the Pharmaceutical Industry*.

Marketing and Consumption at the End of the Twentieth Century

This chapter began with a deconstruction of the transaction through which prescription medicine reached its final consumer, and that provides an appropriate framework for considering the changes that have taken place over the last fifty years and their impact on the transaction. The first aspect of the transaction noted was that the people who consume the medicine, the patients, do not choose it, for that is the prerogative of the doctors. Officially, that is still the case, but it is no longer quite as simple as it was.

There is considerably more information in the public domain about the products of the industry, and more patients, seeing themselves as consumers, feel they have a right to an informed discussion about what is being prescribed for them. Not only does this reflect the growth of consumerism and, in some countries such as the USA, of disease-based organizations;[77] it also reflects a growing ambivalence towards professional authority wherever it is located, and increasing suspicions of large commercial organizations. The relationship between the industry and the medical community continues to raise questions, sometimes uncomfortable. There are doubts about a situation where:

> Pharmaceutical representatives are a welcome fixture at most medical schools and residency programs; their companies – and the meals and gifts they provide – are often relied up as a fundamental institutional context of medical education.[78]

In the 1960s, the thalidomide tragedy certainly created doubts and public concern. In a lecture to the Royal Society of Arts in 1963, Professor Ernst Chain, Nobel Prizewinner for his work as part of the Oxford team who developed penicillin, summarized the public perception of the pharmaceutical industry in these terms:

> The climate of public opinion with regard to drugs is cool – to say the least; the word has acquired an almost derogatory tinge. In the minds of many people – and some of them in high places – drugs are immediately associated with deformed thalidomide babies, and those who take a more lenient view, still consider them as rather expensive, dangerous chemicals of somewhat doubtful value with which they are overdosed, and which are urged on them or their doctors by the persuasive voice of commercial propaganda; and as to drug manufacturers, these are downright suspect, and the picture of nasty, vulture-like, greedy creatures, predatory and thriving on human pain and disease, comes to the mind of lots of people.[79]

Chain used his lecture to stress the benefits offered by the discovery of the antibiotics during the therapeutic revolution and since (he was closely involved in Beecham's

---

77   Daemmrich, *Pharmacopolitics*.

78   J. Greene, 'Attention to Details: Etiquette and the Pharmaceutical Salesman in Postwar America', *Social Studies of Science,* 34(2) (2004), pp. 271–92.

79   E.B. Chain, *Academic and Industrial Contributions to Drug Research* (London, 1963).

development of the semi-synthetic penicillins). However, some of the coolness to which he referred had in fact been created by the evidence revealed in the Kefauver hearings in the USA about the commercial behaviour of the companies manufacturing and marketing antibiotics. Backroom deals on pricing and the fact that 'development and marketing, rather than research, were critical aspects of firm success' revealed a side of the industry that was distinctly 'unsavoury'.[80] Later, the revelation of the pricing policies of Roche with regard to Librium and Valium gave that company unwelcome publicity, as did the evidence which accumulated slowly about the addictive nature of the drugs.

In the 1980s, the anti-inflammatory drug Opren had to be withdrawn two years after its launch in Britain by the subsidiary of the US company Lilley. The withdrawal followed the suspension of the drug, recommended by the Committee of the Safety of Medicines (CSM – forerunner of the MCA, now the MHRA) after several deaths attributed to jaundice and renal failure in elderly patients suffering from arthritis for whom the drug had been prescribed.[81] More recently, concerns have been raised about anti-depressant drugs, the SSRIs. These include doubts about the way in which clinical trials are conducted and reported, and the role and influence of the companies in that process.[82]

Whilst scientists would argue that no drug can ever be considered wholly 'safe' and that the procedures and process created in the wake of thalidomide in Britain involve balancing risks, the publicity which accompanied the high-profile cases mentioned above has had its impact on consumers and others involved in the transaction. It has been suggested that the success of modern medicine (drugs as well as surgery and other medical procedures) has itself generated a 'perplexing four-layered paradox'.[83] The four layers, each paradoxical in itself, are: disillusioned doctors, the worried well, the soaring popularity of alternative medicine, and the spiralling cost of health care.[84] In the twentieth century, medicine, in the widest sense, 'grew conquering and commanding', but it has become 'the prisoner of its won success' and lost certainty about its direction and mandate.[85]

There are questions, too, about the nature and process of medicalization. In the immediate post-war years, the pharmaceutical companies sought to identify market segments of illness, particularly chronic and widespread problems, at which they could target their R&D efforts, secure in the knowledge that if they succeeded, the market would be there and satisfactory returns would be generated. However, demand was seen as a function of the size and composition of the population, the incidence of disease and the standard of living – all factors over which the pharmaceutical

80 Goodman, 'Pharmaceutical Industry'.

81 J. Abraham, *Science, Politics and the Pharmaceutical Industry* (London, 1985).

82 C. Medawar, 'The Antidepressent Web', *International Journal of Risk and Safety in Medicine*, 10 (1997), pp. 75–126; D. Healy, 'Shaping the Intimate: Influences on the Experience of Everyday Nerves', *Social Studies of Science*, 34(2) (2004), pp. 219–45.

83 J. Le Fanu, *The Rise and Fall of Modern Medicine* (London, 1999).

84 Ibid.

85 R. Porter, *The Greatest Benefit to Mankind* (London,1997).

industry had no control. Whilst these are all still significant factors and the standard of living determines the fact that the major markets for prescription medicines are to be found in North America, Europe and Japan, it has been argued that the industry has found ways to create markets for its products in affluent societies, particularly for the so-called 'lifestyle' drugs. At the end of the twentieth century, 'it would be difficult to be unaware of the value to pharmaceutical companies of defining medical problems that their drugs can treat'.[86]

It is clear that discovery, development and marketing do not constitute – if indeed they ever did – a linear process. Since the 1980s at least, marketing managers have become involved much earlier in the process of discovery and development; how influential they are may vary from one company to another. One account of the development by Merck of the cholesterol-reducing drug Mevacor relates how unenthusiastic the marketers were in the early 1980s, when the company's R&D researchers were working on the drug. The marketers wanted the project abandoned since they considered the market for such a drug was small. Within the company, R&D won and the drug was launched late in 1987; the value of sales in its second year had reached $500 million, and were predicted to continue to grow.[87] Some industry observers have attributed the increasing significance of marketing to the industry's failure to develop 'ground-breaking' or really innovative drugs recently. In the USA, of the 10 top-selling drugs in 1997, only 4 rated as offering modest therapeutic gains, while 6 were rated as offering little or no therapeutic gain over existing therapies. In these circumstances, it has been suggested, pharmaceutical companies will have to look to consumer product marketing techniques and strategies, focusing on corporate rather than individual drug brands.[88]

Evidence and analysis of the complex relationships between consumers, the pharmaceutical industry and the medical community at the end of the twentieth century are still at a relatively early stage. Consumers may not choose, but may play a part in choosing, the drug they will consume. Whilst they may still be unaware of the costs of medicine, few doctors in Britain can any longer be unaware of the price of medicine. And the evidence so far suggests that the statement with which we started – 'the researchers find out what the customer needs, and then the marketing people go out and make sure they take it'[89] – may yet require modification.

There is no doubt that techniques for identifying markets and consumers are considerably more sophisticated and manipulative than they were half a century ago. In the USA, the world's largest market for prescription medicine, with the highest growth rate and the home of an increasingly large proportion of the world's industry, direct-to-consumer marketing was formally approved by the FDA in 1999. As yet

---

86   S. Sismondo, 'Pharmaceutical Maneuvers', *Social Studies of* Science, 34(2), (2004), pp. 149–59.

87   Lynn, *The Billion-dollar Battle*.

88   M. Corstjens and M. Carpenter, 'From managing pills to managing brands', *Harvard Business Review* (March–April 2000), pp. 20–22.

89   Lynn, *The Billion-dollar Battle*.

there is no sign that will be permitted in Britain or Europe, but the changes in the industry and its regulation will continue to affect the marketing and consumption of prescription drugs.

Index

abortion 95, 114–15
advertising 22, 30–47, 93, 96, 116, 125
almanacs 30–47, 53
analgesics 247
antibiotics 2, 10, 148, 161, 166
apothecaries 13–27, 52, 56, 64–5, 81–2, 145
Apothecaries' Act (1815) 82
Archer, John 38
'Ask your pharmacist' campaign (1982) 141
Association of the British Pharmaceutical
    Industry (ABPI) 153
astrology 4, 18, 21, 31, 33
Aventis 165

barber surgeons 23
Bath 52, 55–6, 66
bespoke medicines 127
beta-blockers 148, 158
Bevan, Aneurin 143
Bignall, Cumbria 52
blood-letting 14, 49
Boot, John 88
biomedicine 9
biotechnology 163–4
Bolton Benevolent Society 76
Bournemouth 151
Boyse, William 36
branded medicines 5–6; see also proprietary
    medicines
Bristol 84
British Medical Association 108, 144
Brufen 158

cancer 118–19
Cardwell, F. of Wakefield (Chemist) 98
Catholics 54–5
Chain, Professor Ernest 166
charities 75–7
chemist 8–9, 50, 52, 64, 68, 80–104, 141
coffeehouses 44
College of Physicians 5, 19, 20, 25, 37
Commonplace books 69–71

Company of Stationers 33
contraceptive pill 148
coral 26
cortisone 148
Council of the Pharmaceutical Society 109
counter prescribing 101
Crowther, George Henry 88
Culpeper, Nicholas 15

Dangerous Drugs Act (1920) 112
Dickman, Henry 17, 19
diet 18
disease 1
distribution 41–5
Dr Bickerstaff 52
Dr Loxham 74–5
Dr Skelton 88
drinking houses 44
druggist 8, 16, 80–104
Dunlop Committee 158

Elixir Salutis 17
Elliott, John Gartside 103
    R. 97
erythromycin 161

Farwell, John 37
fixed shops 42, 65
Food and Drug Administration (FDA) 157,
    160, 163, 168
Forman, Simon 18
Freeman, Thomas Augustus 69
French National Health Scheme 146
friendly societies 130
fringe medicine 92

Galen 4, 21
Gaskell, Elizabeth 81
Gentleman's Magazine 53
Gillebaud Commission (1956) 152
Gissing, Thomas 100–101
Green Sickness 69–70

Griseofulvin 156
Guillebaud Committee 153-4
Gutenberg, Joannes 32

Haddock, Josiah 65
Hall, George 100
handbills 30–31
hartshorn 26
Harvey, Gideon 14
hawkers 42
Haworth, Mr 64–5
Helmontian medicine 21
herbs 4, 15, 26, 87
Highcliffe Commission (1959) 152
home remedies 106
Huddersfield 83–105

ingredients 25–6

Jarrow 152
*Journal of the Royal College of General
　　Practitioners* 161

King, William 100
'kitchen physick' 3–4, 15

Lancashire 51–78
Lancet 80, 91
Legionnaire's Disease 153
legislation 105–42
Librium 162
lifestyle drugs 137–42
Lincoln 91
Lockwood, W.P. 87
London 13–27, 34, 41, 87, 151

'magic bullet' 147
manufacturing 26, 41
Mason, Richard 19
mastic 26
medical
　　botany 89
　　consumerism 30
　　marketplace 4–5, 55, 77
Medical Times and Gazette 90
Medicines Act (1968) 114
middling sort 20, 59–63
Mildmay, Lady Grace 16
Ministry of Health 140, 153

National Health Insurance Act 130–31
National Health Insurance Scheme 132, 145
National Health Service 107, 120, 143–52
National Health Service Act (1946) 133
National Pharmaceutical Union 134, 141
New Poor Law (1834) 7, 79, 130
newspapers 31
Nickelson, John 52
Northamptonshire 51, 53–78
nostrum 123–5, 128

'off-the-peg' medicines 127
Old Poor Law (eighteenth century) 72
Opium 94–5, 109
over the counter medicines 2

Paracelsus 21
Parker, Michael 52
patent medicine 98–9
Penicillin 110, 114, 146–8, 166
Pepys, Samuel 35
Pharmaceutical Companies 10, 146
　　Abbott Laboratories 151–2, 165
　　Bayer 164
　　Beecham Group 156, 165
　　Bristol-Meyers 165
　　Burroughs-Wellcome 150
　　Glaxo-Wellcome 151, 155–6, 165
　　Johnson and Johnson 157
　　Merck 158, 168
　　Parke-Davis 150
　　Pfizer 165
　　Roche 162, 164
　　Sanofi 165
　　Schering-Plough 157, 164
　　Smith Kline Beecham 165
　　Squibb 165
　　Upjohn 156
Pharmaceutical Journal 98–9, 131
Pharmaceutical Society of Great Britain 8,
　　82, 102, 107, 133–4
pharmacist 115
Pharmacoepia 5
Pharmacy Act (1868) 126, 133
　　(1908) 110
Pharmacy and Medicines Act (1941) 113
Pharmacy and Poisons Act (1933) 113
physick 3
Poor Laws 72–5,

postal delivery 44–5, 66
prescriptions 16, 132,135,141, 162–3
prices 18–20, 41, 52, 55–7, 62–3, 71, 73, 75,
    104, 135, 144
Proprietary Medicines 17, 22, 36–41, 98–9,
    110–11, 125–7, 136
    Andrew's Liver Salts 124, 125
    Bateman's Pectoral Drops 38
        Scurvy Grass 38
    Beecham's Pills 125
    Betnovate 155
    Brande's Bronchial Sedative 98
    Buckworth's Lozenges 39
    Burgess's Lion Ointment and Pills 116
    Butler's Acidulated Cayenne Lozenges
        99
        Pectoral Elixir 99
    Carlyle's Sovereign Elixir Against
        Decay 70
    Carter's Little Liver Pills 125
    Clarke's Scurvy Compound 38
    Daffy's Elixir 6, 17, 39–40, 57, 67–8
    Dr Bright's Pills of Health 98
    Dr Davis's Famous Female Pills
    Dr Locock's Pulmonic Wafers 98
    Dr Turner's Famous Dentifrices 48
    Frampton's Pill of Health 95
    Godfrey's Cordial 94
    Holloway's Ointment 98
    Horton's Famous American Elixir for
        the Rheumatism 70
    James' Powder 59
    Jefferson Dodd's Corrective 115
    Jone's Elixir 70
    McColleys Golden Purging Pills 40
    Martin Sweeting's Toothache Elixir 98
    Marshall's Universal Curate 99
    Mr Lignum's Improved Vegetable
        Lotion 99
    Mrs Lydia Pinkham's Vegetable
        Compound 115
    Nendick's Pills 45
    Nurse Harvey's Gripe Mixture 97
    Nurse Powell's Corrective Pills 115
    Opren 167
    Paris Pill 115
    Parker's Elixir of Scurvy Grass 38
    Pedley's Infallible Cure for the
        Rheumatism 70
    Perry's Essence 99
    Pilulae Londinenses 37
    Pordage's Scurvy Grass 38
    Russell's Spirit of Scurvy Grass 43
    Solomon's Drops 99
    Tagamet 162
    Towle's Pennyroyal and Steel Pills 115
    Velno's Vegetable Syrup 95
    Welden's Balsamick Spirit 41
    White's Composition Essence 97
    Widow Welch's Pills 95
    Woodward's Pills 43, 45
    Woolley's Pectoral Candy 98
    Worsall's Pills 99

quacks 13, 37, 39, 50, 57, 67, 79–80,114
Quakers 54
Quinine 95

recipes 16, 69, 71, 93, 197
Registrar General's Office (1837) 108
regulation 3, 90, 110, 113, 114, 126
Reinhardt, G.B. 97
Report of the Medical Officer of the Privy
    Council (1864) 90
'Rose Case' 5
Rowlandson, William 86–7

Sabine, Edward 61–2
Sainsbury Committee 159–60
Salmon, William 44
Sanderson, J. and W. 87
Saunders, John 18
Select Committee on Medical Poor Relief
    (1844) 90–91
self-help books 17, 53
self-treatment 15, 17, 37–41, 50, 68, 78
Sermon, George 40
Shakespeare, William 13, 26
Sheffield 83, 94
Shorter, Edward 50
Sigsworth and Swan 89
simples 16
spa towns 52, 55–6, 66
Spinks Report (1980) 163
Streptomycin 148
surgeon-apothecary 49, 86
Swift, Thomas North 88

testimonials 40
Thalidomide 160, 166
Therapeutic Substances Act (1956) 114
Theriac 20
tobacco 2, 44
Trade directories 57
transportation 44–5, 53
Tuberculosis 148
Typhus 81

Valium 162
Venereal Disease Act 106, 117
venereal diseases 95–6, 104,106, 117, 147–8

Vitriol 26
Voluntary Price Regulation Scheme (VPRS)
    153–4

Wads, John 36
Wakefield 83–105
Wakefield and Halifax Journal 99
welfare state 140
Wellcome, Henry 150
W.P. England & Co. 97–8

Zantac 149, 162
'zoonoses' 1